HORSE-DRAWN
DRAWN
TRANSPORT
IN LEEDS

William Turton
2 January 1825 – 7 August 1900

HORSE-DRAWN TRANSPORT IN LEEDS

WILLIAM TURTON, CORN MERCHANT AND TRAMWAY ENTREPRENEUR

ANDREW TURTON

DEDICATION

to my paternal grandparents

Felicia Turton (*née* Roberts) 1878–1972
William Turton 1880–1965

In association with Leeds Philosophical & Literary Society

First published 2015

The History Press
The Mill, Brimscombe Port
Stroud, Gloucestershire, GL5 2QG
www.thehistorypress.co.uk

© Andrew Turton, 2015

The right of Andrew Turton to be identified as the Author
of this work has been asserted in accordance with the
Copyright, Designs and Patents Act 1988.

British Library Cataloguing in Publication Data.
A catalogue record for this book is available from the British Library.

ISBN 978 0 7509 6176 9

Typesetting and origination by The History Press
Printed in Great Britain

CONTENTS

PICTURE CREDITS

I acknowledge with thanks the following sources of pictures and copyright permission. Other illustrations are out of copyright or deemed to be out of copyright. Please direct any enquiry about copyright to the author c/o the publisher.

Adam Gordon
Getty
Leeds Art Gallery
Leeds Civic Trust
Leeds Historical Transport Society
Leicester Library
Leodis (Leeds Library Services)
London School of Economics and Political Science
Thoresby Society
West Yorkshire Archives (Sheepscar)
Yorkshire Post
The author is responsible for the tables

PREFACE

Andrew Turton started out to research the life and business of his great-great-grandfather. This would have been an interesting subject in itself, if limited. But what he has produced is far more valuable. By putting the succession of businesses that developed as technology changed and his various ancestors developed new skills, he has created a book that explains and puts into context the development of horse-drawn transport in the nineteenth century.

The detail is fascinating. In my book *The Subterranean Railway*, the history of the London Underground, I explained how omnibus transport was costly to provide and as a result limited in scope. Mr Turton has put this into context in Leeds where the issues were similar. The need to run a transport business with horses was both expensive and risky, as well as creating vast amounts of waste material which, while useful as a fertiliser, earned little money because of its abundance.

Mr Turton points out that the age of the urban horse-drawn transport systems lasted just over three quarters of a century. Intercity transport by stagecoach was killed off by the railways. However, horse-drawn trams survived until the technology of electricity improved to such an extent that four-legged power became uneconomic.

Before getting on to the main focus of his history, Mr Turton takes us through the corn and hay and the coal and mining businesses of the nineteenth century. In the latter he shows some truly shocking statistics on deaths of miners and pit boys, many of whom were aged under 10 and even as young as 5. The fact that this happened just a few generations ago makes the history even more compelling.

The history of systems such as railways or tramways is a series of incidents and inventions which led to a particular technological path. The railways, for example, may never have happened had it not been for the poor condition of roads and the non-existence of rubber tyres in the early nineteenth century. Mr Turton does a good job of giving the back-story to the various reasons why tramways became such a popular and successful invention, albeit for a relatively brief period. Government involvement and regulation – and often lack of it – is always a key factor in these accounts. And, as all my own rail history books show, politics is never far from being one of the determining factors in the success or failure of various enterprises, which is why it is so relevant that one of this book's sections is called 'Society and Politics'. So the local authorities figure large, and, of course, the Leeds Town Hall gets a suitable mention. William Turton himself, like many entrepreneurs involved in transport in the nineteenth century, was involved in local politics.

Mr Turton livens up his in-depth historical account with numerous amusing anecdotes, such as the notice which informed 'Passengers desiring to sleep should instruct the conductor at what time they are to be awakened' – not a service offered on the late night buses and trains of today.

The strength of this book is that Mr Turton has managed to provide a tremendous amount of detail alongside salient interpretations of the facts. By putting these facts into a wider context he has created a fascinating read. Mr Turton has managed to write a transport history book, focusing on his own family, that provides an illuminating and compelling account of an important aspect of Victorian Britain.

Christian Wolmar, Transport historian

ACKNOWLEDGEMENTS

So many people gave me advice, information and encouragement. I wish to thank them all, including those whose names do not appear here.

A very special thanks is due to two of Leeds' foremost historians. First to Jim Soper, Dipl. Arch., Dipl. TP, ARIBA, author of the fine five-volume *Leeds Transport 1830–1986* and a founder member of the Leeds Transport Historical Society. My appreciation of his work and subsequent help is shown throughout the text.

Secondly, Dr David Thornton MPhil.; PhD. Author of some of the best books on Leeds and editor and council member of the Thoresby Society. He was the first person to read the text in draft form.

Other Leeds historians and writers: Raymond Dalton, Robin Dove, Kevin Grady and other members of the Leeds Civic Trust, Peter Hirschman, Martin Wainwright and Penny Wainwright.

The many people of Leeds who talked to me about Chapeltown, Hayfield House and other places and introduced me to people: Robin Corner, Pat Falkingham, Garth Frankland, Tiny Maguire, Graham Pawley, Jenny Samuel, Patricia Turner, Dave Walter.

Those who replied to my letter in *The Yorkshire Post*: John Barton, Harold Jackson and John Steele.

Those most hard-working librarians and archivists, and their staff, at the Leeds Family and Local History Library and Leeds Central Library; West Yorkshire Archive Service, Sheepscar (Stefanie Davidson) and Wakefield (Katie Proctor); LEODIS, Leeds Photographic Archive (Rose Gibson); The Leeds Library; The Thoresby Society (Greta and Peter Meredith); and, in London, the British Library in Euston Road, the Colindale newspaper library and the National Archives at Kew.

For help with the history of the Turton family: my paternal first cousins Norman William Turton, Peter John Turton and Philip Robin Turton who were in touch throughout; descendants of John Turton, my paternal second cousins twice removed the late Lance Turton, Elizabeth (*née* Turton) and David Toulmin, Ann Agar (née Turton), Kitty Turton, David Turton, Ken Turton; Martin Stubbs, Michael Carter-Inman; also members of the Turton diaspora in Australia, Canada, New Zealand and South Africa

Dorothy Turton Bjarnson, Vanessa Blake, Neal Hargreaves, Sharon Livingstone, Tony Turton, Emma Weeding, Kathy Westlake and others.

I owe a special debt of gratitude to the Leeds Philosophical and Literary Society, and its president Antony North and secretary Chris Hatton, for their sponsorship of my research and publication through two grants totalling £1,400.

I am honoured that Christian Wolmar accepted the task of writing a preface.

Amy Rigg, Editor at The History Press, for her professional advice.

To my friends Victoria Glendinning and Roger Jellinek, and my immediate family: my sister Ruth Christodolo, my daughters Clio Turton and Polly Turton, and my wife Antonia Benedek.

Andrew George William Turton, 2015

AUTHOR

Dr Andrew Turton was christened Andrew George William Turton out of respect for his father and three generations of great-uncles (all George), his grandfather, great-great-grandfather and three generations of great uncles (all William). His paternal ancestors were born in Leeds.

His father's death in 1944 as a Flying Officer on active service with the RAF led to a memorial grant which enabled him to attend his father's school, Charterhouse.

This was followed by two years national service in the army as a second lieutenant in the Intelligence Corps and three years at Peterhouse College, Cambridge, reading Modern Languages. His first job was with the British Council, when he spent two years in Thailand.

A sabbatical year at the London School of Economics led to field research in Thailand, a PhD in Social Anthropology and a long career at the School of Oriental and African Studies, University of London, where he was head of the department of Sociology and Anthropology and chair of the Centre for South East Asian Research.

He has written widely on a variety of themes in the fields of ethnography, history and biography. His latest publication is *Manor Gardens Centre 1913–2013: a century of service in community health and social care.* He has been chair, now patron, of this charity for many years.

INTRODUCTION

Trams have a promising future. They are being revived in many European towns and cities. In some they were never out of use; in others they have been rediscovered after a regrettable absence since the 1950s. Even horse trams might be part of this future. They were a key stage in the early development of urban passenger transport. Slow, green and sustainable, they should be remembered in contemporary debates about urban transport.

William Turton, of Leeds, had many of the attributes of a pioneer, entrepreneur, self-made man and transport visionary. He started in 1844 as a small-scale hay merchant and rapidly expanded to include corn (fodder), coal, livery stables, cabs and horse omnibuses. He was a man for his times, uniquely placed to develop tramway systems, first in Leeds in 1872 and then throughout the north of England, including Bradford, Leicester, Liverpool, Manchester, Newcastle, Nottingham, Sheffield and other places.

Horses and horse food were the main forms of urban transport and its fuel throughout the nineteenth century. There was not much that Turton did not know about either. He had been a machine maker's apprentice and kept up with technological developments gaining hands-on experience with tramcar design, steam engines, even compressed air engines and later the electric tram and combustion engine.

By the 1860s he was wealthy and self-assured enough to enter municipal politics. He was an elected councillor during the early years of Leeds Tramways Company of which he was a founding board member and long-time chairman, until its handover to the Municipality in 1895. He never ceased to be a corn and coal merchant, and a bus and cab owner. His three sons continued the corn and coal businesses until it left family ownership soon after 1920.

It was often said that there was no money in horses and that no one got rich from running tramways. Turton's position, however, gave him strength in depth not only as a corn and coal merchant but also through his major shareholding in and board membership of Thomas Green and Son, engineers who made many of the steam engines and tramcars for Turton's tramways in Leeds and elsewhere.

Urban passenger trams had been in operation in the USA since the 1830s. They were to start in England forty years later and very soon had to cope with competition from steam, briefly, and electricity. They were exciting and challenging times for William Turton. In the last quarter of the nineteenth century he became the most experienced and respected figure in urban transport in the north of England.

This book views Turton through the social, political and economic context of Leeds and Leeds through his life and contributions, in mutual interaction, at the intersection of social history and biography. The horse tramways bring the town and the man together at the high point of the development of Leeds and the career of William Turton.

When I formed the intention to write this book early in 2006 I was a stranger to both the city and my ancestor. I rapidly made myself familiar with the archives and libraries of Leeds and the British Library newspaper collection. I paced the streets of Leeds and drove around in the outskirts. I met a number of very knowledgeable and generous people. But the most important find was Soper's *Leeds Transport Vol.1 1830–1902* (1985). The first volume of this now completed five-volume *magnum opus* treats, extensively and authoritatively, horse trams, the Leeds Tramways Company and William Turton. It was largely on the strength of this that I felt confident to propose and receive agreement from the Leeds Civic Trust to have a Leeds Blue Plaque placed in his honour on the now Grade II listed shell of Turton's warehouse. Mr Soper has since been most generous in offering me information and advice, and I have quoted extensively from Chapters 6–10, 13 and 17 (some fifty-two pages) of the first volume. In particular Jim Soper has shared his research references to the Leeds newspapers, which are the only source for the meetings of the Leeds Tramways Company share-holders. Needless to say, I have revisited his sources and am responsible for any errors of fact or interpretation.

I have sought to go deeper into some matters and to use new approaches, information and dimensions. The aim is to use the man to illustrate the town and the town to contextualise the man. The mutualities are even more complex as the two do not merely reflect but help to create each other.

Because of its late introduction and longer use in Britain, it was the electric tram that was so celebrated and mourned when urban trams went out of use. So the literature on the horse tram era is not generally strong. One book on the history of horses and their contribution to human society has no mention of omnibuses or trams. A little book on the horse trams of Britain that bemoans the lack of historical accounts of the horse tram, devotes two-thirds of its pages to illustrations. A book on the trams of Yorkshire has no mention of the horse-drawn tram. A book on the trams of Leeds has no reference to either William Turton or Daniel Busby, his associate. I hope to be able to restore some balance.

My initial ignorance of the life of my great-great-grandfather was more of a mystery. My father died when I was 5 years old, at which age I would not expect my grandfather to refer to his grandfather. But he never spoke of him later and seems to have spoken to no one else in the family about him. Nor did my grandfather ever refer to the fact that his father, John, had died when he was 8, nor to the fact that he had a younger brother. Both my grandfather and his brother worked in the corn business with their

Uncle George until about 1912. They moved from Leeds to other places in Yorkshire. They both served for most of the First World War. By 1923 my grandfather had been declared bankrupt following unwise investment in his motor business in Scarborough in a competitive and economically depressed environment. He moved permanently to live in Bournemouth. His brother continued to live in Yorkshire. My grandfather never saw or spoke to or of his brother again. Recently I have restored contact with this branch of the family.

These mysterious gaps in the family history are not redeemed by any family documents. There are two studio portraits of William Turton (both reproduced in this book) and one item of silver that bears his name. Council minutes bear his signature; newspapers contain letters and statements by him reported at shareholders' meeting. Otherwise we have no personal records of the man. There are two material monuments to his name: the family tomb in St Matthew's churchyard and the external structure of his four-storey warehouse in the River Aire at Crown Point Bridge.

In 1999 the West Yorkshire Victorian Society achieved Grade II listed status for the warehouse, and in 2007 the Leeds Civic Trust erected a Blue Plaque in honour of William Turton. This plaque was sponsored by members of the Turton family. At 3.00 p.m. on Friday 28 September 2007 John Turton gave the unveiling address and the author also spoke. The event was attended by many family members, together with representatives of the Leeds Civic Trust, the Leeds Philosophical and Literary Society, the Thoresby Society, the Leeds Transport Historical Society and the West Yorkshire Victoria Society. Most of these are mentioned in the Acknowledgements.

The Blue Plaque is situated to the right of the great archway that led into Turton's warehouse yard, built high enough to admit the highest-laden hay wagon. The keystone has a fine carving of a horse's head that can be seen on the cover of this book. This is deeply appropriate since, along with William himself, the horse is a principal protagonist of this story.

PART I

LEEDS

Moot Hall, Briggate, 1816.

View of Leeds from the East c.*1700: St Peter's parish church in the centre, St John's top right; Tenterfields in foreground (in Thoresby 1715).*

1

GOLDEN FLEECE

The Leeds that William Turton was born in, on 2 January 1825, was only just beginning to resemble a major English industrial town. It was not yet a city in the full constitutional sense. Nor did it have a cathedral or even the ruins of a castle. But it was a substantial town, productive and wealthy, proud of its civic self-sufficiency. It had also begun to suffer the social and environmental consequences of industrial capitalism. It was ready for take-off into an unprecedented and unknowable development of industry and urbanisation.

William Turton's life ran in parallel with this development. He helped to make it happen. His story is also the story of Victorian Leeds. His family came to Leeds from the Yorkshire countryside before the end of the eighteenth century. Their arrival was one consequence of the expansion of industry, the industrial revolution. At that time almost all the new influx of people into Leeds came from the surrounding rural areas.

The themes and topics of our story demand that we examine the origins and development of the town of Leeds, in the West Riding of Yorkshire, as well as of the man, merchant and transport entrepreneur, councillor and civic dignitary.

THE WEALTH OF LEEDS: WOOL AND WOOLLEN CLOTH

People have lived at the site of modern Leeds for two millennia or more, and for good reasons. It was well watered and at a good river crossing. It had a hilly eminence close by, a defensible space that became the site of a castle and then a manor house. From at least the seventh to the eleventh century AD Leeds was a substantial settlement. Stone crosses of the ninth and tenth centuries have been found on the site of St Peter's church. The Domesday Book record of 1086 tells us that Leeds (Ledestune) had a church and a priest, a mill and meadowland, and a population of 200. Perhaps we can call it a large village already bidding to be a town.

There had been trade between Ireland and the Baltic passing through the valley of the Aire since the Bronze Age. The area had been at the centre of the kingdom of the

Brigantes. It became Saxon in the sixth century AD and by 600–650 was under the Danelaw. The period from the late eleventh century to the early thirteenth century was a time of expansion and proliferation of towns throughout England. These usually grew up according to the needs of State, Church and Trade. Leeds had a castle, but not an important one. Kirkstall Abbey was built by Cistercian monks from Fountains Abbey to the north in 1152 but was dissolved 1539. It also had a substantial 'cathedral like' parish church, St Peter's, which was probably rebuilt in the twelfth century, again in the reign of Edward I (1327–77) and yet again after a fire in 1500. William was to be baptised there.

In the case of Leeds, trade was the main factor in its development as a town. Trade meant wool (especially in the period AD 1200–1600) and woollen cloth (especially 1500–1800). The coat of arms of Leeds city to this day includes a 'golden fleece', whose symbolism needs no unravelling. It had been part of the armorial of Leeds' first alderman Sir John Savile when Leeds received its Royal Charter in 1626. His kinsman Sir William Savile was the Royalist who was defeated by the Parliamentary forces under Sir Thomas Fairfax after a brief battle in 1643 at the western edges of Briggate, where the burghers dug trenches literally in their own back gardens.

Like so many towns of importance, Leeds is well placed in terms of access by various means of transport. There is evidence of several Roman roads meeting and crossing the

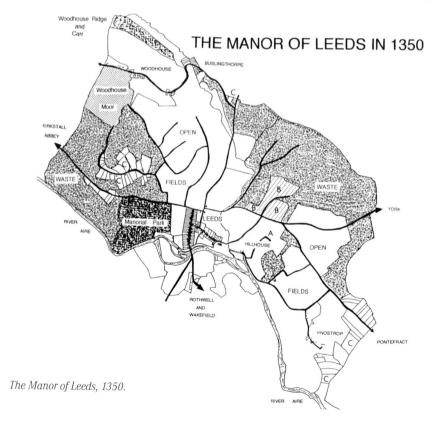

The Manor of Leeds, 1350.

River Aire near or at Leeds, most notably the road from Chester to York. At first there was a ford and later a bridge, probably from the eleventh century or earlier, though the first written record of a bridge is in 1322. A weir, the 'Leeds Dam', was constructed to deepen the port and provide water power for mills. Until 1829 Leeds Bridge was the only bridge over the Aire for many miles. It gives its name to the street Briggate (*brig* meaning bridge and *gata* meaning street in Saxon), which remains the core, the axis, the commercial and transport hub of the city. It was here that William Turton had offices.

Leeds has the privilege of being situated almost exactly half way between London and Edinburgh, and half way between the Irish Sea and the North Sea. The River Aire rises at the limestone cliffs near Malham Tarn, which is to the west of the Pennines. The Aire valley links east and west and at one point it is only about 10 miles from the River Ribble with which it was later to form a canal route to Preston and Liverpool. Seen from the other end, the Aire joins the Calder near Goole and briefly becomes a tributary of the Ouse before entering the Humber. This river route from the North Sea had long been navigable by small craft up to Leeds. With the general development of production and trade from the late sixteenth century, water transport became more sophisticated. The pound lock, which allowed boats to bypass weirs, was widely in use by the end of the sixteenth century. Various canal systems began to be discussed in the seventeenth century, with technical advice from Dutch engineers. After decades of debate, the merchants of Leeds put up their money to build the Aire and Calder Navigation, founded in 1688 and opened in 1689. The main route had few locks and little canal length along the river, so it was faster and cheaper than many such systems. The route went from Leeds to Wakefield and Goole, which became a substantial inland seaport linked with Hull. Goole was strategic enough to be a target for enemy bombing in the First World War. To the south the network extended to Barnsley and Sheffield, to the south-east to Doncaster and to the north-east Selby. It has been described as 'the country's most successful commercial inland waterway'. The system as a whole continued working until late in the twentieth century, and parts have never closed.

Leeds was exceptionally well placed to be a centre of the wool trade. At times it was the most important centre in England. It was close to the sheep rearing, wool producing and weaving districts of Airedale and Calderdale to the west and southwest. These areas were connected to the network of suppliers, variously known as chapmen, hucksters and (wool-) broggers, who bought wool and cloth from small producers at village fairs and farms. These traders sent the wool and cloth on packhorses, combining with river transport when possible, to merchants in Leeds. Leeds also had its water-powered mills and a fulling mill. The rural producers began to add value to their products by spinning and weaving their own wool. Certain districts specialised in worsted (long staple, fine cloth) or kersey (short staple, coarse cloth), and in dyed ('coloured') or undyed and unbleached ('white') cloth. Leeds became more of a finishing centre in the chain of production, shearing, raising the nap, dyeing and so on. By 1534 the historian John Leland visited Leeds on his travels and declared that 'The Town standith [*sic*] most by Clothing'.

At first the export had been of wool, unspun and unwoven. In 1331 John Kempe of Flanders is recorded as having come to England and started to develop woollen cloth weaving. There were others, possibly before and certainly afterwards.

For some time exports of woollen cloth were small. In the period approximately 1375–1420 wool prices were high. Even by present standards Cotswold wool at £4–6 pounds a sack (c.AD 1400) sounds high. In the sixteenth century woollen cloth exports expanded and seem not to have looked back for another 300 years or more.

The first town charter for Leeds was granted in 1207 when it was already trading in wool. The quality of English wool had a high reputation, even higher than that of Spain. By the end of the twelfth century and early thirteenth century there were considerable exports of wool, especially to Flanders, which is roughly equivalent to modern Belgium. The annual export of wool amounted to some 30–50,000 sacks. It has been estimated that 50,000 sacks, the equivalent of the wool of 6 million sheep, was the commodity used to pay the ransom of King Richard I (the 'Lionheart') in 1194, which had been set at 300,000 livres. Leeds became the wealthiest town in West Riding after Wakefield and Pontefract. By 1470 wool production in England was concentrated in the West Riding of Yorkshire.

The Manor of Leeds, 1650.

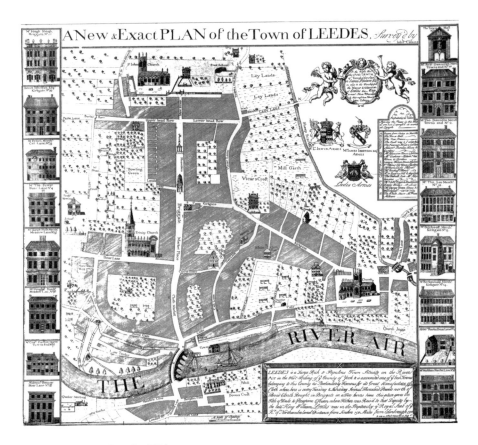

John Cossins Plan of Leeds, 1726.

Leeds had an important market by 1258 and Briggate became the town centre that had formerly been Kirkgate and St Peter's. In 1615 a new Leeds auction market was built. Leeds Moot Hall, or Town Hall, was completed in 1618. Leeds was granted a Royal Charter of Incorporation as a 'free borough' in 1626 by King Charles I. The chief purpose and value of this status was to protect its cloth production and trade. Leeds was now the fourth largest town in England. This epoch was epitomised by the very wealthy and civic minded cloth merchant, mill and landowner John Harrison (1579–1656). He paid for the building of the moot hall (1615–18) and built St John's church, the second church in Leeds, in 1634. He also built almshouses and a small grammar school (founded 1552) in 1624. He was an alderman. One of the most famous figures in Leeds' history, he served as a kind of model for the merchant prince philanthropists of the Victorian age. It is of note that the history of Leeds is not marked much by the participation of great lords and aristocrats.

Two generations later Ralph Thoresby (1658–1725) continued this bourgeois benevolence and civic pride. He too was wealthy from the woollen trade and industry and also inevitably a member of the Town Corporation. He helped raise funds for both the first White Cloth Hall in 1711 and Leeds' third church, Trinity, which was completed in 1727 just after his death. The Leeds Tramways Company was to have its main offices in a yard facing this church. Thoresby was primarily a scholar and antiquarian and he was elected Fellow of the Royal Society. His diaries cover more than forty years of life in Leeds. His collections and scholarly example were honoured in the setting up of The Thoresby Society in 1889, which still flourishes. His book *Ducatus Leodiensis* (published 1715) is the first historical account of Leeds and is another sign of the growing pride and self-consciousness of the town.

Thorseby commented on the corn market at Leeds as being 'very profitable; and the more so, because the Populousness of the Places makes it yield greater profit to the Husband-men than other markets do'.

The town doubled its population during the seventeenth century, despite severe mortality in the plague of 1666 when the parish record listed 1,325 deaths. At about 6,000 in 1700 it was not of great size. Nonetheless, Celia Fiennes (1662–1741) writing of her travels to Yorkshire in 1697–98 says that it was 'the wealthiest town of its size in the country'. And she had visited almost every county in England. Its merchants lived in fine houses of stone and brick. But as in the nineteenth century, both rich and poor could suffer from terrible epidemics such as bubonic plague in 1604, 1644 and 1645. A civic response to health needs was the provision of piped water, one of the earliest systems in provincial England. Many of the town's wealthy citizens had adopted Puritan paths of Christianity and when the political climate allowed, the first 'non-conformist' meeting house was established.

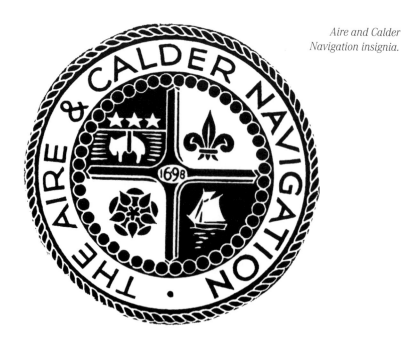

Aire and Calder Navigation insignia.

Benjamin Gott's woollen mill 1792, the first in Europe.

The wool trade expanded throughout the eighteenth century. It was now chiefly woollen manufactures: white cloth, coloured cloth and broadloom, a mixed weave. The grand first White Cloth Hall was built in 1711 and a few years later, 1724, Daniel Defoe saw the market in action and wrote that it was 'a prodigy of its kind unequalled in the world'. A new Coloured Cloth Hall was built in 1758; a third cloth hall was added in 1776. This was in Calls Lane, close to what is now the Corn Exchange; it had 1,000 stalls.

Woollen manufacturing industrialised early. In 1792 Benjamin Gott opened his Bean Ing factory on a 16-acre site to the west of the town. This concentrated all processes under one roof for the first time. It was not only the largest in Leeds but was the largest single employer of industrial workers in Western Europe at the time, with a work-force of 1,200. In 1792 John Marshall (1765–1845) moved his woollen factory to Water Lane in Holbeck, just south of Leeds. His collaborations in developing machinery for both wool and flax manufacture led to important advances, especially in mechanical spinning. By the end of the century, in 1797, Leeds had 130 woollen merchants who controlled the major share of the Yorkshire wool trade. In 1800 Gott expanded and built Armley Mills to the south-west, which is now an industrial museum.

Marshall powered forward the flax industry, using home grown and imported flax. This was a major diversification of the Leeds economy, the first of many, and made Leeds the centre of the flax industry.

This commercial and industrial development of Leeds placed demands on transport systems, and helped to stimulate their development. The Aire and Calder canal served them well from 1699. It is still in use after 300 years, for most of which barges were towed by horses, or horses alongside steam tugs. The Leeds to Liverpool canal was started in 1777 and although its 127-mile length – the longest in Britain – was not fully open until 1816, some stretches were usable from the start. From 1758 a four-mile 'horse railroad' delivered coal from the Middleton colliery to Leeds. The packhorse continued to be essential in the capillary stages of transport of cloth and other goods to distribution points on the canals.

THE GROWTH OF CIVIL SOCIETY

In terms of 'civil society', in just about any sense of the term, Leeds was on an improving curve in the eighteenth century. The new Town Hall, or rather 'moot hall', a perennial index of the development of Leeds, was rebuilt in 1710 and a small marble statue of Queen Anne was erected on its façade in 1713, the year before her death. In 1787 the moot hall clock was added. Public meetings, however, even those called by the mayor and council, often took place in pubs, a tradition still in use in Turton's time as a councillor. Cossin's cartography of 1726 literally put Leeds on the map. This map is illustrated with eighteen drawings of the façades of the house of the most prominent merchants. None of these survive. It is interesting that the general scale and proportion of these town houses are similar to those of the house William Turton built for himself at the height of his career. Civic infrastructural improvements resulted in the introduction in 1755 of street lighting and paving in some central parts of the town. The Leeds Infirmary was inaugurated in 1767 (expanded twice in the 1780s and again in the 1820s). It moved to Great George Street in 1868.

The eighteenth century was largely peaceful for Leeds. The threat of a Jacobite army attacking Leeds in 1745 led to the town preparing its defences and levying volunteer soldiers. Even worse to contemplate, in 1793 a French invasion was thought to be imminent. Once again Leeds braced itself, and once again the threat was not realised. This led to the forming of the Leeds Volunteers, a paramilitary unit. This was also in part a precaution against a perceived threat by the élite that the English lower classes might emulate their revolutionary neighbours in France. There had been a number of popular protests and riots during the century. In the corn riots of 1715 there were three deaths, but there was nothing on the scale of nineteenth-century militancy to come.

The rise of non-conformism was furthered by the advent of Methodism from 1742, but the established Church of England was still the predominant form of Christian association, a position it was to lose by the 1830s. But in the middle of the eighteenth century St Peter's, still 'the Parish Church of Leeds', had a congregation of 3–4,000 and was reportedly packed for services, with wooden galleries being added to accommodate the faithful. Various forms of Methodism together constituted a plurality of all religious sects in the nineteenth century. John Wesley had visited Leeds several times. On the last occasion, among weightier matters, he is said to have held a nine-month baby on his knee and blessed him. This was Richard Oastler, the 'radical Tory' whose campaigns against 'child slavery' in Leeds and nationally we shall return to later.

In common with other substantial English towns, the middle classes in Leeds – in effect they were the urban upper class – began to have new tastes and aspirations to a 'genteel society', a civil society, in both social and more political terms. This period corresponds roughly with the long reign of King George III (1760–1820). Education was largely for the middle classes. They read the newspaper the *Leeds Intelligencer*, which started in 1754, and its competitor *The Leeds Mercury* (1718). The latter, which is to play a large part in our story, was bought by Edward Baines in 1801. His family was to dominate the newspaper scene for most of the nineteenth century. In 1768 the Leeds Library opened. This library, rebuilt in Commercial Street in 1808, is the oldest continuously operated private lending library in the country. One of the founders was Joseph Priestley, who was for many years minister at the Mill Hill Unitarian chapel in Leeds. In 1776, when the New Cloth Hall was opened, the Leeds Assembly Rooms opened its membership to the upper and upper middle-classes for social gatherings, dancing, cards and so on. As a sign of the times, in 1858 it became home to the Leeds Working Men's Association. The Theatre Royal (1771) in Hunslet, and the Music Hall (1792) also served the new middle classes.

This social tendency and 'society' required new comfortable and fashionable housing. In 1772 some 3,000 new houses were built and by 1792 a total of 6,000, thereafter increasing at a rate of 5 per cent of housing stock per annum. In 1793 Park Square was begun, with its typical 'Georgian' style, just west of old central Leeds, but was not completed until 1815. It was soon to fall victim to that paradox of the 'social limits to economic growth' (Fred Hirsch, 1977) – you can't keep the smoke, pollution and disease out of 'the west end'. Working people were fortunate if they could occupy the new two-storey 'back-to-backs' built especially for the factory workers. There was much worse on offer, but the new houses themselves soon became the overpopulated and foul dwellings of the mid-nineteenth century.

Sir Frederick Eden (1797, Vol.III) reported on Leeds Township in 1775. It had a population of 17,117, with 7,000 families of which 1,836 paid the 'window tax'. Land was extremely expensive at from £2–5 to £300 per acre but up to £1,000 for land adapted to building. In general the cost of living in Leeds was the highest in the north of England. Wages were 2–3s per day for artisans and wool workers, 1s 3d–1s 6d for labourers.

William Turton's grandfather, Richard Turton, was working in Leeds in Black Bank at the end of the eighteenth century. We do not know what his profession or calling was. Since his name does not appear in the earliest directory of this time, he might have been a small artisan, shopkeeper, or small farmer. But it is most likely he was at least in part a corn or hay merchant, since that was already the trade of his son John when he married at the age of 20. He would not have been immune to the economic fluctuations of the times. In the 1790s there were bad harvests, which combined with the exactions of the war with France to depress living conditions for the majority.

As early as 1797 we begin to hear reports on the conditions of the working classes: 'Cellars, Garretts and such like Places exhibit ... abodes of human Misery, the wretched

Inhabitants are frequently found either exercising the last Efforts of Nature to support themselves ... or languishing under the most powerful Influence of the most complicated Disease.' These comments would still be apt and echoed fifty and a hundred years later.

Mutual Benefit Clubs were formed. Employers such as Gott donated blankets and soup kitchens. The noble Earls Cardigan and Cowper gave sparse support to the poor of their estates. The Middleton Colliery miners went on strike in 1796. London viewed Leeds in clichéd terms as a 'hotbed of sedition'. The works of Thomas Paine spread like wildfire, stronger than the patriotic fires that burnt his effigy in public places. What would the nineteenth century hold for the people of Leeds?

2

'UNHAPPY ABODES OF FILTHY MISERY'

The Aire below is doubly dyed and damned;
The air above, with lurid smoke is crammed;
The one flows steaming foul as Charon's Styx,
Its poisonous vapours in the other mix.
These sable twins the murky town invest,
By them the skin's begrimed, the lungs oppressed.
How dear the penalty thus paid for wealth;
The joyful Sabbath comes; that blessed day,
When all seem happy, and when all seem gay!
Then toil has ceased, and then both rich and poor,
Fly off to Harrogate, or Woodhouse moor.
The one his villa and a carriage keeps;
His squalid brother in a garret sleeps,
High flaunting forest trees, low crouching weeds,
Can this be Manchester? or is it Leeds.

Anonymous epigram, late eighteenth or early nineteenth century, read to the Leeds Philosophical and Literary Society on 20 January 1857 by William Osburn Esq.

'It is hard to over-emphasise the diabolical misery of the early Victorian city.'
(Hunt p. 16, 2004)

Sykes Yard off York Street 1901; at No. 10, there were twenty residents on two floors and a cellar.

The Poor Man's Friend *by John Leech (180–64), from* Punch *February 1845; death portrayed as more welcome than the workhouse seen through the window. Leech later painted portraits of William Turton and his first wife, Sarah. These and other paintings are referred to in Turton's will.*

THE POOR MAN'S FRIEND.

SURVIVAL

Survival, against the odds, is one of the wonders of any sort of early family history and never more so than in nineteenth-century Leeds. William Turton was born, on 2 January 1825 in the eastern part of the town. His parents John and Elizabeth were young and healthy. His mother was nineteen, and it was almost certainly her first pregnancy. She lived until her early forties, he to thirty-eight, which was above the life expectancy at birth for their class. They had five children who survived beyond infancy, and as far as I can tell, into adulthood. Even so, on average a woman was likely to have as many or more children die soon after birth or in infancy as survived. Elizabeth had gaps of rather more than two years between her children, so this cannot rule out some early 'perishers', but perhaps she was fortunate.

William's father, John, had been born in 1804. He had grown up in a Leeds that was not only industrialising fast but had reached the age when steam power had begun to be the driving force in industry. In turn John's father, Richard Turton, was born in c.1769 and lived at 'Black Bank' off Marsh Lane in the east of Leeds. He and his wife had six surviving children, two girls and four boys. The eldest was born in about 1798. John was their fourth child.

Since our story is about a merchant who supplied food for the horses that drew the transport for an increasing urban population, demographics are of special interest. We have quite accurate population census records for each decade of the nineteenth century. These figures are used for many purposes and calculations, so a brief introductory word may help. The population of Leeds is given for the municipal area of the town borough and separately for the outlying townships. In some accounts of Leeds it is not clear which figure is being used, though more often than not it is the larger total. Thus in 1801 the population of Leeds town was 30,669 and together with the townships 53,276. In 1901 the figures were 177,920 and 428,968 respectively. The relevant units are, first the old manor, which is more or less coterminous with Leeds township, and more loosely with central Leeds. Then comes the Parish of Leeds, which contained the Manor and the out townships. Later other townships or neighbouring villages were added to Leeds Borough and the most recent entity, the Leeds Metropolitan Borough, extends further still to Otley, Wetherby, Rothwell and Morley.

The townships are mainly to the north, west and south-west. In order of size in 1901 they are: Hunslet, Headingley, Holbeck, Armley, Wortley, Potternewton, Bramley, Chapel Allerton, Farnley and Beeston. The order of size remained fairly similar over the years, with notable exceptions of Headingley and Potternewton in the north which expanded faster.

As we shall see, the story of the development of urban passenger transport, especially the horse tram, in the last quarter of the nineteenth-century is largely about the connecting of the townships with central Leeds.

Despite the steady increase in population, the death rate was high, infant mortality especially high, and life expectancy at birth incredibly low as seen from the twenty-first century. We have the following much cited piece of information about the average age at death in 1842, the year after John Turton, William's father, a corn dealer, died aged 38. The figures must be considered as 'literary' rather than strictly 'statistical' evidence, but they are part of a comparison made between several parts of England urban and rural, north and south. For Leeds the average life expectancy was given as: Gentry, 44; Tradesmen, 27; Labourers, 19, with an overall average of just 21. This is hard to assimilate. It includes of course all deaths from the earliest neo-natal (though maybe not all these were recorded). Bear in mind that as recently as 1911 the number of infant deaths in Leeds was 123 per thousand. This compares with one of the worst boroughs in London, Islington, with 115 per thousand in that year.

The population of Leeds was increasing spectacularly due to immigration from rural Yorkshire and Ireland. Leeds came to have the largest Irish population in Yorkshire: 5,000 in 1841, 10,000 in 1851 and 15,000 by 1861, which was then 12 per cent of the total population. Most of the Irish lived in the poorer eastern parts of Leeds where William grew up and where he traded.

Population naturally increased from within. Nevertheless at times of crisis, such as after the spring floods of 1839, when sewers were choked and cellar dwellings were inundated, there were three deaths for every two births in the eastern part of town.

Epidemics of contagious and infectious diseases had catastrophic effects in some years. The cholera epidemic of 1832 came at a time when much attention was being focused nationally and locally on the conditions of the people. Seven hundred people died in Leeds. St Peter's church, at that time still the old medieval building, was the main parish church of Leeds. It had to extend its graveyards and buried 642 people during the 5 months June–October and 453 in just August and September at the end of a long, hot and terrible summer. Twenty-one people died of cholera in Marsh Lane alone, close to William's birthplace. His wife Elizabeth had three small children and gave birth to another in that year.

There were further epidemics: in 1847 typhus; in 1848 cholera, with 2,000 deaths in Leeds; and in 1849 small pox. These were the first five years of William's youthful enterprise. Even as late as 1889 an epidemic of typhus fever occurred, sparing people of no social classes. Alas typhus fever was sometimes referred to as 'Irish fever'.

The death toll was due to a large extent to new circumstances in social history. The old ones – dearth, disease and epidemics, relative lack of medical knowledge and care and its provision – continued. But now there were new dangers from industrial pollution of air, water and food, and of accidents caused by industrial machinery. The famous Leeds surgeon Dr Turner Thackrah had a strong concern for occupational health. He recorded that some 450 deaths occurred each year in Leeds from machinery accidents. He also expressed doubt as to whether as many as 10 per cent of people in Leeds enjoyed 'full health'.

LEEDS FROM THE OUTSIDE

We have many subjective accounts of the quality of urban life in Leeds in the early nineteenth century. The writers are often well travelled in England and Europe and many are aware of official reports and so on. They are thus in a position to make well-observed comparisons. They give a telling and not at all pleasant picture.

One might expect the earlier accounts to be more favourable. John Dyer, who has been described as 'the poet of English business', wrote in 1757:

> The ruddy roofs and chimney tops:
> Of busy Leeds upwafting to the clouds
> The incense of thanksgiving; all is joy.

'Incense of thanksgiving' must be the cruellest irony. William Cobbett in his *Rural Rides* (collected 1830) writes of 'this fine and opulent town, which may be called the London of Yorkshire'. Perhaps this does not rule out the worst. But already in 1820 William Hazlitt sighed 'Oh! Smoked city! Dull and dirty Leeds!'

A detailed account of 1819 contrasts the east, William's home zone, with the still fairly fashionable 'west end':

> In the eastern parts (Sheepscar Beck) [a stream that runs close to William Turton's birthplace] the houses are mean, and the streets and lanes dirty, crooked and irregular, emitting disagreeable smells from the dying houses and different manufactures, while the discoloured and dirty torrent puts a person in mind of Styx and Cocytus .... The southern edge of the town, along the banks of the Aire, is almost equally disagreeable, and although containing some good houses, has, in good measure, the appearance of a prison.

Barclay Fox, a Quaker visitor from less industrialised south-western England, wrote in 1836:

> Leeds amongst all others of its species the vilest of the vile. At a mile distant from the town we came under a vast dingy canopy formed by the impure exhalation of a hundred furnaces. It sits on the town like an everlasting incubus, shutting out the light and the breath of summer. I pity its poor denizens. London is a joke to it.

His judgement was shared by a German traveller with wide experience of England and towns of continental Europe: 'The manufacturing cities of England are none of them very attractive or pleasing in appearance, but Leeds is, perhaps, the ugliest and least attractive town in all England' (1842). Charles Dickens visited Leeds in the company of George Stephenson and described it as 'The beastliest place, one of the nastiest I know.'

UNEVEN DEVELOPMENT

Leeds was in the vanguard of the industrial revolution in England, from the start-up years of about 1780–1800. And of course, with hindsight we know that England was in the vanguard of industrialisation in the wider world. In fact even as late as 1848 it was the only fully industrialised economy in the world. In addition to England in the 1820s only France and the USA had any great number of steam-powered machines. The Stockton to Darlington steam passenger railway started operation in 1825 and in the next thirty years the production of iron and coal in England tripled. This supplied the railways; what fed the horses will be a major theme of this account. In Leeds the textile mills, wool and flax, and ancillary industries, such as dying and tanning, were still the main driving forces and employers. At Crown Point, on the river just east of St Peter's and close to so many of the scenes of William's life, there was a mill in 1794 with a rateable value of £100 and in 1801 a steam engine owned by Snowdon and Hodgson's Mill with a rateable value of £600, insured by Sun Insurance Co. The seven-storey warehouse on the north-east corner of Leeds Bridge built by 1826 was the tallest in Leeds – if not nearly as extensive as Gott's Mill – and may have given a 'prison like' feel to the urban landscape.

The condition of the river Aire was of constant concern, but little was done to improve things. An article in a newspaper of 1841 gives a detailed description:

> In that part of the river, extending from Armley to the King's Mills [a distance of maybe three miles or so], it is charged with the drainage and contents of about two hundred water-closets, cesspools, and privvies [sic], a great number of common drains, the drainage from dung heaps, the infirmary (dead leeches, poultices from patients, etc.) slaughter houses, chemical soap, gas, drug, dye-houses, and manufactures, old wine wash, with all sorts of dead animal and vegetable substances, and now and then a decomposed human body; forming an annual mass of filth equivalent to 30 millions of gallons.

Twenty-five years later, in 1867, another report on pollution of the Aire referred to similar, perhaps worse conditions. It again refers to waste from hospitals and dye-works, and specifically mentions that fifty dead animals were taken *daily* from the river Aire in central parts of Leeds.

In the very early years of the nineteenth century the waterworks company had supplied only about 2,000 households with piped water. For household purposes most people used water from the Aire, together with wells and bore holes. Water carriers sold drinking water from their carts, but the great majority of people would be most unlikely to pay even for their drinking water. This puts the consumption of tea and beer into perspective. As William Cobbett notably complained, domestic consumption of weak beer for adults and children alike had been undermined by longer working hours for women, the widespread availability of cheap tea and the rise of industrial-scale breweries. By 1830 the Aire was said to be completely unsafe for drinking. The Leeds Waterworks Company nonetheless continued to use water from the Aire from further upstream, until 1841. The waterworks was the first utility to be municipalised in 1852.

These environmental conditions affected most people. But the more intimate environment of housing was much more variable and for many people constituted terrible risks. Most people spent little time at home, and almost none in daylight hours. Walking to work for a sixteen-hour day six days a week did not allow for much other than sleeping. Some children slept in the factories where they worked; perhaps they could find a warmer corner and some cloth waste to sleep on.

Housing conditions became a national issue from the time of the reforms starting in 1832, and the amount of detailed information available is remarkable. Frederick Engels was a young, wealthy textile manufacturer in Manchester, influenced by the heady new philosophy and politics coming out of Germany and France. At the time he published his *The Condition of the Working Class in England* in 1844 he was just 24 years old, the very year William started in business on his own, aged 19. The title page says it was 'from personal observation and authentic sources'. Engels had visited Leeds. He cites extensively from the Chartist journal *The Artisan* of October 1843. Amongst many detailed observations are:

> ... the disgusting state of the working-men's districts about Kirkgate, Marsh Lane, Cross Street and Richmond Road ... all this taken together is explanation enough of the excessive mortality in these *unhappy abodes of filthy misery.* In consequence of the overflows of the Aire the houses are often so full of water they have to be pumped out.

Very few people in Leeds owned property. In the East Ward in 1839 only 1.8 per cent of households had owner-occupiers, and the figure for the town as a whole was only 3.8 per cent. Landowners had filled just about every corner of space to provide basic dwellings; alleys, lanes, courts, yards and cul-de-sacs were crammed together. A typical 'cottage' or single dwelling was a cellar and two rooms above on an area of five square yards. Back-to-backs could mean stacks of four storeys with 'blind-backed' dwellings on each side of one room only in depth. Cellar dwellings were the worst (including to some extent the cellars of the richer households, where servants might live) and often cited as a cause of ill health. Blocks of houses might share a cesspool, with dangers of methane gas poisoning. 'Privies' were rare, and in one instance two 'simple privies' were shared by housing occupied by 386 persons. Not until 1899 was it compulsory for houses to be connected to the town sewers. People kept chickens and even pigs in their dwellings. Bacon was probably the most important luxury in the working-class diet. When municipal efforts were made to discourage this, a 'Leeds Pig Protection Society' was established in 1867 to protect the rights of domestic pig owners, if not exactly the pigs themselves!

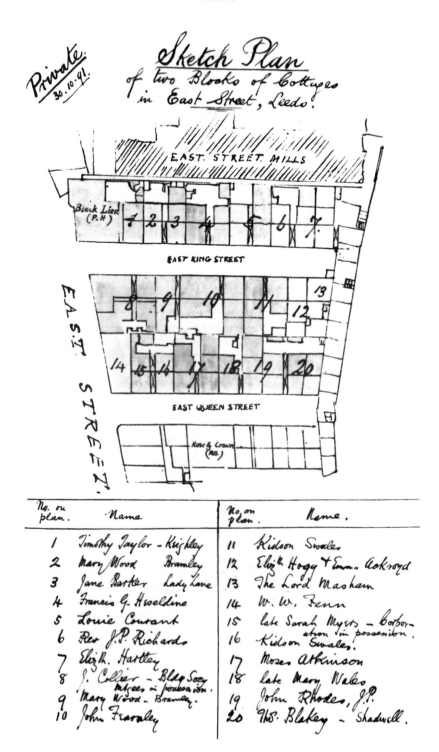

Sketch of 106 back-to backs, East Street, built 1788, given to Beatrice and Sydney Webb in 1891.

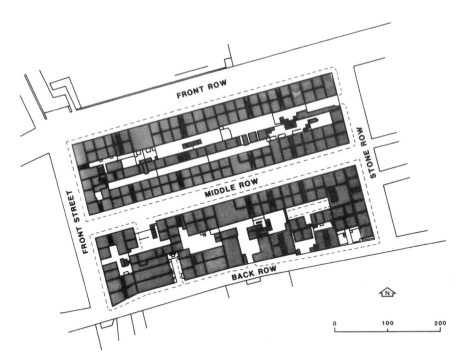

Plan of back-to-back housing c. 1807.

Almost every room would be used for both sleeping and other uses. People of different sexes, generations and indeed families might sleep in the same room, often on straw. Light and ventilation were minimal. 'Furniture' might be at most two or three three-legged stools and a couple of tea chests for tables and storage. Many lived in 'common lodging houses' with two to six lodgers in addition to the householders.

Housing space and quality in itself was not the main problem. It was pollution of the air by industrial gases, smoke and particles, and of the land and water from every sort of waste product of human, animal, vegetable and industrial origin. Leeds had its tradition of medical care but it was incapable of keeping up with demands. The Leeds Dispensary opened in 1822. A Medical School was founded in 1831. In 1833 a report by six physicians and thirty-eight surgeons highlighted the importance of drainage, sewerage and general cleanliness. A few years later Leeds Infirmary was completed. In 1842 a new Leeds Improvement Act, one of many enabling acts of similar name, authorised three new rates and a public loan of £100,000. These beneficial acts were often unpopular not only in the view of those required to pay the rates, but for perceived infringements of various popular rights and freedoms.

The Reform of Parliament Act of 1832 enfranchised the middle class – a term which had been in use from about 1812. At least if you paid rates to contribute to the welfare of the deserving poor, you had a vote. You also had a vote if you were 'a £10 householder'. This meant paying £10 or more per annum in house rent, which was an assessable measure of urban economic status. If we turn again to the East Ward of Leeds, an electoral unit established precisely by the 1832 Reform Act, we find that in 1837 the average house rent was £5.38, and in some streets as low as £3.50. Most would be 'sub-let'. The average for the 'west end' of town was £9.00. And you needed to be paying £10.00 or more to get the vote. So the government did not need to be too worried about opening the floodgates of popular democracy. In 1842 some 93 per cent of the population of East Ward was working class. Beresford's fine book *Leeds East and West*, making good use of Robert Baker's statistical and cartographic reports of the period, offers further contrasts between these social zones. The east contained a larger pro-portion of the town population; it was denser; it had poorer housing stock; it had a far greater chance of epidemics. There are also some interesting contrasts in types of houses and households:

Types of household in Leeds 1842	East	West
Common lodging houses	38	nil
Beer houses	135	34
Inns	76	26
'Houses of ill fame'	72	12
Irish heads of households	915	48

Humphrey Boyle, a shopkeeper in Meadow Lane calculated an average family budget in 1832 as follows:

Weekly household budget for a family of five in 1832	£	s	d
Rent 2/-, fuel 9d, candle 3d		3	0
Soap 3d, soda 1d, blue and starch 1½d			5½
Sand, black lead, bees wax etc.			2
Whitewashing a cottage twice a year			½
1½ stone flour for bread – at 2/6d per stone		3	9
¼ stone flour for puddings – at 2/8d per stone			8
Eggs 2d yeast 1 ½			3 ½
1½ pints milk per day at 1 ¼		1	1
¼ stone oatmeal at 2/2d per stone			6 ½
1lb treacle 3 ½d, sugar at 7d per pound		1	2
1½ oz tea 5d, 2 oz coffee 1 ½			10½

5lb meat at *6d* per pound		2	6
Vegetables 1*d* per day			7
Salt, pepper, mustard, vinegar			2
7 pts beer at 1½*d* per pint			10½
Water			1
Schooling for 2 children			6
Reading			2
Wear and tear in beds, bedding, brushes,pots, pans and other household furniture			6
Clothing: husband ½*d*, wife 8*d*		1	10
each child 4*d*		1	0
Total	£1	0*s*	3*d*

Summary			
Food and drink		12*s*	7*d*
Clothing		2*s*	10*d*
Rent		2*s*	
Fuel and light		1*s*	
Cleaning			8*d*
Education			8*d*
Wear and tear, furniture, utensils etc.			6*d*

Many were forced into the workhouse and others met an early death, 'the poor man's friend'. Even if one other member of the household contributed, there would have been little chance of saving or of occasional 'luxuries' such as oranges for a celebration. The better-off and 'prudent' poor might pay a small subscription to a Friendly Society such as The Foresters to cover sick pay, medical treatment and funeral expenses.

These are some of the conditions in East Leeds at the time when William was growing up there. As we shall see his sister Mary, like so many of the children from the area, worked in a mill as a factory hand. So it is appropriate to conclude this chapter with a look at some of the conditions of work for the young.

An article in the *Leeds Mercury* on 16 October 1830 had a resounding impact on the political classes of Leeds. It was entitled 'Yorkshire Slavery' and it described and deplored the hours, conditions and remuneration of work by children. Young children, especially girls from the age of seven, were required to work a thirteen hour day, including a notional half hour meal break, between the hours of 6.00 am and 7.00 pm. For this work they received 2*s* a week. Many families depended entirely on the income from the labour of their children. The author of this broadside against the

Leeds merchant élite was Richard Oastler (1789–1861), son of a Leeds cloth merchant. Many Liberals and Whigs, and Tories such as Oastler, were supporters of the anti-slavery movement, which had already ended the slave trade, if not entirely slavery, in the British colonies. He urged them 'not to forget that Britons have common right with Afric's sons'.

Several towns in the North including Leeds set up 'Short-Time Committees'. They urged candidates in the 1832 election to support a Ten Hour Bill. The movement was linked to Parliamentary reform, opposition to the Corn Laws and resistance to the new Poor Law. A Ten Hour Act was passed in 1847 and revised in 1850. The author of the standard biography of Oastler summarises the law as follows:

> The law now protected three classes of workers: children aged 8–13, young people 14–18 and women. No children under eight to work in factories – this was in effect a factory act not a general law. Children to work no more than six and a half hour day. Young people and women to work ten and a half hours, exclusive of mealtimes, and only up to 2,00 pm on Saturdays, effectively a 60 hour week. Enforcement of the law was quite different matter, and the campaign for a universal ten-hour day continued throughout the century.

Oastler was a deeply religious evangelical Christian. He was a strange mixture of deference and rebelliousness. He was steward on the Squire Fixby's estate at an annual salary of £300 for eighteen years, during which he led a successful tithe revolt of tenant farmers against a greedy Anglican incumbent. He is said to have 'created that most striking of all English paradoxes – the conception of Tory democracy'. He was a patriotic Tory who defended the social hierarchy, yet a radical Tory. The Radicals in and outside the Liberal Party called him 'a supple and reactionary Tory'. The Whiggish Liberals regarded him as a dangerous socialist. The Huddersfield Short-Time Committee had indeed said that 'The root of the trouble was the unrestrained competition which led to repeated wage cuts and the simultaneous intensification of labour'. While lacking an explanatory theory, this analysis has some resemblance to Marxian socialism. Many of his supporters were Chartists, but he was opposed to revolutionary Chartism. He was known as 'the Danton of the factory movement', and also with folkloric irony as 'the Factory King'. Yet eventually Disraeli was to take up many of his themes.

William Turton knew about Oastler; almost everybody knew about Oastler. Even Edward Baines, a strong opponent, wrote after Oastler's death that 'His name was once a household word in every working man's home in Yorkshire and Lancashire.' It will be interesting to consider what themes in Oastler's Toryism might have resonated with William Turton. As the only direct connection we can show is the tenuous one that Turton owned properties in humble Oastler Terrace, off North Street, now no longer on the map. And in 2005 a Leeds Civic Trust Blue Plaque to Oastler was placed in St Peter's Square by the leader of the Labour Council. This was two years before Turton received his Blue Plaque, not so far away.

PART II

INITIAL CAPITAL

1844–1870

Leeds Corn Exchange soon after opening in 1863.

S. Peter's
(Parish) Church
from the River

PERCY ROBINSON DEL. 1894

St Peter's parish church from the Aire 1894, drawn during rebuilding on the south side of The Calls. Built by R.D. Chantrell 1837–41 and Vicar Walter Farquhar Hook (in Leeds 1837–59), with voluntary contributions of over £29,000. A church has stood on the site since the early seventh century.

3

WILLIAM – APPRENTICE MECHANIC; MARY – FLAX MILL WORKER

What were William's early experiences from his birth in 1825 until say 1840, when his parents were still alive and he had four younger siblings? When I started this enquiry I half suspected I might be dealing with a 'rags to riches' story. How can we assess where and what he started from? His father, John, gave his occupation as 'corn miller' on his marriage certificate in 1824 and again on the registration of William's baptism in 1825. This suggests a degree of wellbeing and success. But he was only twenty and maybe his father had started him off. This man, William's grandfather Richard, lived in East Leeds, which was mainly agricultural at the time. He might have been a small farmer. If he helped John, he would certainly have helped his older son George. George was a corn dealer of some sort. He is often also listed as keeping a 'beer house' from the 1830s, after the Beer Act had allowed householders to make and sell beer from their homes or premises.

The annual directories of professions, trades, private residences and other municipal information are a helpful source for our period. One refers to Turton as a 'corn dealer' in 1837, and then a 'shopkeeper' in 1839. Census categories may not be too reliable or consistent. But this could suggest a move into smaller scale retail trade, or a decline in fortune, and possibly in health? This would still make him a small trader and so presumably not to be counted among the 93 per cent 'working class' population of East Ward in 1842. But none of his younger children of school age in 1841 (Joseph 11, Elizabeth 9, Martha 6) are listed as 'scholars' (i.e. at school), so they may have worked for wages. As we shall see William was an apprentice and his younger sister Mary was a 14-year-old factory worker.

When John Turton died of consumption (tuberculosis) early in 1841, his wife Elizabeth was left with a rented accommodation at No. 122 York Street, which was also a trading address. She remained there until at least 1843. She had no resident servants or employees. But neither did she have any lodgers. She had five children, of whom only one received a very low wage. Elizabeth continued to run the shop – whatever that was – on her own. Young Joseph would be beginning to help, together with William and Mary in whatever time they had to spare after long working hours. And girls aged 9, or even younger, can be pretty handy at helping keep shop.

William would have begun to be aware of his environment beyond the immediate family from the early 1830s. This, as we have seen, is the period in which two reliable witnesses refer to Leeds as 'the vilest of the vile' (Fox, 1836) and 'the ugliest town in England' (Kohl, 1842). He was no stranger to the local people and the local streets that were the 'unhappy abodes of filth and misery', situated in just about the worst part of the town.

At the same time Leeds was a place of superlatives, of 'improvement', 'reform' and all manner of 'advancement'. For some contemporaries, however, it was already clear that this progress, this amazing story of the growth of industrial capitalism, was precisely the cause of the misery as well as the triumphs and the glory.

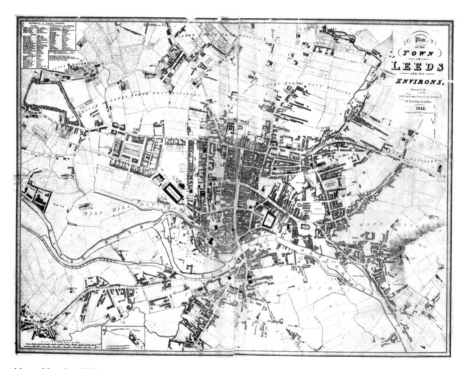

Map of Leeds, 1815.

The accession to the throne of Queen Victoria in 1837, aged just 18, and her marriage three years later to Prince Albert probably did not cause much of a stir among the people of Leeds. One might say that popular monarchy had not yet been invented as an institution. But William's attention, his imagination and excitement must have been stimulated by the rebuilding of St Peter's parish church (1837−41), the building of Crown Point Bridge, central Leeds' second major bridge in a millennium (1840−42), and Clarence Docks (1840−43). They were all massive and expensive projects. Transport was at a watershed. Steam trains had arrived. Borough Station in Marsh Lane was opened in 1835 providing Leeds' first passenger train service, to Selby in the east. It was still the heyday of the stagecoach for intercity routes, with 130 arrivals and departures daily in Leeds. The horse-drawn omnibus was the main new feature of inner-city transport in the 1830s.

William lived close to people in far worse conditions and with far worse life chances than himself. He would be aware of the considerable numbers of people newly arrived from Ireland who settled most densely in that part of town. They would be quite distinctive and visible as part of the work force needed by these new construction projects. He would know something of working conditions in the factories from what his sister told him. He used the same streets, breathed the same air, felt the same effects of the River Aire on his doorstep. He must have had a memory of the cholera outbreak in 1832 when he was seven and a half years old. Surely he would recall the little boxes being carried shoulder high and the carts trundling towards St Peter's graveyard. He would not forget his mother's dire warnings of where not to go and what not to do to avoid the plague.

Leeds and the River Aire from the east c.1830; Leeds Dam in centre, Lock on the left; St Peter's on the right.

William would have been brought up to have views on people's religious ideas and practices. He would have been exposed to the animosities and social exclusiveness that often go with such divisions, since Christians of all kinds regularly called the others 'godless'. There is no suggestion at all that this became an issue for him. He was baptised, aged 4 months, in St Peter's parish church, the established church of Leeds that had occupied the site for a thousand years. We can be fairly sure that he was to some degree a 'practising' or 'church-going' Anglican all his life, and members of his family would have been too. The new Irish were Catholics, but the main, and by the 1830s preponderant, tendency was non-conformism, from Unitarianism to Methodism of various hues.

Education and literacy are useful indicators for assessing William's background. At marriage his father signed his name and his young mother 'made her mark'. At this time about 60 per cent of women 'made their mark' on registers, and about 40 per cent of men. William attended St Peter's Parish School. The Sunday school movement had taken off in the 1780s, and by 1817 most churches had their own Sunday schools. In the 1830s there were some fifty Sunday schools in Leeds Township, of which fourteen were Anglican and which had an average of about 300 children each. The few other public or private schools educated a very small number of children. At least William's parents would not have been among those who are said to have been too ashamed of their children's clothes to send them to Sunday school. We must bear in mind that Sunday Schools were not only a religious 'top-up', as we might think of them now.

Leeds Grammar School.

For most children Sunday was the only day available for schooling. Children may or not have enjoyed it but it was at least an occasion of a couple of hours or so when they might sing hymns, say prayers and listen to strange but optimistic stories. The outings were popular. Children seldom spent more than a year or two at Sunday school and left by the age of 11. Basic literacy was by no means the rule, though for many it was the only chance to begin to learn how to read and write. William seems to have had a lasting respect and affection for the Sunday school, as he left sums of money in his will to St Peter's and another Sunday school.

I would not say that young William never wore clogs – they were an almost universal form of footwear – but a sure sign that he did not go in a 'clog-wise direction', as a family wit has quipped, was that he attended Leeds Grammar School (LGS). What does this tell us?

William is recorded as having attended LGS at the age of eleven for six months from 16 January 1837 to mid-summer 1837. His cousin William, son of John Turton's older brother George, went with him, aged just 9 and remained for a full eighteen months.

LGS was a school for the male offspring of the Leeds urban middle class, or at least those who had aspirations and did not prefer a non-conformist education. The school in North Street was refounded in the seventeenth century by John Harrison. It was expanded in 1823. The headmaster from 1830–54 was Rev. Dr Joseph Holmes DD, who received one of the largest salary incomes of anyone in Leeds. It was rare for any boy to stay at the school for more than three years and a good two-thirds left within two years. This puts William's very short stay into perspective. In 1837 there were thirty-three pupils of whom:

Length of enrolment at Leeds Grammar School 1837
6 left after 6 months (including William)
18 left after 6 months to 2 years (including his cousin)
6 left after 2.5 to 3.5 years
3 left after 5.5 to 10.75 years

Despite such short stays, we are told that in the period 1820–1901 as many as 64 per cent of all leavers later entered the professions (medicine, law, the clergy, military and others).

My best guess is that at the time Uncle George had decided to send his son William aged 9 to LGS and William son of John accompanied him. The editor of the LGS Admissions Books wrote in 1901:

It is to be feared that many parents thought that they were doing the best they could for their children by sending them to [Leeds Grammar School], but took them away when they found that what they were learning would not help them much in after life.

Throughout the century many well-known Leeds families, including Methodists, sent their sons to LGS. These included families into which Turtons were to marry and with whom William had important business and political dealings: Maude, Pegler, Thomas Green, Kitson, Baines, Lupton, Nussey and others.

The decision to apprentice William was taken by his father not long after leaving LGS, perhaps aged 12. He was well placed to be nominated for a parish apprenticeship, otherwise an apprenticeship could cost as much as £40. What did John have in mind for his son? Was it an apprenticeship in engineering ('a machine maker's apprentice'), which was a rapidly advancing trade, seen as a means of becoming a high wage earner, or a self-employed artisan? Was it to provide a training that would serve him well if he was to continue in his father's business? Was it to give him the option? Or, in a pessimistic reading, was it because the family business or John's health had declined? In any case it improved his basic numeracy and literacy. It gave him an understanding of machinery and engines that would become increasingly relevant as his career developed. He was always able to keep up with the head-spinning progress of technology and invention.

Apprenticeship had for many years been deregulated after centuries of tight legal restrictions. In the old days apprentices usually started before their fourteenth birthday and worked for some four to six years depending on the trade and other factors such as form of sponsorship. William's father's death, in early 1841 when William had just had his 16th birthday, must have affected his plans. The next three years are crucial, watershed years. At the end of them William is a mature young man and had started, in no doubt a modest way, as a 'hay dealer'. For some of those years his mother continued to run the 'shop'. It is safe to assume that this was a small retail dealership in corn and hay. She died in 1846. After his father's death William continued as an apprentice, but maybe not for long. Mary continued to work in the flax mill, now over 14 and perhaps working a thirteen-hour day. How much longer she worked as a factory hand we do not know. In any case it was not, as we might now say, a 'sustainable' occupation. Both William and Mary were most probably helping their mother considerably in the shop in 1843. By then he had accumulated some knowledge of the business and was widely known among the customers and suppliers.

In sum it seems that William was intended to become a skilled worker and artisan, able to earn an above average wage. Family circumstances and perhaps a reading of the wider economic situation and opportunities within it, led to him to choose to be self-employed. But let us consider before moving on what the world of the wage earner was like. After all, some members of his family continued as wage earners, and he himself began to employ labour.

A telling indication of the effect of industrialisation is the downward spiral of average weekly wages for weavers in the West Riding of Yorkshire:

Wages of weavers in the West Riding 1795–1834		
1795	33s	approx. £75 per annum
1815	4s	approx. £35 per annum
1829–34	5s 6d (4s 1½d after taxes)	approx. £14 per annum

In the 1830s a labourer might earn 1s 6d per day (9s for a six-day week). And this work was often intermittent. The wage earner suffered disproportionally from numerous commodity taxes which were levied on, for example, malt, sugar, tea, coffee, vinegar, hops and oranges ('the poor child's luxury'), cloth, tallow, horse food, paper, bricks, windows and dogs. As the weavers pointed out, they did not include power looms. There were frequent protests against commodity prices and low wages.

Factory work literally crippled children, whether from the sheer deformation of immature bodies from the pattern of work or from disabling accidents. Most of the factory work force was under 21 years old and of these the majority were women and children. The labour auctions of the 1830s screened Irish immigrants, preferring women and children as in slave markets of old, or even not so distant memory. On the other hand, relatively healthy, younger male Irish labourers were valued precisely because factory workers were often unemployable after their twenties. At the same time Irish labourers were considered not up to the more advanced demands of factory work and routine.

William's sister Mary was a factory worker. In the 1841 census she is listed as a 'flax doffer' aged 14. This is such an important index and factor in the young Turton family at this time that it calls for some reflection. Flax processing and weaving was a major industry in Leeds. It had been encouraged by the state from the sixteenth century onwards. From flax, linen is made and also other special cloth such as cambric and lace. It can be combined with wool and cotton.

A flax doffer is a worker who 'doffed or tied up the full spindles of linen thread and quickly replaced this with a fresh empty spindle'. The job was done by women especially and young girls. Since it may have required an extra degree of responsibility and co-ordination, older girls may have done it. Conditions of work were generally wet, hot, dusty and dangerous. Mary started work in the factory before her father died. Recent legislation had forbidden the employment of children under nine in factories and restricted their working hours to twelve per day in a six-day week. So possibly Mary started work in about 1837 aged 12, the same year as William may have started his apprenticeship.

It is a safe bet that Mary worked in Marshall's mills. John Marshall (1765–1845), son of a linen draper, began the industrial spinning of flax in 1788. His became the largest employer in Leeds and it is highly probably that Mary Turton worked in his Temple Mill in Water Lane, just south of the Aire in central Leeds. It was an easy walk from home. Mary may well have attended the opening of Marshall's new Temple Mill in 1840 when 2,600 workers sat down to a 'Temperance Tea'. The building was lavish and extraordinary.

Marshall's mill in Leeds c.1840.

Marshall's Temple Mill for spinning flax c.1810.

Girls and young women leaving the flax mill c.1840.

It was modelled, at least on the exterior, on the old Egyptian Temple of Horus at Edfo. It had a chimney resembling Cleopatra's Needle. The flat roof had glass domes to admit daylight and was also laid with turf and grass on which sheep grazed, a remarkable example of the 'greening' of industrial Leeds *avant la lettre*. Disraeli refers to this as 'A Temple of Industry' in his novel *Sybil*.

Marshall developed machinery that benefited both wool and flax industries. He was a Unitarian and had a utilitarian social consciousness. He is known for his provision of some schooling for factory-workers – 'well-behaved' boys and girls aged 11–12 – on Monday mornings. For some he was always a rapacious capitalist, and was burnt in effigy by opponents in Leeds. He was also a 'reformer' in the spirit of the times and introduced some improvements in working conditions, such as forbidding corporal punishment and regulating the temperature of the mill. He personally retired from the fray, but his sons succeeded him after 1830 and his mills ground on.

The wages of workers in Marshall's mills in the period 1837–41 are recorded and are worth a look, if only for the extraordinary sight of weekly wages being calculated to the nearest farthing:

Average weekly wages in Marshall's flax mill 1837–41	
Men	19*s* 10*d* to 21*s* 9*d* 3 farthings
Women and girls	5*s* 11*d* 1 halfpenny to 6*s* 3*d*
Children	2*s* 4*d* 3 farthings to 3*s* 2*d* 3 farthings

The average annual wage of all workers at Marshall's had declined from £20 10s in 1810 to £17 in 1843.

Marshall became grotesquely wealthy, especially in the early years. In the years 1805–44 the average range of his annual income was £15,000–£30,000; in one year it was £65,000. Between 1804 and 1815 he increased his capital from £40,000 to £400,000. He bought a Parliamentary seat for 5,000 guineas in 1825 and built Headingley Lodge for one of his children for £6,000 in 1829. Even more than many such men, he despaired of being able to turn wealth into social status. In the last thirty years of his life he spent 1 million pounds in a quest to raise his social status. He spent a third of this on household expenses, entertaining and so on. Another quarter of a million pounds was spent on 'paintings, patronage and politics'. We shall return to this when considering William Turton's far smaller fortune.

It is clear that a family with a comfortable and steady income from trade, even a small enterprise, would not wish or need to send its oldest daughter to work in a factory at that time. The social and economic historian Eric Hobsbawm bluntly states the options for those confronted by this new industrial capitalist system that had deprived them of such traditional pre-modern economic and social support systems as may have existed, 'They could strive to become bourgeois; they could allow themselves to be ground down; or they could rebel'. William himself was not to be 'ground down'. Could he have rebelled?

Leeds township had a long history of working-class organisation and resistance. Consider for a moment the period from the French Revolution to the Chartist 'general strike' of 1842. These were the generations of William's parents and grandparents. The mood in Europe occasioned by the French Revolution led, among other things, to some very radical groups who sympathised with their French counterparts across the channel. Indeed they sometimes held out hopes for French involvement in domestic struggles in England and Ireland. There were 'the United Irishmen', which notably combined both Catholics and Protestants, and 'The United Englishmen'. Religious, trades union and political reformist groups emerged and intermixed.

In 1792 Thomas Paine's pamphlets and *Rights of Man* were 'sold and given away in profusion' in the houses of journey-men, cloth workers in Leeds; though a 'loyal mob' could also be found to parade and burn him in effigy. There were protests about the price of corn. In 1801 Leeds magistrates feared that 'an insurrection was in contemplation among the lower orders' who were 'combining' to seek lower prices and taxes for basic necessities and to increase wages. Gott's mill workers went on strike in 1802 and in that year the mayor of Leeds expressed his dismay at 'the momentous shape, which the spirit of combination was taking among workers of almost every class'. There was a proliferation of secret committees and other popular organisations, marked by quite extreme forms of oath-taking, and sometimes millenarian and syncretic religious ideas. Violent action was on the agenda. In 1812 there were Luddite riots in Leeds and evidence of people organising for armed revolutionary activity. Specifically, there were raids on arms stores and widespread theft of lead. This sense of secrecy and efforts to exclude patronising and co-opting influences may be felt in an account of a meeting in the late 1790s, at a Methodist chapel in Leeds, of the radical 'Kilhamite' sect, 'There was a company of 500 people, a dense poor and unruly population at the top of Ebenezer Street where strangers of the middle class could not reasonably be expected to go.'

Eight days after the Peterloo massacre in Manchester on 16 August 1819 when 15 demonstrators calling for Parliamentary reform were killed and 300–700 injured, 4,000 Leeds people expressed their solidarity on Hunslet Moor: 'We mourn our murdered friends in Manchester.' In 1842 the Plug Riots (referring to the smashing of steam boilers) was part of a national strike inspired by the Chartists. In Leeds the demonstrators met with overwhelming force:

    1,200 constables
    181 infantry with fixed bayonets
    17 Lancers
    Horse Artillery field gun.

There were of course many efforts to co-opt and control the rising tide of popular discontent and its forms of expression and organisation. The continued development of the notion of 'civil society' was evidenced in the rebuilding of Leeds Library in 1808, the founding of the Leeds Philosophical and Literary Society in 1819 and, in order to spread enlightenment to the artisans, the Leeds Mechanics Institute in the mid-1820s. John Marshall and other wealthy industrialists and middle-class allies helped to promote and sponsor these institutions.

In the 1840s the Chartist movement was at its height, and on occasions at its most violent. Forty-one thousand people in Leeds signed the Chartist petition, three and a quarter million in Britain as a whole. One of its principal news organs was the *Northern Star*. This was published in Leeds and sold 40,000 copies of each issue. These were widely read. Often copies were bought by small syndicates and shared and read aloud in pubs. A militant song, a kind of secular hymn, entitled 'Oppression' appeared in the *Northern Star* of 2 September 1842, written by 'D.C.'. Selected lines read:

    Shall we for ever bear the scorn
    Of heartless wealth and fancied power?
    Bequeath to ages yet unborn
    Our abjectness – a galling dower?

    Shall we behold the festive halls,
    Where the loud laughter of revelry
    Echoes along the tinselled walls
    In mocking of our misery?

> Forbid it God! The dignity
> Of manhood must awaken'd be;
> Justice demands, and Liberty
> Proclaims we must and shall be free!

William did not rebel. As a machine-makers apprentice he was not a natural Luddite. As a member of the Church of England he was less likely to be influenced by the radical, non-conformist Liberals. Some Anglicans were, and William was briefly to express an interest in the Liberal cause. He decided to become a small self-employed trader. As we have seen this was most likely triggered, and in part enabled by, the death of his father and then of his mother just a few years later. Did he have the 'minimum entrance fee of some property and education' for it to be a clear-cut decision? Hardly. Careers they said were open to talent. All you needed was energy, shrewdness, hard work and a hunger for something better. William did not lack the attributes of energy, shrewdness and hard work, and he never lost his appetite for self-improvement. He achieved wealth, and a degree of social power through his dealings as a merchant capitalist and entrepreneur. He was to know some of the pleasures of 'festive halls' and the 'laughter of revelry'. Heartlessness and mockery, in terms of personal characteristics, we shall not find. His record on justice and freedom, both broadly and in particulars, will be considered.

4

WILLIAM TURTON, CORN & HAY MERCHANT

We only have William Turton's word for it, but he chose to have 'established 1844' carved in stone when his new premises were built in 1876. Let us take stock of him and his family and household economic circumstances in the year 1844, the year he started off on his own.

William was 19 years old. He had been an apprentice machine-maker possibly from the age of 12 to 17. So we need to account for a year or two before he started on his own. His father had died when he had just turned 16; his mother continued to live at No. 122 York Road. We know this was John Turton's trading address in 1839 and Elizabeth's in 1843, both as 'shopkeepers'. It is likely that William was diverted from any career in machine making and helped his mother in the shop between 1842 and 1844. We can be reasonably certain that the shop was the front room of their dwelling house. They retailed hay and straw, and possibly corn on a small scale.

He was strong and healthy. There is no evidence that he suffered any serious injury or maladies until bronchitis took him off quickly in 1900. He was a fair-haired Yorkshire speaking young man of promise. He was literate and numerate, and with some training in technological skills, he understood machinery and mechanics. He may well have had some basic accounting or bookkeeping ability, at least enough for 'shopkeeping'. I do not want to anticipate assessment of his character or personal and social attributes, but there seem to have been no serious defects or distortions, no obstacles to progress. My hunch is that he had a fair amount of shrewdness and charm. He had considerable awareness of the society and economy of Leeds and the industrial environment, and the fuels it needed. He had begun to acquire some experience of horses.

William had five younger siblings who in 1844 were aged: Mary 17, Joseph 14, Elizabeth 12, Martha 9 and Sarah 6. Mary might still have been a factory worker. Joseph and Elizabeth might have started to earn. All or any of them must have helped their mother in the shop from time to time. Joseph and Mary may have helped William in his early years. Mary married in 1847 and may have died in 1858, aged 31. Joseph was married by 1850 when he is described as a 'cartman'. He died in 1868 aged 38.

William's mother, Elizabeth, died early in 1846, so by the middle of 1846, aged 21, William was head of the family. He and his siblings were all unmarried or not of an age to marry. He had responsibilities towards them. Whatever he inherited as eldest child and eldest son, and whatever the family income at the time, there were still two little sisters who would need 'parenting' for several years to come.

The family shop was still a 'going concern'. There was some stock and some simple equipment, maybe scales, sacks, trolleys, sacks, shovels and other tools. It is just possible there may have been a pony and cart. Most importantly there was the good will of customers and suppliers. And William and his siblings had some experience of running the shop.

He rented their house, which was probably a small terraced 'cottage', even as small as one-up one-down and a basement. Fewer than 2 per cent of houses in the area were owner-occupied. Even the electoral franchise was based largely on house rent rather than ownership. The rent still had to be paid.

Within a year of his mother's death William had taken the bold step of moving to No. 31 East Street. This move is loaded with significance for his life. It underlines his desire to develop his own kind of business independently, and to move beyond the shopkeeper end of the scale of trading. It coincided with his meeting and marrying Sarah Ann. It was probably a slightly larger house, two-up two-down and basement, but still a terraced 'cottage'. This would allow space for his younger sisters, his own children and a servant girl of about 12 years old at first. It was closer to the site at Crown Point that soon became the centre of his trading operations.

East Street runs from just near St Peter's church, always a pivotal feature in the landscape of our story, eastwards and a little south along the banks of the Aire below Leeds Dam up to the point where Timble Beck (or stream) flows into it. Crown Point Bridge, about a mile east of Leeds Bridge, had been open for about four years. William would have been fascinated by its advanced engineering design and beauty. The north-east end of the bridge soon joins East Street. First it passes on the west the corner of The Calls – the site of Turton's warehouse to come – to arrive close to The Palace Inn (No. 148 East Street, still trading) and its neighbour St Peter's. To the right of this junction the northern side of East Street starts at No. 1 and not far down was No. 31, the Turton home.

On the 1834 map the northern side of the street is not fully built up, so it would be quite a new house. Its neighbour at No. 32 was The Waterloo Inn. Maybe it had a handy yard and stable that William could make use of. Over the years William bought several other houses in East Street: Nos 4, 16, 18, 20, 22, 27, 29, 30 and 33. These were not speculative investments but accumulated as part of the infrastructure of the firm for the use of the more senior staff. He later bought a number of other nearby properties, some of which were later the subject of slum clearance; others were part of the residuary estate and sold as late as 1959 when No. 9 Oastler Terrace and No.13 Leeds Street sold for £46 17s and 2d, while No. 22 East Street, no doubt needed for large scale redevelopment, fetched £1,500.

William had moved but he was still in the East End. He was not to move out of the area until about 1860, after he had begun to be seriously well off. He did not flaunt his money or spend it unwisely. By 1849 his worth as a citizen as measured by rentable value was such that he was a borough and municipal elector. He later became councillor for East Ward and continued trading there all his life. His new house may have been an improvement, but he could not change the environment, the pollution, the threat from flooding. The area contained some of the most dense and worst housing in Leeds. These were terrible and dangerous years for the people of Leeds. There was a typhus epidemic in 1847, a cholera epidemic in 1848 that killed 2,000 people, and epidemics of smallpox, scarlet fever and typhoid fever in 1849. The Turtons came through but possibly William's mother had been an early victim of one of these infectious diseases.

How did William Turton manage to take off? Most enterprises of the time were family affairs, and it is to the family that we turn. William had an uncle, his father's older brother by two years, George Turton (1802–84). He was to outlive his younger brother by more than forty years. Uncle George had a son, William (William George), who was approximately William's age mate; he was the one William went to the Grammar School with for a few months. In 1848 his cousin is listed as a 'corn dealer' at No. 7 Elland Road. In 1851 George was trading as a 'corn dealer and beer seller' at No. 12 Elland Road.

Uncle George was not a wealthy man. He traded all his life as a small corn miller or dealer from a single shop front in Elland Road, not far south of Water Lane in Holbeck. It is highly probable that after his brother's death in 1841, and even more so after his sister-in-law's death in 1846, he gave his nephew a helping hand. William was a self-starter and a good bet. He had responsibility for two families and so was well

——— HAY CART ———

Hay mercahnts cart, mid-1880s.

deserving. I am sure William repaid any debt. He also remembered his cousin's son in his will. So Uncle George was a generous man, since he had to help his own son as much or more. His wife, Aunt Harriet (née Nichols) (1799–1872), had three younger children almost exactly the ages of William's youngest sisters. She very likely helped to bring them up. It may not have been coincidental that William was to name four of his children after the names his uncle had given his children.

William did not start with nothing; but he did not start with much. With this, and his own wits and energy, the young man had to meet family obligations and make an uncertain launch into an unknowable future, an uncharted sea of fortune.

This is a good moment to emphasise the importance of women in our story, especially the family members. William had the example of Elizabeth, a strong mother who for five years ran a small shop and raised a family of five after the early death of her husband whom she had married at 19. He also had the example of his sister Mary, younger by only two years, who had gone to work in a flax mill at the age of 12. When his mother died he had two little sisters aged 11 and 8 who must have looked up to him as more like a father than a big brother. William was soon to marry, and by this time Mary and Joseph at least would have been more or less independent.

We know all too little about Sarah Ann his wife, who was just six months younger than him. They had five healthy children. She was with him throughout the major part of his career, sharing hard times and good. When she died in 1877 William set up an impressive tomb and monument to her in the graveyard in Chapel Allerton. It is a tribute to her and a memorial of his affection for her. We shall return to this. We shall also meet his daughters and daughters-in-law a little later.

Let us return to the progress of Turton's career as a corn and hay dealer. In an 1847 directory William Turton is listed for the first time as a 'haydealer' at No. 31 East Street. In 1847 the Charlton's Directory for Leeds lists eleven hay dealers (amongst whom William Turton), nineteen corn merchants, fifty corn and flour dealers, and twenty corn millers. The hay dealers and corn merchants and factors would have been most likely to deal in horse fodder. Not all corn merchants would deal exclusively in 'horse corn'. The terms may have been used loosely but my assessment is that a hay 'dealer' and a 'shopkeeper' would be at the smaller retail end of the scale. Corn and hay merchants were likely to operate on a larger scale. The larger number of corn and flour dealers suggests this smaller scale. Flour implies food for human consumption. Corn milling would be more specialised and capitalised and at the larger end of the spectrum. Turton's business certainly involved some milling though he is seldom referred to as a miller. In any case, it was a busy, thriving and competitive sector.

In 1851 the census records that he was a corn dealer at No. 4 East Street and that he employed two men. One of his employees might well have been his younger brother Joseph, who worked as a 'cart-man'. William would need a cart or wagon and someone to load and unload, and to drive it. There would also be a fair amount of manual work, carrying on backs and on trolleys, sorting and chopping, bagging and baling. So at the age of 26 he had expanded his trading premises and had taken on two workers.

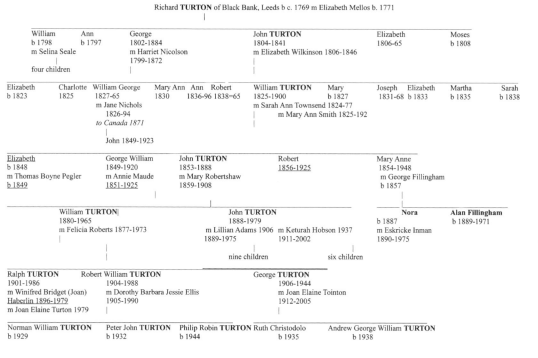

Select paternal pedigree of William Turton.

During the 1850s he bought or rented new properties at Nos 4, 10 and 30 East Street and at No. 13 Canning Street. In 1853 he is listed for the first time as 'hay, corn and straw merchant'. The inclusion of corn implies the diversification and expansion, which continued to be features of his business practice.

CORN

The terms 'corn' and 'wheat' were used interchangeably in nineteenth-century Britain. Originally corn had a meaning of any kind of grain or cereal. Maize or Indian corn was not much grown in Europe in the early nineteenth century outside the western Mediterranean fringe. It was grown more extensively in Africa and the Americas. Today, of course, in the USA corn is synonymous with maize.

Food for horses may be termed fodder, forage or provender whatever its components of grains, grasses, pulses or legumes. In the wild, horses graze almost continually on the move. They have a small stomach. They eat and digest small amounts at a time, and are not able to go for long periods without eating. Hence the 'nose-bag' that enables a horse to eat during the working day. Horses are fed a mix of cereal and other vegetable products to replicate their natural diet and give them a special advantage for the kind of hard work they are required to do. The better the horse is fed, the more work it can do.

The term corn merchant or corn factor draws on the nineteenth-century usage since a merchant such as William Turton certainly dealt in oats, barley, rye and various pulses and so on. Oats included various types such as white, black, English, Russian and Old Russian. Horses were also fed beans (Königsberg, English) and peas (Canadian). Linseed meal was given for extra strength and for sick horses. Linseed, oats and barley were often boiled before feeding. An interesting local product was furze (as it is known in Yorkshire), or gorse. This is a leguminous shrub that grows wild on moorland. The less woody tips are picked and rolled and beaten to soften the prickles and it then used as forage for horse and cattle. It is a locally abundant natural resource, but labour intensive in its processing. There is only one reference to it in our story when in 1911 one of William's grandsons lists himself as a 'Corn, Hay and Furze Merchant'.

HAY

Hay is cut and dried grasses, usually greenish when fresh. Hay may include some legumes and flowers. Hay with clover is a high quality sort. Hay was often chopped before sale, the feed then being referred to, in Yorkshire at least, as 'choppie'.

The price of hay varied considerably as shown by these figures for Leeds in October 1870:

Price of hay in Leeds 1870	
	Cost per quarter
Prime old hay	127s 6d –135s
Inferior old hay	116–120s
Prime new hay	115–125s
Inferior new hay	100–110s
Prime clover	130–140s
Inferior clover	115–125s
Prime new second cut	120–130s
Inferior new second cut	110–115s
Straw	30–34s

William Turton also sold hayseed, which he advertised weekly in May in the *Yorkshire Post*. There is a related but distinct product called 'dried grass', which was cut when green and dried by hot air. It contained grass, clover, lucerne and sainfoin.

Straw makes up about half the product of the grain crop by volume after the grain, of any sort, has been removed. It is used as bedding for larger animals and as roughage in horse and cattle diet, but only as a part of it. Straw is slow to digest and low in nutrition but is valued for low maintenance care and cold weather diets.

GRAIN PRODUCTION

Most of these items of fodder were grown and supplied by local farmers, from whom Turton would buy whenever possible and when prices were competitive. Two who are mentioned are John Revis of Scarcroft, just north-east of Leeds beyond Roundhay, and John Rollins of Halton near Ilkley, between the Aire and the Wharfe. In a bad harvest year hay was imported from Ireland (e.g. 1876). It was not until 1890 that hay began to be imported from Europe.

Yorkshire was then divided into the ancient Ridings, North, West and East. Each was the size of many other counties. West Riding was not a particularly aristocratic county, but the nobility and gentry nonetheless owned about one-third of cultivated land. MPs who were members of these landed families tended to oppose the repeal of the Corn Laws:

Land ownership in Yorkshire c.1870			
Social status	Number	Total land owned (acres)	Average
Peers	19	236,181	12,430
'Great Landowners'	66	442,031	6,697
Squires	101	171,700	1,700

The following summary figures for agricultural production are taken from the Victoria County History of Yorkshire. They give an idea of overall production and importantly of the relative scale as between the Ridings. West Riding is preponderant in all categories, in all selected years:

Land under crops and grass in Yorkshire 1867–1906			
Total land under crops and grass			
	1867	1886	1906
West Riding	1,144,530	1,210,824	1,187,488
East Riding	626,793	665,433	675,697
North Riding	773,977	856,616	866,230

Order of frequency by volume of crops grown: wheat, oats, barley, beans, peas, rye.

Horses ownership in Yorkshire 1886–1906		
	1886	1906
West Riding	52,577	61,661
East Riding	37,715	41,766
North Riding	40,315	45,130

These tables illustrate the importance of the grain production in Yorkshire and especially West Riding. There is a steady expansion but this by no means kept up with demand. Counties of origin in England were Yorkshire, Lincolnshire, Norfolk, Suffolk and Essex, and barley also from Scotland. Wheat was the most likely to be imported for fodder (with domestic wheat being used for flour) and was the most expensive. Trading at the Leeds Corn Exchange in 1870 showed the following prices:

Prices of grain in Leeds 1870		
	Amount sold	Price per quarter
Wheat	88,786 quarters	47s 3d
Barley	76,581 quarters	36s 5d
Oats	2,915 quarters	22s 2d

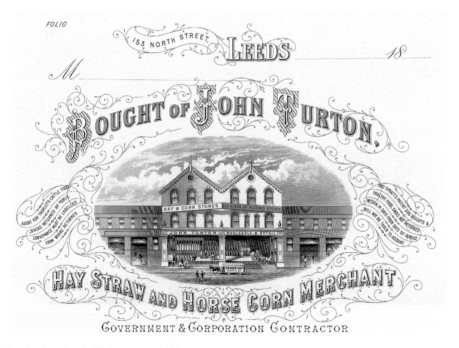

Invoice letterhead of John Turton, 1880.

Old Corn Exchange at top of Briggate c.1820.

Interior of Corn Exchange showing corn trading c.1920–25.

The price of wheat declined throughout the century by a factor of about four. In the period 1800–19 the average price per quarter at Liverpool of 'good red foreign wheat' was about 88s per quarter, with prices boosted by wartime conditions. Between 1820 and 1899 prices of between 60–75s per quarter were reached in only fifteen years, including a surge during the Crimean War (1854–56), which would have benefited Turton. The average figure for 1880–99 was as low as 33s per quarter. But as the cost of fodder decreased, the cost of horse transport lessened proportionally. So Turton benefited either way. He had a special interest in viewing an exhibition of 329 photographs of the Crimean War in the Music Hall in May 1856.

However, it was not until late in the century that the cost of transatlantic transport lessened sufficiently to make it particularly attractive. Turton regularly bought corn imported from northern Europe and Russia, and to a lesser extent from Italy, USA and Canada. Whether it came from Alberta or the Ukraine, the corn arrived by canal to his wharf on the Aire. Turton traded entirely in the period after the repeal of the old Corn Laws in 1846 when imports were no longer penalised by tax.

Yorkshire expressed itself, so to say, through the annual agriculture shows of the Yorkshire Agricultural Society, which had been founded in 1837. Shows took place in Leeds in 1839, 1849, 1879 and 1898. It is quite probable that even as a lad Turton had attended this great annual event. He certainly attended the ones in Leeds and probably a great many of the others. He helped to organise the invitation and plans for the show in Leeds in 1879. He may well have had a stall or some other representation at the shows but this information is not available. He must have renewed contacts with suppliers and customers, looked knowledgeably and critically at the horses, and maybe did a few deals. He would have been in his element.

MARKETING

Turton dealt as a wholesaler and at the higher end of the retail trade. His success must have depended greatly on his skill in buying in the right place at the right time, and of course at the right price. Sometimes he would buy direct from a farmer, or a factory working solely for a farmer on a large estate. At other times, and when local harvests were insufficient or prices unattractive, he would buy at the Corn Exchange. Here corn dealers could inspect samples on the stalls, which were small tables with sides to them. Most business took place between 10.00 a.m. and 2.00 p.m. helped by the superb natural lighting designed by Leeds' most famous architect, Cuthbert Broderick. Core samples could be taken from sacks with a harpoon-like iron rod. If the core were black, the corn was unripe, wet or rotten. They could feel the grain, smell and inspect by sight. Specialist buyers are said to have a flair such as that of a wine or tea taster.

Lance Turton, the last of the children of John Turton by his first wife, reminisced in 2010 (then aged 86). He had been a farmer in the days just before combine harvesters (which could thresh as well as reap and bind) and motor vehicles were generally in use. Spring-planted grains varied in the seasonality of their harvest. They were often cut before being fully ripe to avoid wastage. August and September were the busiest months. The reaper-binder cut the crop into 'sheaves', which were gathered into 'stouks' and pooled into 'stacks'. They could keep for a few months in this state. The grain was left on stouks until almost ripe. They were then carted on wagons called 'rullies' to the 'thrashing' machine (as they say in Yorkshire). The grain was then 'riddled' and 'cleaned', chiefly to remove weeds.

William Turton would send two of his own men and his horses and wagons with 10 stone sacks (140lbs). If the grain was sent by LNER (London North East Railway) they used 'railway sacks' of 12 stone. Turton would take the grain to the railhead. There was little transport available for coal during the height of the corn season.

Turton sold to an urban clientele of factories, workshops, municipal and other public institutions, and to retailers who sold on to shops and householders. Turton also sold to local agricultural users. This is certainly the case in his dealing with branded cattle food. The front cover of this book has a copy of one of his invoices. It is a beautifully designed 'letterhead' full of information and a good bit of advertising. At the bottom it has the legend 'Sole Agents for Thorley's Cattle Food'. His agency was begun in 1861.

There was an excellent market for superior cattle food or growth and health enhancing additives. This was due to the great interest in breeding and exhibiting livestock of the

Thorley's livestock food, publicity beer mat.

highest quality, ever improving breeds and greater profitability. Thorley's Cattle Food Merchants had been established by the 1850s. They had their national headquarters, Thorley's Cattle Feed Mill, in London at Victoria Wharf, Battlebridge Basin, just east of King's Cross Station on the Grand Union Canal. William probably saw this when he came to London on one of his infrequent visits to the capital.

Extensive advertising fanned Thorley's fame. Its product was 'an additive that ensured perfection'. Even in 1930 Thorley's Food was advertised as 'A Condiment for All Stock'. In the middle of the nineteenth century the old fashion of painting pedigree animals was still in practice. The animal painter A.M. Gauci, of No. 24 Stephen Street, Tottenham Court Road, was the foremost such painters. A typical example is his lithograph of 'Kate, Poled Heifer, fed on food seasoned with Thorley's condiment'.

The caption boldly states that it had won first prize at the Smithfield Show in 1867. Turton's franchise of the Thorley product would have been an asset to both parties.

By the end of the 1850s Turton had expanded his base in Leeds and begun trading at 114 North Street. North Street runs north from Vicar Lane and is joined by New Briggate an extension of old Briggate leading from Leeds Bridge. It continues north towards Sheepscar where it becomes Chapeltown Road, now the A61 to Harrogate. In the 1850s it was still only just within the northern limits of Leeds and was not fully built up. No. 114 North Street was quite close to other streets that will become significant in the Turton story: Harrison Street, Sheepscar Yard, Templar Street, New York Road and others. Turton was also soon to buy the buildings at Nos 149, 151 and 153 North Street to set up his second main centre of trading.

He was still living modestly at No. 31 East Street and trading from various premises in that street and at some point or points near Crown Point Bridge. The area just north and to the north-east and north-west of Crown Point Bridge had long been called Crown Point, and precise locations there are sometimes hard to distinguish. By the time Turton started working here the whole riverside bank from Crown Point Bridge to Leeds Bridge, about a kilometre long, had been built up with wharves, factories and warehouses. The first date that we have for Turton operating from The Calls at the corner of that street and Crown Point Road is 1861..

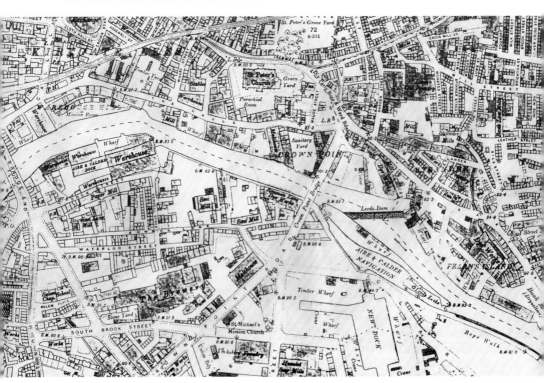

Map of Crown Point area c.1875.

The Calls runs eastwards from Leeds Bridge following the northern bank of the Aire. More precisely it leads off Call Lane, which goes from the bottom of Briggate, between the river and St Peter's churchyard. The land south of St Peter's was for centuries church land and not built upon. The area closest to the river was known as Church Ings on eighteenth-century maps. Ings is a regional term for flood meadow. The commercial and industrial use of the waterfront extended gradually eastward from the early nineteenth century and a road, The Calls, was made along it, with buildings on either side. It reminds the author of Wapping High Street in London's Dickensian docklands. Crucially it ends at Crown Point where the new bridge was built in 1842. There are various claims for the etymology of the name. According to a member of the Victorian Society of West Yorkshire, The Calls is 'a curious street name possibly derived from the Latin *callis*, meaning a beaten earth track, or Anglo-Saxon *cawls*, meaning low lying marshy ground'. Between Turton's land and the bridge itself there is 'a long flight of steps, dark and ugly, descending between the houses, long known as Jenny White's hole; and here ... Jenny White, finding "marriage vows as false as dicer's oath", ended her unhappy life.'

The Calls was a busy commercial and industrial street. It had warehouses and mills, tanners and dye-works, boat builders, builder's merchants and a maltster, all trades dependent on access to water and the supply of bulk goods. Like many such waterfront streets it had a reputation for bad and immoral social behaviour. The Calls was a marginal zone in a sense. It was on the edge of old central Leeds. The close presence of St Peter's church redeemed it. To the east was some industry and more penury. But to the west it was close to the old White Cloth Hall, the Assembly Rooms and, above all, the new Corn Exchange (1862).

There had been a mill at Crown Point since 1794 at the latest. By 1834 there were substantial buildings on this corner site. They vary as to size and disposition on different maps. Simon Hartley Spence (1807–56) was a corn factor at No.64 The Calls in 1845 and again in 1851 living with his wife and a servant on Town Street, Potternewtown, a smart address in a pleasant village some 2 to 3 miles north of Leeds town. His occupation was 'wharfinger', a wharf owner and manager. It is significant in that it suggests that along with his place of residence and the earlier mention of him as a corn factor, he probably owned or rented the whole corner site and that his corn trading involved and co-ordinated large scale water transport and waterfront warehousing.

William Turton's small hay dealing business grew up in the shadow so to say of this well-established and wealthy merchant. Perhaps he had worked with Spence early on or had some dealing with him as a broker of his products. Spence died in 1856. William is at the address by 1861 and trading already in coal, and this needed a wharf. So he acquired the site on a lease, by 1860 at the latest. He is therefore likely to be the direct successor, in a sense a beneficiary of Spence's enterprise. By this time his staff had increased considerably. The variety of his products increased the number of processes and hence machinery: grinding of wheat, rolling of oats, chopping of hay,

Aire and Calder warehouses, Leeds Bridge.

crushing of pulses, boiling of linseed and so on. He began to invest his surplus in more machinery and steam power. The area must have pulsated and puffed with sound and smoke from the engines: on land the steam cranes and winches, the hammers and cutters and pumps; on the water the tug boats, barges and dredgers. We shall see later that it was here that he was to build his great warehouse, mill and wharf-side operation, which have left their trace to this day.

Turton bought some of the land at Crown Point from John Denison, one of the wealthiest men in Leeds. Turton eventually owned the entire site known as Turton's wharf and warehouse, or Nos 64–66 The Calls, between the Aire, Crown Point Road, The Calls and his neighbour to the west, a town council yard. He also owned considerable plots of land on the Aire to the east of Crown Point Bridge where he ran his coal operations.

Leeds archives have conserved a document relating to the warehouse at Crown Point. This is of a 'Plan of Alteration and Completion of Premises situate at the junction of Crown Point Road and Calls belonging to and occupied by Wm Turton'. It is by 'Thomas Gaines, No.92 Elmworth Street, Leeds.' Gaines was chief clerk to William Turton. It bears a council date stamp 11 June 1875. This shows planned elevations on four floors. We do not know the name of the architect. There is some resemblance to the style of a distinguished architect Thomas Ambler (1836–1920) who was working at the time, including warehouses and the Crown Point Printing Works.

The site to the east is given as 'Corporation stone yard'. This later became a night-soil deposit and at the end of the century a generating plant that provided electricity for the borough trams.

Most of the space is marked as being some variant of corn, hay and straw chamber, or just warehouse. Several areas have clearly marked stables, at least forty with stalls for horses and carriages. In the centre is an open yard. To the east of the entrance arch are offices, on the floor above are a sitting room and kitchen and above that two bedrooms.

Various store rooms and a larder are shown. The ground-floor plan is much concerned with drainage which starts at the base of what is now the extant brick. By this is a lavatory. This suggests that one function of the tower was as a ventilation flue.

There is no corner view of the building at The Calls and Crown Point Road and no sign of the carvings of dates and Turton's name which remain today, nor the horses head sculpture. Tantalisingly, there is no indication of owner or use of the area towards the River Aire. The plans are for the building alone. It can be safely assumed that he did in fact own at least part of the wharfside.

His warehouse was as much a factory given the amount of processing involved. It had a staff of considerable size. He, and later his first son George, ran it. They had managers who included cashier, chief clerk and foreman. Then there was the senior technical staff: engineer, stable overseer, transport overseer, crane operator and blacksmith. Turton provided housing close to the warehouse for some of these. The rest of the workforce, on lower wages, would include drivers, machine operators, stable staff, clerks, carpenter and carriage smith, wheelwright, saddler, painter, stokers, cleaners and of course a large number of shifters, humpers and heavers.

RISKS

A chief defence of capitalist entrepreneurs against charges of exploitation is that they bear considerable risks. These are many kinds. We shall see later how Turton dealt with such risks as conflict of interest, accidents and compensation, consumer criticism, lawsuits and so on. Since he was successful in his business dealings, we can assume that he survived and emerged strong from various kinds of competition, ups and downs in markets and larger economic swings. Our account tends to flatten out any troughs and peaks. From the eighteenth century the insurance industry and the legal system had begun to rationalise and compensate for problems of disaster, misfortune and failure.

FIRE

Turton designed his building at Crown Point to minimize risk from fire. He zoned activities and had a stone staircase at the wharf end and an iron spiral staircase. But the hazards of oil lamps, forges and sparks and flames from machinery were great, especially with so much dry hay, straw and vegetable oil about. The design of the warehouse, offices and milling areas allowed for some functional zoning and safety features. According to Goad's insurance map amended 1954, the riverside area was for milling and there was a stone staircase. The offices on the first floor overlooked The Calls to the north and had an iron spiral staircase.

The round brick tower is a bit of mystery. It now contains a stone spiral staircase to a platform with iron railings and a few windows lower down. It is nearer the stable area (east) than the area where steam engines would be, so it is doubtful if it was ever a chimney. Peter Brears writes, in 1993, of 'A local tradition states that he [William Turton] built the tall round minaret which rises above his warehouse as a look-out tower, from where he could see his vessels coming and going along the Navigation [Aire and Calder Canal].'

One fire was reported in the *Yorkshire Post* of 20 October 1870:

Fire in a stable in Leeds

Yesterday afternoon between 2 and 3 o'clock, a fire broke out in the stable occupied by Mr Turton, omnibus proprietor, Harrison Street, Leeds. The hose from the Town Hall and engines of the Liverpool, London and Globe [insurance company] were speedily on the spot, and succeeded in extinguishing the fire in about forty minutes. There were 14 horses in the stable at the time the fire was discovered, but they were all got out alive, five of them however being seriously burnt. The premises are insured by the Liverpool, London and Globe, but the extent of the damage is not at present known.

The most serious fire occurred at Nos 64–66 The Calls in 1884 as reported by the *Leeds Mercury* on 18 March:

Though through the exertion of the firemen much valuable property was saved, the fire was so destructive that we understand Mr. Turton estimates the damage at between £8,000 and £10,000. The loss is partly covered by insurance at the Royal Insurance Office. The fire was overcome at about three o'clock Tuesday morning; but it was five o'clock before one of the steamers belonging to the Corporation Fire Brigade could be withdrawn, outbursts of flame occasionally taking place. Yesterday the scene of the conflagration was visited by a large number of people. Several firemen remained on duty so as to prevent any fresh outbreak.

FRAUD

Theft and fraud were other serious risks.

In January 1861 a bag of gold and silver coins worth £28 was stolen from an open and unattended safe in Turton's Crown Point business.

Reynolds Weekly Newspaper (London) carried the following report on 23 August 1868.

Central Criminal Court
Extensive Fraud by the "Long Firm"

Samuel Israel, 36, dealer, and William Barnes, 33, baker, who were remanded from last session, were indicted for unlawfully obtaining by false pretences from William Turton, a quantity of corn seeds, with intent to defraud. Barnes pleaded guilty to two charges; Israel 'Not Guilty'.

Prosecutor was Mr William Turton seed merchant, Leeds. In the month of March he advertised for sale a quantity of hayseed, in the Yorkshire Post. In reply he received a letter from Barnes, requesting samples to be forwarded. A card was enclosed, headed 'Larkhall Manor Farm Dairy' with royal arms underneath, and describing Barnes as a 'purveyor of farm products, dealer in fresh butter, new-laid eggs etc. and finally stating that a liberal discount was allowed to hotels and schools. Samples were accordingly forwarded, upon which an order was given, and Mr. Turton sent twenty quarters of seed in forty new sacks. The seed was taken by a Great Northern Railway carman to Angel-place. The carman there saw Barnes, and in accordance with his directions the seed was taken to Israel's house in Long-lane Bermondsey, and it appeared subsequently to have been disposed of to a person in Hendon.

To summarise, Israel's landlady informed on him. Inspector Potter searched the house and found property obtained by three other members of 'The Long Firm' of which Israel was the leader. The property was worth £2,000 of which goods to the value of £500 had come to Israel in the past nine months. Israel received a sentence of two years imprisonment with hard labour, a sentence the judge said was too light but the maximum he could impose. The sentence on Barnes was deferred. In this case Turton had not asked for a reference, but in a similar case heard at the same time, a plaintiff had been given a bogus address for a solicitor.

ENTREPRENEURS

No one would object to Turton being called an entrepreneur. In his day it would have been a 'self-made man'. The term entrepreneur was current at the time but was not used on anything like the scale on which it is currently employed. There are nowadays many books on what makes an entrepreneur or how to be an entrepreneur. The experts can still say that 'entrepreneurship is one of the least understood forms of economic behaviour'. A retrospective book on *Entrepreneurship in Britain 1750–1939* interestingly cites John Marshall of Leeds as an example. It points out that he inherited £9,000 from his father in 1787. Recent scholarly analysis also emphasises what is perhaps common sense, that access to capital is likely to be the chief factor in the making of an entrepreneur. Most successful small businesses start with their own or family money rather than a bank loan. A gift or inheritance of £5,000 (in 1990) is said to double the likelihood of a young person starting on a self-employed business. This figure is roughly equivalent to £50–100 in Turton's time. £50 was the sum that the young Michael Marks, co-founder of Marks and Spencer, was lent to start his first enterprise as a travelling salesman based in Leeds.

One can make extensive lists of other characteristics and acquired skills of successful entrepreneurs. They require a special fusion of imagination, vision, energy and skill in the service of combining knowledge, technology and resources in new ways in order to develop new products and services. The entrepreneur need not be running a business for profit. The skills and attributes could equally be employed in the work of non-profit social enterprises.

The successful entrepreneur may expand or develop the range of products, improvement in products, or the geographical range of sourcing and marketing. Leeds at the time provided a rich ecology for Turton's achievements and range of ambitions. He expanded his portfolio of business interests. We shall soon consider his involvement in the coal trade and in transport. He operated well beyond Leeds in his corn and coal dealings. He operated across the whole of northern England in his tramway business. This was the extent of his empire. Through his involvement in Thomas Green and Son Engineers, he was linked to markets in all continents and in all parts of the Empire. He had wide horizons.

The early 1860s were to see him scaling new heights. His corn business flourished and he was a founding member of the new Leeds Corn Exchange (1862). A second major peak was to come in 1865, when William became an omnibus proprietor.

5

NEW KING COAL

There is a saying about Leeds that 'Coals [*sic*] and Water made this town'. Perhaps the sheep go without saying. It is especially true of more recent centuries. The first recorded significance of coal in the West Riding for smelting iron and burning lime is in the thirteenth century. Wood and turves were the main types of fuel until the sixteenth century, together with the more expensive charcoal.

Leeds literally sits on top of its coal. The Victoria County History of Yorkshire records succinctly that coal is concentrated in the West Riding, 'The Yorkshire Coalfield forms part of the Great West Midland Coalfield, which stretches from Leeds and Bradford in the north to a few miles south of the town of Nottingham.' Wakefield and Sheffield are the two main districts. West Riding was rather slow to develop its coalfields. In the middle of the seventeenth century, the Newcastle and Tyne area produced about half of all the coal in England most of which was shipped south by sea.

Horse and coal cart on rails, late eighteenth century.

At the beginning of the twenty-first century we have rather fallen out of love with coal. I am one of the generation of those who grew up with the wonders of a coal fire with its particular colours and gases, and the 'soldiers', the sparks that flew up the chimney or burnt in pretty, evanescent patterns on the sooty fire back. Even as young as 6, I recall shovelling buckets of coal to bring into the house, and then the inevitable shovelling of clinker and ash that later generations had to be warned not to put in their plastic dustbins. I remember too the excitement when the 'coalman' came with a delivery. There were two of them with a horse and flat-backed cart. Their faces were black with red eyes; their caps were of an indescribable shape and on their backs they had a thick leather pad on which they humped the hundredweight sack down to the coal shed at the end of the side passage. It was not always the best coal, the good lumps of shiny stuff, but sorry looking slack and coke and furnacite for the boiler.

We need to make a special effort to bring Turton's coal dealing business into the centre of our story, into the front line of his progress. The task is not made easier by the almost complete absence of direct information about his coal business. And it may seem a far cry from corn and hay, horses and horse-drawn vehicles. But consider that his corn mill machinery used coal-powered steam engines. It was coal and coke that refined the iron and steel to make the tramlines, the carriages and the depots. His tramway networks ran through many of the towns and outskirts of the densest coal mining areas. He was also a major shareholder and director in an engineering firm that specialized in coal-fuelled steam engines.

Industrial development often has a simple logic. A useful material is found in quantity in an area that also provides the means to process it and transport it to places that lack and need it: the iron ore, the coal, the clay, the canals. Local inventions arise to meet local needs: the spinning and weaving machines, the development of mass

Middleton steam train approaching Crown Point area.

production of clothing; the progress from axles for carts and springs for stagecoaches, to whole railway engines and rolling stock, that could help you go by steam from Leeds to Calcutta; from ancient edge tools such as the scythe to Thomas Green's patent lawn mowers that graced not only the best golf clubs round the world, but also the royal gardens of Emperors and Empresses, in London, St Petersburg and Tokyo. All these were 'Made in Leeds'!

IRON AND COAL

Coal and iron go back a long way together. They are found in the same mineral deposits that also often include limestone, clay and ironstone and other minerals with useful affinities.

Coal had largely replaced wood and turf, and wood transformed into charcoal, as the basic fuel by the nineteenth century. Colliers were aware that coal was non-renewable and limited but it was used as if it were limitless. Wood, though potentially renewable, had become in short supply as early as 1600 as forests receded before the agriculturalist, pastoralist and shipbuilder. The early expansion of coal production can be roughly indicated by the following estimated figures:

Tonnage of coal produced in Britain 1560–1780	
Year	Tonnage of coal produced
1540	200,000
1640	1,500,000
1780	10,000,000

Charcoal had been used for centuries to smelt iron. Wrought iron also needs limestone and ironstone. Coal and iron ore were often mined in close proximity and using the same type of shallow 'bell-pit' or the 'adit' cut into the side of a hill. A team of just twelve people was the norm: six adult face workers ('getters') and six boys ('hurriers') who moved the coal to the surface or exterior of the mine. 'Coal trams' were pushed and pulled by two boys.

Invoices for 1896 show a variety of types of coal by quantity, use and price. In approximate order of value they are:

Robin Hood (name of colliery, deep coal)
Lofthouse (name of colliery, deep coal)
Seconds
Thirds
Smithy coal
Cobbles

Nuts
Slack (engine, furnace)
Smudge
Riddlings

Coal then began to be used not just to produce the iron and the steel, but also to fuel steam engines that at first were largely used to pump water from the mines. They were heavy, static machines, such as those of Newcomen's piston engine of 1712. These were not in common use and we should not over-emphasise the role of coal and steam power at this time. Eighteenth-century industry was characterised chiefly by hand working in small workshops or at home. Even the early factories simply reduplicated hand power by using hand-worked machines that could do the work of twenty people. Waterpower remained essential in the textile industries (for fulling, dyeing etc.) and for milling foodstuffs and minerals. Steam pumps were auxiliary to watermills when used to pump water from the millrace back up to the dam in order to conserve water. On such 'railways' or 'wagon ways' as there were, it was horses that pulled the coal wagons. The new canals were not yet primarily for the transport of industrially produced goods.

By the 1790s a few Leeds industries began to leave records in the insurance company archives. The size of the steam machines was at first quite small, averaging about 24-horse power in a range of 10–40. The rule of coal and iron had begun. Coke had become cheaper than charcoal. Iron rails had become cheaper than wood, such as oak and beech. Nevertheless ships and many forms of conveyance by land continued to be made from wood, sometimes imported from the Baltic and later from the newer colonies of Asia and Africa (teak, mahogany etc.)

A piece of anonymous doggerel from the turn of the nineteenth century catches the feeling of the new dominion of iron:

Since cast iron is now all the rage
And scarce anything's now made without it,
As I live in a cast iron age
I mean to say something about it.

We've cast iron coffins and carts
Cast iron bridges and boats.
Corn factors with cast iron hearts
Which I'd hang up in cast iron coats.

TRANSPORT OF COAL

Coal is heavy; well, we all know a ton of eiderdown weighs as much, but the relative transport cost by value is a lot less. Carrying coal on packhorses was far too expensive for long distances. Hence the strategic location of the Tyneside fields with their sea route to London and the southeast. With the extension of canals after 1700 the price of coal fell dramatically. From 1812 coal began to carry itself, so to say, as the steam traction engine was introduced.

The pit price was likely to be about half the final delivered price. The cost of freight to William Turton might have been about 20 per cent of the total, leaving him the costs of unloading, storage, bagging, delivery and unloading, clerical and insurance and other overheads. This might yield no more than about 5 per cent profit.

Turton had a large stable of horses for the transport of forage and coal. The horses might be interchangeable but of course the sacks and wagons and other equipment had to be dedicated. In London in 1890 there were at least 8,000 horses engaged in the coal trade. A horse could make two to four journeys per day depending on length. On average they could pull about one ton per trip at about 2.5 mph. We shall discuss later the cost of keeping horses, but we can anticipate by saying that the cost of horse food was always the key element. Here, of course, Turton had an advantage.

DENABY MAIN COALS
Direct from the Colliery.

PRICES FOR CARTING ACCORDING TO DISTANCE.

Weight guaranteed by delivery note with each load bearing the Railway Company's Stamp.

PRESENT PRICES AT THE DEPOT.

G. N. RAILWAY, WELLINGTON BRIDGE, LEEDS.

Denaby Best Silkstone House Coal	... ...	12/9 per ton.
„ Seconds „	... ...	11/- „
„ Nuts—Brewers' Coal	... ...	9/6 „
„ Smithy Coal, Selected	... ...	10/6 „

Agent in Leeds :—Mr. S. MERRITT.

Offices :— 41, Cookridge Street, and Wellington Bridge.

ALL ORDERS PUNCTUALLY ATTENDED TO.

Advertisement for coal from an almanac of 1889.

Coal dealer's cart.

'Tom Puddings', a train of steel coal barges on the Aire and Calder Canal.

MIDDLETON COLLIERY

The Middleton Colliery situated about 5 miles south of Leeds is worthy of a vignette as it plays such a prominent part of the story of Leeds and coal. It illustrates so many of the themes we have touched on. For many years it was the chief and even the only supplier of coal to the town.

In 1646 Sir Ferdinand de Leigh owned a coalmine at Middleton. A Tyneside collier, Ralph Brandling married into the De Leigh family in 1697. It would be tempting to say this marked the time of the coming of age of the Leeds area coalfields. His family was to run the mines for the next two centuries. In order to remain competitive he needed to reduce the cost of bringing coal from pithead to user or merchant. On 9 June 1758, in response to Charles Brandling's plans, an Act of Parliament was passed giving him permission to build a railway or wagon way from the Middleton colliery to Leeds. This was the first authorisation of such a railway in Britain. The key precedent was that it crossed the land of other people. Of course he had to bear the costs of various bridging and fencing. Railway it was, but it was neither made of iron nor carried steam engines. The rails tracks were made of oak spiked to a transverse sleeper every 3ft. The sleepers were then covered with gravel and cinders. The rail had a renewable beech strip along which the flanged wheel could run, anticipating what was to become the standard edge rail. Wheels were also of beech with a metal tyre and flange. The line reached 4.5 miles in length. It ended at a coal staith just south of Leeds Bridge on Water Lane. Staith is an old term for a coal terminus, for unloading and distribution. When the first train arrived in Leeds bells were rung and cannon fired.

The original Act of Parliament, which of course had to be agreed by Leeds Borough, required the colliery to provide a specific amount of coal to Leeds and only to Leeds, at a specific price. At first this was 240 corfes (or corb, basket, about 210 pounds weight) at four pence three farthings per corfe. There were several subsequent Acts, each one authorising a greater quantity at a higher price.

Technological changes came in quick succession. This led in 1787 and 1796 to strikes and machine breaking by the miners. John Smeaton, engineer, of Leeds made steam pumps for the mines in the 1780s and in 1793 new pumps were bought from Boulton and Watt. Brandling's agent, Blenkinsop, patented a rack rail method of traction in 1811 and commissioned the leading Leeds firm of Fenton, Murray and Wood to design a steam locomotive to use the system. Matthew Murray (1765–1826) reckoned that £2,000 operating costs per annum could be saved by using steam engines rather than horses. He worked fast. His engine was tested on 24 June 1812 and a regular service started on 12 August 1812. The engine had been built at the Fenton, Murray and Wood works at Holbeck, just yards from the railway terminus.

The 5-ton engine could do the work of sixteen horses pulling coal. Horses were still used extensively for shunting and other work at the colliery, and for onward wholesale and retail distribution. The engine could pull twenty-seven wagons (or 'trams') with 94 tons at 3.5 mph on the level. On a one in eighteen gradient the load was reduced to as little as 15 tons. Ten miles per hour was the maximum speed possible. This was a big step at the time. It may seem very modest now but it was the first commercially successful steam-worked railway in the world.

USE OF COAL IN LEEDS

In earlier days in Leeds, coal would be seen only in the houses of the wealthy. It was a common sight in the furnaces and forges and the blacksmith and the whitesmith. By the age of Queen Elizabeth many merchants and entrepreneurs became rich from mining tin and coal, and some of the aristocrats under whose land the minerals lay. In the Leeds area this included the estates of the Earls of Cardigan, Harewood and Mexborough.

London was a great consumer of coal brought down from northern coalfields by sea. New dwelling houses, and more especially those of stone or brick, were installed with chimneys and chimneystacks. The role of domestic fires in the production of smoke was noted in 1810 with mocking accuracy by Sir Richard Phillips, a famous satirist and commentator of the times:

> The smoke of nearly a million coal fires, issuing from the two hundred thousand houses which comprise London and its vicinity ... Half a million of chimneys each vomiting a bushel of smoke per second.

———— COAL WAGGON ————

Coal merchants cart.

Many of us today live in old houses that still have several fireplaces and chimneys and maybe a coalhole in the street outside, but most fireplaces are no longer used to burn coal. A hearth was an attractive indication of wealth and consumption for taxation. So we have a Leeds Hearth Tax List dated 1672. Many families would probably not have had a proper fireplace, but the list tells us that of those who did two-fifths had one hearth, two-fifths had two to three hearths and one fifth had ten or more. The latter category was no doubt the double-fronted, three-storey houses of stone and brick of the wealthy merchants. These would have had fireplaces in upstairs rooms and servants to service them all. The historical record is lacking in the field of the domestic use of coal and also of the retail end of coal marketing.

At the time Turton was trading there were 102 collieries in the borough of Leeds. None of the surrounding moors had been substantially built over. Their depth did not exceed 300ft and none could compete with the Middleton Colliery for output, but their proximity to place of use ensured their viability. As the economy and population grew in tandem so did the need for coal. A new factor was the production and use of coal gas for heating, lighting and power. The first Leeds Gas Company started business in 1818, soon joined by one other firm. The council took over in 1869, and Turton was to serve on the Gas Committee.

William Turton, as we have seen, was trained as an apprentice mechanic. He knew the basics of machinery and the steam engine; coal and gas were familiars. As a boy he had seen the first train depart from Leeds. As an apprentice he had seen the construction of Crown Point Bridge, a triumph of iron and the steam engine. His house no doubt burnt coal but would not have had gas lighting. Nor at first did his business use steam-powered machinery.

The developments we have sketched made the distribution of coal, the logistics of coal, more complex and we can see a growth in the number of related trades in successive commercial directories. There was room for more coal merchants. Who could be more ready, better placed in every sense, than William Turton? We do not know in which year he started; by about the mid-1850s would be a fair guess. The first directory entry for him as a coal dealer is 1860. He was then at a wharf in Water Lane, south of the river, close to the colliery terminus, Kitson's engineering works, Tetley's brewery and other major works. He later set up also at Crown Point, with a staith on the northeast corner. The cost of moving coal was enormous; anything over a few miles had to done by water. Leeds was connected by water to the Irish Sea and the German (North) Sea. The Aire and Calder Navigation linked Leeds to many coalmining areas in all directions. In 1861 a new type of barge was introduced in response to competition from the railway, which had extended from Leeds to Goole in 1848. These served until well into the twentieth century. These were known as 'Tom Puddings', steel containers. 'Compartment boats' that measured 25ft x 15ft x 9ft deep, carrying 25 tons, could be linked in a long row of up to fifteen containers like a string of puddings or sausages. They could come right up to Turton's wharf at Crown Point where he had the storage space, the wagons, the horses, the workforce, sacks, winches, scales and cashiers.

He was used to breaking down cargoes, baling and sacking, storage and delivery. In modern terms he was not just a corn and coal merchant, he was a 'logistics specialist'.

Turton's business was, as we shall see more clearly later on, crucially influenced, and on the whole enabled, by political developments, both national and regional. He was well aware of this. The Leeds Council take-overs of water (1852), roads (1866) and gas (1869) all had an effect on the improvement of markets for coal. An Act of 1832 comprehensively regulated the sale of coal. In particular it required sale by weight and not by the very varied and contradictory local volume measures that had been used previously. This was passed in spite of objections that the practice of watering sacks to reduce dust could add weight and cost.

The number of middlemen in the marketing of coal could be quite extensive. Collieries might employ or contract a factor to deal with all the output. Turton was almost certainly not such a factor or sole agent. He probably bought from several collieries and probably more local ones. He would have visited the mines and have been familiar with conditions. After all he supplied them with fodder for the pit ponies, to which we shall return. No 'dead mileage' for Turton's wagons there.

He sold to some large customers. The workhouse is one that we have a record for. The largest of coal users almost certainly had their own arrangements for resourcing their fuel requirements. The railways, gasworks and major factories all had their own wharves for coal deliveries.

Turton did not advertise much in newspapers or directories, yet many coal dealers did. This was at the smaller retail end of the market trail, with amounts of coal and cash given on a scale that would allow the careful householder to maximise choice. Just as for millennia people have gathered coal for free from the seashore and open cast deposits, so the poorer dwellers in the urban jungle devise their own methods and sources. Thus at the end of the fuel chain we have the Leeds 'tricklers', the young boys who followed the coal carts collecting the 'trickles' of coal that fell – or perhaps had been encouraged to fall – off the back of the wagon. The practice of having a pair of wagons coupled together made this practice easier to do unseen by the driver.

This reference to a traditional form of 'gathering winter fuel' permits an observation that coal could be used as a medium of gift exchange. I will allow that my ancestor was careful with money, cautious and not spendthrift. And yet it would be bad anthropology to lapse into so-called Yorkshire stereotypes. But he was neither a Puritan nor a Scrooge. He shows himself to be a kind and generous man. I relish the hint of ambiguity in his obituary comment that 'the extent of his unobtrusive generosity' was not to be known, but that 'many a poor family will remember with gratitude the timely relief which a sack of coals or some other seasonal gift has brought them'.

Could Turton have foreseen the great expansion of production and use of coal during his lifetime? He saw what was going on around him. He read the conservative *Yorkshire Post* for choice and no doubt the *Leeds Mercury*. Most importantly he met and talked with many men in all the major industries and professions. It is part of the nature and talent of men such as William Turton to be thinking ahead of the game. He knew how to assess risk and he was not a gambler. But as a coal and corn merchant he acted alone. His decisive early decisions were made without benefit of elder relatives, sons or partners.

Let us for a moment take stock of this phenomenon of growth from the second half of the century. Even after the expansion of housing in Leeds by 1860, which began to include building on the moors, there were still 83 collieries in the borough producing 2,459,000 tons of coal per annum. Moving up to regional and national levels of production, the following, admittedly rather fragmentary, figures tell the story:

Coal production in Yorkshire and Great Britain 1854–1914		
Year	Tons, all Yorkshire	Tons, Great Britain
1854	–	64,666,000
1870	11,545,400	–
1900	28,250,679	225,181,000
1909	38,578,878*	–
1914	–	287,666,000
* 1909 West Riding		
mines**	398	
workers (underground)	111,342	
workers (surface)	29,683	
** 1909 largest mine: Condesby Main		
seam	10ft	
gallery	16ft	
depth	763ft	
workforce	3,228 (all adult males)	
annual output	1,000,000 tons	

MINING ACCIDENTS

Two human costs of coal that I shall consider are first the conditions of production – the human, socialised labour used in the extraction and transport of coal. Secondly I consider what we now call the environmental costs. Everyone used or benefited from coal. Most households bought some form of coal. William Turton made a trading profit from the sale of coal. He was, as we shall see, concerned about public health and well-being. He was well informed about social conditions, from intimate experience and the best available statistics. He engaged, as a citizen and councillor, to try doing something to improve these conditions, within the ideological and institutional constraints of the times.

The work of a coalminer must be one of the most demanding and dangerous of all. How much more so in the days before safety lights, trade unions or employers' responsibility? Yet it provided much employment for people in mainly agricultural areas. Families sent successive generations 'down the mine'. These included children from the age of 5, girls from 7–21. Women and children were especially employed to transport coal from seam to surface. They were cheaper than horses.

The increase in use of steam engine industrial processes from the end of the eighteenth century had its specific effects on labour. Self-employed labour, notably weavers who worked at home, saw a big decline in income. Factory staff wages were lowered and there were lay-offs. The situation in coalmines was different. Pits might become exhausted and owners bankrupt, but miner's wages were high relative to other workers. A daily wage of 2s 6d was a longstanding norm, in range 2–4s. Middleton Colliery workers were able to demand a wage increase by threatening to strike, a technique well developed by the end of the eighteenth century. A mining family's joint income could be quite considerable. Exceptionally, given the conditions of work and the high value of the product, miners often worked an eight-hour day.

As usual, working conditions were both improved and threatened by the relentless introduction of new technology. William Firth, a Leeds entrepreneur who later became a councillor with whom Turton would have dealings, introduced a new coal-cutting machine in 1863. At the coalface it had a 75-pound weight pick that could strike at seventy blows per minute. It was superseded five years later by a disc cutter that had a longer life.

News of accidents in deep mines continues to horrify us. We tend to hear of them in countries where coal production is on a large scale and where best practice safety conditions may not be in place. The Turton family were no strangers to news of pit disasters, usually deep mine explosions. In the month of William Turton's birth there was an explosion at the Middleton colliery near Gosforth. Twenty-five men and boys were killed. The oldest was a man in his forties, an age not reached by a majority of working miners, who left a widow and ten children, no doubt some of them already down the pit. The youngest to die was John Amber, a 5-year-old boy.

The catalogue of mine disasters is horrendous. They vie with shipwrecks and railway crashes in the graphic pages of the *Illustrated London News*. The use of children in underground mines was one of the early subjects of reform legislation.

Some notable pit disasters that affected the people of Leeds include the following: 1833, Halifax, thirty children killed in six pits, seventeen aged 5–9 years old; 1857, Lundhill, 189 died; and 1866, Barnsley 361 died (the worst incident until 1910). Over the period 1851–96 in just fourteen Yorkshire pits, there were 1,149 fatalities.

More miners died as a result of inhaling coal dust and gases at the coalface than from explosions. Even more lives were shortened by the end products, smoke and particulates from the chimneys of factories, public buildings and houses alike. It was not just the content of the smoke that was dangerous. Combined with other air conditions, it blocked out sunlight. De Toqueville's described the sun as seen in industrial England as a 'disc without rays' It could not penetrate to provide the Vitamin D that was needed to prevent the pervasive occurrence of rickets and malformation of the limbs of children.

At almost the final end of the process of production and consumption, literally before the smoke left the chimney, there was the task of sweeping clean the chimney to prevent soot blocking the flues or falling into fireplaces. A combination of social outrage and Victorian sentimentality has ensured that the image of the 'little chimney sweep' remains an icon of the times. A child sweep might have to climb ten or more chimneys in a day. An incident in Leeds in 1825 is just one of countless tales. Joseph Haddock, master sweep, employed several boys whom he sent up chimneys for a few pence a day. In one legal case it was reported that he had repeatedly sent one of his boys to climb another chimney after he was exhausted. The boy, a vulnerable orphan son of an African woman, ran away and was taken into the care of the workhouse. An Act of 1875 finally made it illegal to send any person up a chimney.

SMOKE

Smoke is a player in many episodes of our story. The tall brick chimneystack, built as high as possible, or as the law required, to disperse the smoke, is a perfect icon for the steam age of the industrial revolution. Engines had to be developed that 'consumed their own smoke and vapours'. Coke, which is partly burnt and purified coal, became increasingly the fuel of choice after about 1872.

Visitors described with a mixture of awe and horror the smoky landscape of Leeds well before the end of the eighteenth century. Industrial zoning was not a requirement in the early phases of the industrial age.

The attempt in Leeds to create a salubrious 'West End' of fashionable housing failed because some of the chief factories and mills were already sited to the west. The largest was the firm of Gott and Sons, woollen cloth manufacturers. They were brought to court in 1824. The charge was that 'you did emit divers noisesome, unwholesome and offensive smells, stenches, smokes and vapours from ten stoves and ten furnaces consuming coal, charcoal and coke'.

The case was brought by people who not only shared the general 'dread of smoke', but had bought land or houses in the newly developing 'West End', reaching west from Park Square and Park Place. The evidence of the nuisance and the danger was clear. Dairymen had to wash their cows before milking; the ladies' dresses were besmirched with soot from shrubs and hedges. But the judge ordered the case stopped and directed the jury to find for the Gotts on the grounds that the residents could well have known what to expect before they made their investments.

Before long the strategy for those who could afford it was not to go west but north, and uphill. Even moving as far as North Street and Sheepscar, about one mile north of the Aire, was at first a move to a kind of suburbia. In 1845 Mayor Darnton Lupton said, 'everyone who can is going out of town'. The Turton family moved to the north end of

The last pit pony died, aged 40, in 2011; this photograph c.1980.

North Street in about 1860 and by 1870 were living 1 mile further north, and further uphill, on Chapeltown Road (the Harrogate Road) at the southern end of Potternewton and Chapel Allerton. This area was close to open spaces and in due course the largest of all, Roundhay Park. William Turton himself spent most of his daylight hours in Leeds city centre and in numerous other, equally smoky northern towns. He survived in generally good health for seventy-six years. In the end smoke must have contributed largely to his death from bronchitis.

Only after the 'killer smog' of 1952, when at least 4,000 people died in the London area, did Parliament deal with this environmental catastrophe by passing the Clean Air Act of 1956.

We might say that corn and coal, between them King Coal and Ceres, goddess of grain, fuelled the nineteenth century. Turton's trading in these commodities certainly made him wealthy. Even in the age of the petrol and diesel turbine and on the threshold of nuclear power, the coalmines of northern England were still using pit ponies for the underground haulage of coal. As late as 1940, old William Whalley, who had started to work for Turton on 14 February 1876, becoming secretary, manager and director, said in an interview with the *Yorkshire Post* that the firm of 'William Turton, Leeds, Corn & Hay Merchant' was still providing forage for some 2,000 pit ponies in a West Yorkshire colliery they had been supplying for nearly seventy years.

Even when electricity had replaced the horse, the steam tram and the gaslight, it was still coal that produced most of the electric power. In 1896 the City Council started to operate a coal-fired electricity generating plant on its site next to 64–66 The Calls. Metal boundary markers – WT 1896 – suggest that Turton may have sold land to them for this. He may also have supplied the coal.

In his will, Turton left all his coal business to Robert, the younger of his two surviving sons. He left all his corn and hay business to George, the elder son. This division suggests that the latter was the more important in scale. At the same time it suggests that the division would be seen as fair and balanced. In any case the two sons had largely been in charge for some years back. Robert developed the coal business successfully and traded in other mined products. This part of the Turton empire was bought out by a larger mining company, which became part of the Limmer group.

6

HORSEPOWER

Turton's corn warehouse at Nos 64–66 The Calls stands at a focal point on the northern bank of the Aire by Crown Point Bridge. The visitor or passer-by first notices a massive four-storey structure, well ordered in decent brick and stone. Closer viewing reveals two notable features. The first is Turton's name and the date of the building carved in stone above the corner doorway. The second, just down into The Calls, is a huge archway, broad enough to permit the passage of the largest wagon loaded as high as possible with straw and hay. The keystone of the arch is carved with a fine and attractive horse's head. The only figurative detail on the whole building, it is emblematic of Turton's entire enterprise.

Pack horse c.1815.

We have already introduced Turton's involvement with animal fodder and the start of his interest in horse-drawn transport. It is now time to put the horse before the cart. The horse has of course been used for human transport for millennia. Long before the invention of the wheel for transport they were used for riding and as pack animals, as they are to this day. They can also pull wheel-less vehicles, such as sledges and boats, on appropriate surfaces.

To this day the horse remains a creature of beauty, value and usefulness. It is prized for its contributions to sporting and leisure activity, to ceremonial and high status occasions. Anyone may ride a horse. Few people in Britain would be likely to eat horse-meat by choice, though we know well that in many countries it is valued for human consumption.

Strangely, I have no evidence of William Turton riding a horse, but I am sure he did. His son John won a silver tankard as a prize for the best-kept horse in an annual Yorkshire Yeomanry gathering. His grandson, my grandfather, told me, more than once, that he himself refused to go to school unless he was given a pony. This was an excuse for us children insisting that he showed us his crooked right arm, broken and badly set after a fall from a horse.

We still celebrate the strength of a horse in the term 'horsepower', though I doubt we know what that really is. I recall as a child seeing an Austin 7 hp car and assuming it must be like being pulled by seven horses. How grand for such a small car.

Curiously horsepower started life as a measure of the power of steam machines, namely the ability of a horse to raise a weight vertically over time. The original and most used formula was based on the work of London dray (Shire) horses, which is probably about twice that of an average horse. James Watt developed this measure experimentally. His famous name was used in turn as a measure of electric power. And so we have the hybrid Imperial Unit of one horsepower equivalent to 745.7 watts. A horse might have the manpower of about eight men; a tram steam engine that of 8.5 horses.

Despite the mythical and iconic, the glamorous and nostalgic associations of the horse (man's second-best friend?) this animal has not to my mind been given due historical respect as a transport animal. Maybe the iron horse has blinkered us.

The point to be emphasised here is that the use of horses and horse-drawn transport increased enormously throughout the nineteenth century. Horses continued to be a critical economic resource until the mid-twentieth century in Western Europe. The horse had been the fastest means of human land transport until the steam train, by the mid-1820s. Canals brought a new use for their haulage, as the towpaths still bear witness. A horse at walking speed can move approximately fifty times its weight pulling a boat as it can a cart on a road. The Aire and Calder Navigation used horses to draw barges at Dewsbury until 1950.

Horses used in freight haulage 1851–1911	
1851	161,000
1891	500,000
1901 *	702,000
1911	832,000
* Pulling passenger transport in 1901	450,000

The steam train rapidly made the horse-drawn carriage redundant for long distance, intercity travel after the 1850s. But trains did not reach everywhere: not the inner city, nor most of the countryside, nor the coalmines (for underground transport) nor by and large in military use. Trains were part of a highly integrated transport system, as we might call it nowadays. In fact they increased demand and depended enormously on horse-drawn transport to link up with the termini, the stations in towns and the rural halts, and the canal system. In 1902 there were some 3.5 million horses in the UK and about 15 million acres of arable land used to support them. In the USA the total number of horses was 30 million, which consumed the grain product of about one-third of the area planted to crop.

It was to be the combustion engine that replaced the horse, not the steam train.

BUYING HORSES

The horses used in Leeds would have been mainly bred in Yorkshire of local and Irish stock. There had long been a specific 'Yorkshire coach horse' bred for that trade. Soper describes the horses that drew omnibuses and trams as:

> ... principally Irish, short, clean-legged, powerful, 15.5–16.5 hands high and about five or six years when bought. They had a useful turn of speed for their moderate weight and had a higher, more stylish action than the heavy draught horses still used by breweries today.

Leeds Tramways Company (LTC) experimented with mules for a period of exactly one month. On 9 June 1879 they purchased three mules for £114 4s and sold them on for £117 on 9 July. Mules, as has been shown over and over again, are, to say the least, 'unpredictable'. It was an inexpensive experiment that took place under the chairmanship of William Turton. He did most of the selection of horses for both his own buses and the trams.

Soper judges that 'The LTC was fortunate in that its chairman, William Turton, and manager, William Wharam, both had a good eye for a horse. Turton was particularly skilful in the purchase of sound horses ...' Horses were sold at Leeds Fair, off Camp Road, on 1–12 July, formerly at Briggate. There were a dozen or so regular horse deal-

Shire horse and Shetland pony.

Brewery dray horse and wagon, 1889.

ers who brought their animals to the Hunslet depot in south Leeds in what was at first still in rural surroundings. In 1896 the Leeds Council Tramways went as far as Boroughbridge Fair in the Vale of York to buy thirteen horses at competitive prices. Prices remained fairly constant. The bus and tram horse cost on average £30, which was probably about the median in a £25–£35 range. The common term 'pony' is no doubt based on the lower value of a small horse, typically purchased for £25 pounds.

Horses were subject to being requisitioned or compulsorily purchased by the military. Under the Military Mounts Scheme of 1888, 200 LTC horses were registered with the War Office, which paid 7s 6d per horse per year for the right to claim them at any time. It seems they did pay for them. Leeds horses served in the Transvaal War of 1876–81. In 1899 forty tram horses were sold to the army at £45 each, and in 1900 sixty-one horses, at £50. These were good prices considering that 1900 was the last year in which Leeds bought any tram horses. In January 1902 they held a clearance sale of most of the rest.

When the horses ceased to able to do the hard work of drawing trams and buses they were sold for about £5–6. They were then used for lighter work in town or on the farm. Horse dung was sold for 2–5d per horse per week; at least this achieved the regular removal of great quantities of manure from the city. A standard price was 2s per wagonload. Nationally some 42 million tons of horse manure was produced annually. Horse manure was important enough for Turton to advertise in the *Yorkshire Post* (15 February 1875). In terms of renewable energy, the horse was a champion:

To Farmers. A quantity of good HORSE MANURE to be sold cheap. Apply Turton's. Omnibus Proprietor, Harrison Street, New Briggate, Leeds.

At death a carcass was worth £1 10s: bones made fertiliser and buttons; oil and fat were used in leather dressing and stearin wax for candles; horseshoes were sent to the farrier, tails and mane to the upholsterer; hides were used for carriage roofs and whips, and the remaining flesh for cat and dog food.

I shall not attempt to estimate the number of horses in Leeds in these times. It was very large, though nothing compared with today's ownership of motor vehicles. The owners included those of higher wealth and status who owned horses for riding and their personal transport, their traps and gigs, Broughams, Landaus and Phaetons. There were professional carters and carriers, with their cabriolets and hansom cabs, coaches, waggonettes and buses, fly-vans and wagons and all manner of carts. There were other specialist users such as brewers with their drays, undertakers and their hearses, scavengers (or refuse collectors as they were later known), builders, merchants of bulk goods, provision merchants and wholesalers of all sorts. The number of associated trades attests to the importance of this sector of the town's economy: saddlers and harness makers, blacksmiths, whitesmiths (for brass-work etc.), coach makers, wheelwrights and axle makers. There were related occupations such as coachman, conductor, lamp boy, stable-keeper, groom and many other forms of labour.

FEEDING HORSES

Given a £30 initial cost and working life expectancy of five years and a sale price at the end of £5, then £5 is the annual capital cost of the horse. However, the annual cost of feeding and maintaining the horse was more than £50 a year. Of this sum £36 was spent on corn, hay and straw. It is immediately clear that as a corn and hay merchant and an investor in horses for transport, William Turton was 'onto a good thing'. This assertion will be examined in the chapters to come.

Soper gives a detailed break down of the weekly cost of keeping the horse:

Weekly costs of horse maintenance			
	Pounds	Shillings	Pence
Corn and hay		15	6
Straw and moss litter			6
Wages for stableman, foreman and Utensils such as brushes		3	11
Shoeing and wages of blacksmith		1	3
Veterinary surgeon and medicine			3
Weekly total for one horse	1	1	5
Annual total	55	13	10

We have already introduced the various kinds of horse and cattle food in Chapter 4. The average weekly need of the LTC was 5 tons of meadow hay and 5 tons of clover and seed hay. Tenders for hay were invited every six months. The bus and tram horses might consume about 25lb of fodder per day, which is about four tons each year. This might comprise about 2.5 tons of oats and 1.5 tons of hay. A Shire horse might consume 30lb per day or 5 tons per year. The Tetley brewery dray horses are recorded as being given other treats such as sugar beet pulp, treacle and occasionally beer. A small horse or pony might need about three tons per year.

In view of the importance and relative cost of horse fodder, 'The Tramways Company was again fortunate in its chairman, Turton, who was in business as a corn merchant and gave good advice'. We shall consider later whether he managed to avoid conflicts of interest, and if so how. Turton was to be successful in reducing the cost to LTC of both horses and their fodder. But the cost of horse energy in the late nineteenth century was to make it inefficient in the face of massive increase in demand, for transport and profit. Whether the horse was working or not, it ate 20 per cent of receipts.

STABLING HORSES

The depots and stables for omnibus and tram horses differed mainly only in scale. They both depended on the needs of horses and the need to avoid 'dead mileage' of horses and cars returning to base. They were at first makeshift and rented, but on the more important routes were often newly commissioned, even architect designed, and substantial. These were built of brick and steel with slate roofs, and often had an imposing clock on the roof or front wall. The terminus was the chief site of course. The inner-city termini served several routes. Dispersal of stables was necessary also to diminish cross-infection of horse diseases. The termini were invariably at or close to an inn or hotel of some size and reputation. In fact inns and their many services were a main ancillary to the urban transport system. A number of innkeepers became bus and carriage owners. As we shall see, William's son John married the daughter of an inner-city innkeeper.

A large depot might have stalls for a hundred or more horses, with additional stalls for sick horses. There would be a large space for the cars and at one end the manure pit and privy. There were offices for the cashier and foreman, space for drivers, conductors etc., a waiting room, workshops for the blacksmith and mechanics, stores for fodder, grit and salt, and a lamp room, situated as far as it could be from the straw and hay. The foreman would have a detached cottage nearby as part of the ensemble. The owner or company built cottages for others key workers.

THE WORKING HORSE

As a corn merchant Turton sold fodder to users of horses in many trades: the collieries which used up to 73,000 pit ponies by 1914, municipal services (refuse collection, fire, police etc.) and private carriage owners. About one-third of horses were worked in towns, which suited Turton's market. Some of the chief users in London in about 1890, out of a total of 300,000 horses, were:

Private carriages: 40,000
Cabs: 22,000
Tramways: 10,000
Railways: 6,000
Pickford's removals: 4,000
London breweries: 3,000
Coal transport: 3,000
Carter Paterson removals: 2,000
Refuse collection: 1,500

It is of interest to note that while the use of private horse-drawn carriages declined dramatically after the First World War, the number of horses employed was made up for by a great increase in horses for riding and hunting.

In the war itself Turton's grandson William was a captain in the Army Service Corps (in 1918 Royal Army Service Corps, now the Royal Logistical Corps), in charge of supporting the horses of the 62 West Riding Division. Many more horses were used for transport than in cavalry units as such. Some of the specialist uses included:

Ambulances
Ammunition
Cookers
Forage
General Service wagons
Offices
Pigeon lofts
Pontoon carrying
Stores
Veterinary horse ambulances
Water
Wire laying

Horses were of greatest value as general transport and drawing heavy artillery, rather than cavalry as such. The weight of fodder sent to the front exceeded that of all munitions. Nearly half-a-million transport animals were killed on war service.

The bus and tram horse was fully mature and broken in when purchased. Some additional training might be needed on the job. Horses were famously intelligent – sagacious is a word often used – and quick to learn their trade. Soper cites a description of the London tram horse from an article in the *Yorkshire Post* of 1885:

I see them start when the bell rings, and I see them stop when the second bell rings, even when it does so within two seconds. Yet when the bus is in full roll, the conductor rings twice to show the driver he is 'full inside', and the horses knows the double ring and never pause in their stride. I am driving down Oxford Street. At the corner of Bond Street an old lady wants to cross the road. The policeman holds up his white-gloved hand and the horses stop – automatically, not pulled up by Jehu. The lady is safely across; the policeman jerks his thumb forward, and the horse starts again. A heavy dray is in front. Without a sign the horses swerve to circumvent. I sometimes think the conductor might drive by merely pulling his bell cord, and so save the driver's wages.

The life span and working capacity of a horse cannot be assessed with certainty when purchased, though the buyer was allowed a trial period. A few died within weeks of starting. Most could be expected to give four to five years' service pulling heavy passenger vehicles before a kind of semi-retirement. Ten to fifteen years in service was possible. The record seems to have been held by horse No. 262, purchased in about 1877 and sold in January 1900 – after more than twenty-two years' service. This was about the term of Turton as chairman and director of the company that bought and was served by this animal.

A fully loaded double-decker horse tram weighed about 5 tons. If it had to climb gradients it would need three horses. Most routes used two horses. A horse might work four to five hours per day. Six hours seems to be the limit for any horse work. This probably meant a distance of some 12 to 14 miles. Soper estimates that 'To keep a three-horse car on the road with a daily mileage of 70 miles needed 16 horses, five teams on duty plus a spare.'

The tramline reduced friction, which allowed the horse to pull twice the weight with the same effort compared with wheel on road surface, with an obvious gain in return. If the formula was not in practice as exact as this and the horse expended less effort for a given task over time, there was nonetheless a 'lengthening of the working day' for the horses. So they were required to make as much or more effort. Their rewards remained the same. It could be seen as a kind of animal slavery, echoing the distinction the Romans made between *instrumentum mutum* (tool or machine), *instrumentum semi-vocalis* (horse or ox) and *instrumentum vocalis* (human slave).

There are photographs and numerous reports of worn out horses in harness. It was a hard life. But tell that to their human counterparts, the 'wage-slaves'. The better owners and managers certainly included William Turton and the LTC. Stung by a letter to a newspaper that alleged mistreatment, the LTC took the case to court and won. The RSPCA actively monitored the treatment of horses. The use of salt on the lines was in particular held to be detrimental to the horses. We sometimes still see stone 'horse troughs' at the roadside to provide water for horses (and other animals). These are often charitable gifts from individuals and societies. Interestingly, Leeds was praised even at the very start of the nineteenth century for its plentiful supply of these welcome items. Inconveniently tram horses could not reach them.

Horses occasionally died in harness in the streets, which was bad publicity for the owners. The knacker's cart was fairly prompt to come and winch the carcass onto a cart and take it to the knacker's yard. Veterinary surgeons were employed to care for sick horses. For the public there was Oddy's Hospital for Horses and all kinds of Cattle at Water Lane run by Mr Samuel Oddy, veterinary surgeon. A kind of horse flu was especially infectious and dangerous. In 1890 the LTC lost six horses and some bus owners lost almost all of their animals from disease. This is a reminder of one major and specific uncertainty in the use of horses on this scale. It was no doubt an important contributory factor in the failure of a number of transport enterprises.

There was an aesthetic of the tram horse, not to mention the car. The Tramways Company and some of the omnibus proprietors, notably Barmfitt, Turton and Walker, prided themselves on their horses. The horses were to be seen, carefully groomed, matched for colour and gaily caparisoned on May Day and other parades. The tram horses were generally considered to be the best in Leeds. There are photographs of trams decked out for occasions such as royal jubilees, royal visits, recruiting drives, victory celebrations and so on.

Horses had numbers for administrative purposes; when they died their numbers were re-allocated. So too were names, though this was less systematic. The five horses on Turton's Meanwood bus-line when he sold it in 1878 were Tom, Charlie, Jet, Duke and Polly. Another owner, Elizabeth Riley, named her Hunslet bus line horses Doctor, Jimmy, Paddy, Prince, Johnny, Roger and Barney. Stable-keepers and their staff could become very fond of their charges. There is a touching anecdote of one who prepared his old horse for the knacker by blacking her hooves and brushing her coat. He broke down in tears on the way to the yard.

7

TURTON'S BUSES

'The age of the train' is often given as the period 1830–1914. This is much celebrated and rightly so. But for inner-city and inner-suburban transport the period 1825–1903 is 'the horse-drawn era', a not so dissimilar epoch. This has had fewer champions. It neatly coincides with the life of William Turton.

LEEDS TRANSPORT FROM THE 1820s

What was transport like for people in Leeds in about 1825? The previous year had seen a 'Leeds Improvement Act' that required all 'hackney carriages, cars, gigs, and sedan chairs to be licensed'. Most of these had stands in Briggate or nearby. This was the beginning of municipal regulation of urban transport, which was to increase greatly later in the century.

The size of the town and locations of surrounding villages and industrial sites were such that most people could quite easily walk to work and to places of local entertainment. This was travelling by 'shank's mare' or 'shank's pony'. Newer metaphors included 'Walker's bus', and if you had no means of locomotion you travelled 'under your own steam'.

The crowded narrow inner streets were shared by cattle, pigs and other creatures, especially on market days. The upper classes had their private carriages. This entailed ownership of a coach, at least two horses and probably a coachman and groom, and stables. Elegant ladies and some gentlemen might require a sedan chair to save their costumes from the mud and prevent them arriving out of breath. The sedan chair, a French invention, was in use in Leeds from the beginning of its modest 'Georgian' period in about 1767. They were one-person vehicles, a small covered carriage on two poles and a stand, carried by two 'chairmen'. These were in use in the 1820s but became increasingly rare in following years. Of course many people would ride from outlying villages and suburbs, to market and, on other occasions, on horses, with pony and trap and on all sorts of four-wheeled 'wagons' that were mainly designed for the transport of goods and produce. There were also various passenger wagons or carts, also sometimes called 'cars'. There were modified goods vehicles that might carry six to twelve people. Entrepreneurs, especially innkeepers, ran these on market days to bring in people from the villages.

A still quite new and fashionable form of transport for one or two people was the hansom cab. The general term for these vehicles was 'hackney carriage', hackney being a name for a horse and so denoting a horse-drawn carriage for hire. Mr Hansom invented an advanced form known as 'Hansom cabs'. Here cab is short for cabriolet, a two-wheeled enclosed carriage for two passengers. The driver sat behind with the reins going over the roof. They were not cheap. The following is a schedule of prices for the period:

Vehicle hire charges
Hackney carriages
First 15 minutes 1s, then 6d (i.e. 2s per hour)
Per day (12 hours) 18s
Cars, gigs etc. (up to four passengers)
First 15 minutes 8d, then 4d (i.e. 1s per hour)
Per day (12 hours) 12s, double for midnight to 7.00 a.m.

Wagonettes, Leeds Terrace, 1902.

The first hansom cab, 1834.

London cab, 1823.

In 1875 there were 4,000 cab drivers in Leeds for whom forty-three cabmen's shelters had been erected.

In 1830, before the advent of railways, Leeds had 180 'carriers', small businesses dealing in the transport of goods, with various wagons and fly-vans. They operated by land and 'coastwise and by canal', as the brochures of the time said. There were no fewer than 122 principal destinations with daily or weekly services. Some routes had several carriers competing; some were monopolies.

There were thirteen Leeds carriers who specifically linked up with canals and river navigation systems. Some carriers advertised fast boats to Hull to connect with 'steam packets to Holland and Germany'. Journey times by water continued to improve; the journey by canal from Leeds to Liverpool took only two days. It is very clear that there was an extensive, integrated and systematic combination of forms of transport at this time. Until steamboats became widespread, horses were employed both for road and canal transport. The primary fuel was therefore corn and hay.

Here is an example of the connectedness and efficiency of the passenger transport system in the early nineteenth century. Major Cartwright, aged 70, was a member of the Hampden Club in London, a Whig (or 'Liberal') group for radical Parliamentary reform. He undertook several politically 'evangelising' tours of England in 1812, 1813 and 1815. In January and February 1813 he visited no fewer than thirty-five places in barely thirty days: Lutterworth, Hinckley, Leicester, Loughborough, Chesterfield, Sheffield, Huddersfield, Bradford, Wakefield, Leeds, Preston, Wigan, Liverpool, Bolton, Manchester, Lees, Stockport, Newcastle, Birmingham, Worcester, Tewkesbury, Gloucester, Stroud, Bath, Shepton Mallet, Bridgewater, Taunton, Wellington, Bristol, Calne, Marlborough, Newbury, Hungerford, Abingdon, Reading.

This was long before the train and the telegraph; the horse was still the fastest thing, the best way to travel. All these journeys were done by horse-drawn carriage.

A BRIEF HISTORY OF THE STAGECOACH

There are several reasons why it is appropriate to review the development of coach transport as part of the history of the horse-drawn omnibus and tram. Although the stagecoach as the prime form of intercity transport had ceased to operate by the year Turton started up (1844) such coaches were still to be seen working in smaller towns and suburbs, and for summer outings and visits to the 'watering places' or spa towns of Yorkshire until the end of the century. The nine principal coaching inns in Leeds continued to be termini for the new bus routes and the stabling of horses. The Atkinsons of Leeds and Greenwoods of Manchester, with whom Turton had close dealings, were all veterans of the coaching days.

Before 1600 only the aristocracy and very senior figures travelled by coach, and it was not a comfortable experience. Horses were hired by the stage. Some women and sick people might be carried on horse litters. Subsequently broad-wheeled stage wagons, drawn by eight to ten horses with the driver riding alongside on a separate horse, were introduced. The stagecoach as such appeared by about 1640 in which year there just six stage coaches in the country. By 1658 there were three departures weekly from London to York. In 1678 Ralph Thoresby travelled home from Holland via Hull and stagecoach to York; from there he took a horse since coaches to Leeds did not operate in winter. Thoresby also visited London by coach taking four to six days each way.

Leeds has long played a supra-regional role in passenger transport. An extraordinary census taken in 1686 of the inn accommodation in the whole of England, a sort of Michelin guide of its time, ranked Leeds fifth in Yorkshire for its provision of stabling and services for 454 horses and 294 guest beds.

The stagecoach service was only as good as the roads it used. The period 1740–60 saw the introduction of a national network of turnpike roads – privately owned toll roads – and consequent improvement of road surfaces and maintenance. Many rate-payers and other local road users saw this as a disadvantage. In Yorkshire in 1753 there was one of the most serious 'turnpike riots'. Turnpike buildings and gates were destroyed. Soldiers were called out from Leeds and eight protesters were killed with forty wounded, some of whom later died.

The next fifty years or so saw regular improvements in speed, comfort and price. From 1765 coaches left Leeds on schedule from the New King's Inn in Briggate (later the Royal Hotel). The newer, faster coaches, 'flying machines' on steel springs, could do the journey from Leeds to London, a distance of about 192 miles, in two days, with just six passengers, four to six horses, a driver and postilion. But the cost was high at £2 6s. The Leeds Royal Mail in 1785, the fastest of all services, took only twenty-six hours but charged £3 3s, 3 guineas, a smart sum. These rates were equivalent to some airfares or full first-class rail fares today. The slow coaches charged £1 11s 6d inside and £1 1s outside. Whatever the fare the discomforts, delays and accidents were not too dissimilar. There was also the risk of hold-ups. Even Highgate Hill, now very much part of northern inner London, within sight of St Paul's Cathedral, was known as a black spot for highway robbery. Press gangs sometimes operated on main routes, another form of extortion.

The expansion of the stagecoach service can be shown in the following approximate figures for the number of coaches arriving at and departing from Leeds daily:

Year	Arrivals and departures
1800	40
1816	80
1825	110
1838	150

There were direct services to London, Birmingham, Manchester, Liverpool, Newcastle, Hull and Scarborough (via York). Connections could be made to the furthest parts of the kingdom. The interest in their movements gave rise to the first 'coach spotters' in transport history.

The train dramatically shortened the time from Leeds to London. Between about 1785–1830 the fastest coach could travel the distance in thirty hours or so. In 1845 the train took eight hours and in 1910, a mere four.

In Leeds one of the leading stagecoach proprietors was Matthew Outhwaite. He started in 1815 with services from the Bull and Mouth in Briggate and the Royal Hotel (from 1823). His stagecoach service continued until 1846. For several years he teamed up with the Atkinson brothers who had a service that ran from the Albion in the years 1836–42. Like Turton, Outhwaite diversified his transport interests and maximised his opportunities. He was also a freight carrier, and after the start of the railways was among the first to introduce a 'railway bus' to provide a service to the new railway station.

In July 1840, the year of the introduction of the Penny Post, the North Midland Railway opened, and the 'Express', a Leeds mail coach that had started in 1817, ran its last trip to London from the Royal Hotel. In areas not yet served by rail, new stagecoach services were still being started, for example from Ilkley to Leeds in 1841, and from Harrogate to Thirsk in 1842.

Coach routes had to be served by coaching inns, the stage posts. They were responsible for one stage in each direction. These were usually at a distance of 12–15 miles depending on the terrain, in a range of about 7–17 miles. Horses, usually in teams of four, were galloped for much of the distance. It was highly competitive and there were many accidents due to racing, let alone road conditions and drunken driving. The innkeepers were frequently also farmers who might breed their own horses and grow their own corn. They also fed, watered and accommodated the travellers. This provided work for all the family and a good income.

Briggate in the 1850/60s before the arrival of the tram.

Six-horse stagecoach outside the Old King's Arms.

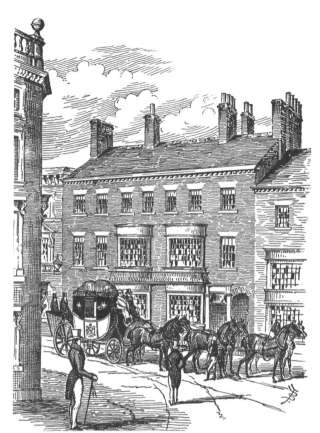

The Rockingham served the Leeds–London route from 1781 until 1841.

The Royal Hotel, Briggate.

In Briggate alone there were twenty-six inns and, in addition, five temperance hotels and nine eating houses, so the traveller was well catered for. The Royal Hotel in Briggate, where Turton was to have one of his bus termini, can serve as an example. It was an eighteenth-century inn, formerly known as the New Kings Arms. It started as a coaching inn in 1765. It had fifty post horses and boys. Some large inns might have one hundred horses and ten post boys. The post 'boys', usually senior men, were crucial to the efficiency and speed of the turn around. Hence it was the operators who paid them in fees and tips. They were not paid by the innkeepers. This was the kind of job that stayed in the family.

Tom Bradley's fine book, beautifully illustrated by himself, *The Old Coaching Days in Yorkshire* (1889) describes the stable at the Royal Hotel:

These stables were below the level of the ground, and were approached from the yard by a sloping subway. The natural conclusion is that they would be stuffy,

103

ill-ventilated holes, but such was not the case. They were roomy, airy places enough, with stone archways and groined roofs, the masonry of which is a strong rebuke to some of our present day jerry construction.

THE HORSE OMNIBUS

The earliest innovation in an urban transport service with fixed routes and schedules was the horse bus known as the 'five sous carriage' (*carosse à cinq sous*). This appeared in late seventeenth-century Paris, where it had a short and unsuccessful life. With greater demand and better-surfaced roads, Paris took them up again in 1826. A certain Mr Omnès devised the motto *omnes omnibus* (Latin 'for all'). London followed soon in July 1829 when George Shillibeer started the first bus service in England, the famous Paddington to Bank route. In a sense this was an early 'railway bus' linking the new Great Western Railway terminal with the heart of London. Up north by the 1850s John Greenwood had 64 buses and 387 horses in Manchester. The London General Omnibus Company had 567 cars and 5,879 horses in 1857. At its peak in 1905 LGOC had 1,1418 cars and 17,000 horses. They were withdrawn in 1914. By then fares of a halfpenny and one penny were common. But in a hundred years speeds had not exceeded about 8 mph.

The omnibus is by definition a long-bodied four-wheeled covered vehicle, with a rear entrance, designed to carry passengers, usually between fixed stations. Seats were at first lengthwise with passengers facing each other or later in rows, sometimes back-to-back in so-called knife-board seats (a term first introduced in 1851). Double-decker buses, at first with open tops, were introduced later. The larger buses could carry thirty to forty passengers with a usual maximum of eighteen on top. The lengthened covered carriage, or car, of the omnibus (or *bus* the term I shall mainly use from now on) was a distinctive departure. Early designs continued to influence the shape and style of many kinds of horse-drawn vehicles including the trams. Many larger towns and cities

Shillibeer's first omnibus, 1829.

had the resources to develop their own carriage-building capability, and Leeds in particular became an important centre for their manufacture.

A new form of public transport calls for a new code of behaviour, as notices in the buses of our own day continually remind us. In 1834 *The Times* published this guide to behaviour in omnibuses:

Omnibus Law

1. Keep your feet off the seats.

2. Do not get into a snug corner yourself, and then open the windows to admit a north-wester [*sic*] upon the neck of your neighbour.

3. Have your money ready when you desire to alight. If your time is not valuable, that of others may be.

4. Do not impose on the conductor the necessity of finding you change; he is not a banker.

5. Sit with your limbs straight, and do not let your legs describe an angle of forty-five, thereby occupying the room of two persons.

6. Do not spit upon the straw. You are not in a hog-sty, but in an omnibus, travelling in a country which boasts of its refinement.

7. Behave respectfully to females, and put not on an unprotected lass to the blush because she cannot escape from your brutality.

8. If you bring a dog, let him be small and confined by a string.

9. Do not introduce large parcels; an omnibus is not a van.

10. Reserve bickerings and disputes for the open field. The sound of your voice may be music to your own ears – not so, perhaps, to those of your companions.

11. If you will breach politics or religion, speak with moderation; all have an equal right to their opinions, and all have an equal right not to have them wantonly shocked.

12. Refrain from affectation and conceited airs. Remember you are riding a distance for sixpence which, if made in a hackney-coach, would cost you as many shillings; and that should your ride elevate you above plebeian accommodations, your purse should enable you to command aristocratic indulgences.

A Coates three-horse bus.

The importance of horse-drawn transport for the new railway system must not be underestimated. The first passenger train service out of Leeds was inaugurated on 22 September 1834. The train left from Marsh Lane terminus in East Leeds, just a short walk from William Turton's home. The train went to Selby, on the Ouse just before it flows into the Humber. Two weeks later Leeds' first bus service was started from the western end of Kirkgate to the station. They were known as 'railway buses' and were sometimes run by the train companies themselves. One of the early operators was the firm of John and William Atkinson. William Turton was just a lad at this time. He was familiar with the sight, and noise, of Atkinson's buses, even if he never could afford to ride on one. The suggestion that he might one day own the firm would have been met with great laughter and ridicule.

June 1838 marks 'the real beginning of suburban transport in Leeds' with the opening of a bus service on the Leeds−Headingley route. The destination, Headingley, was a well-to-do and 'salubrious' outlying village, barely yet a suburb. It remains to this day a favoured suburb (and home of the Yorkshire County Cricket Club). This address and the fare of 6*d* indicate that the 'omnibus' was indeed not for all. At first they were very much for the prosperous middle class, and a few aspirants. It was not until the end of the century that the penny and halfpenny fares came in.

By the end of the following year, 1839, the Atkinson brothers were competing on the Headingley route, and by 1845 they were running twelve services per day from the Black Swan in North Street. William Atkinson (1792−*c*.1868) and his brother John

(1787–1855) had been operating cab services in Leeds since the early 1820s or sooner. They worked from a livery stable that hired out horses and carriages for a variety of purposes. They began to open new routes and services and became major players in the Leeds omnibus business. They moved their livery stable to Harrison Street, which was to become a base for William Turton. They also continued to run a hackney carriage service and, for a while longer, a stagecoach service. But by June 1841, in common with many a transport operator at this time across the country facing increasing competition from railways, they gave up their stagecoach business.

The profitable Headingley and Chapeltown routes continued to be shared between Littlewood and Atkinson from about 1840–1863. This seems to have been an example of a beneficial co-operation rather than strong competition and to have led to a better, more comprehensive service. The Atkinsons were shrewd businessmen and skilled at pricing. They bankrupted one competitor who charged 6d on a route that they divided into two 4d stages.

On some other routes competition was fierce. There are many examples of racing between drivers and owners, 'furious driving' as it was known. This endangered passengers, who were quick to complain. It also wore out buses and horses. And inevitably it led to a number of prosecutions. The Atkinsons, it has been said, 'displayed a kindly image unlike some competitors' (Soper). There were other risks. Horse flu was one. The short depression of the late 1840s combined with the competition from the railways on stagecoach routes led to the downfall of some proprietors. Bus and coach ownership was by no means a risk free investment.

The period 1847–63 did not see much expansion of bus routes and services in Leeds, with the exception of the Chapeltown route. However, there were some developments. In May 1852 the first cross-town bus service was introduced. Previously the routes had gone out in spoke-like fashion. It was now to become more of a web or network. These cross routes were to remain important in linking with the tram system that used the principal radial roads. A new lower fare of 2d came in about 1860, when the double-decker bus permitted a differential lower fare for outside passengers on top. John Atkinson died in 1855 leaving his younger brother William, aged 63, to continue to run the business on his own, which he did for the next ten years.

These were good years in terms of the general economic development of the country at large, of Leeds and the private fortunes of William Turton. He had by now accumulated a surplus from trading in horse fodder and coal that he could invest elsewhere. For William Atkinson too it seemed to be going well. He began to expand his business in the early 1860s, but by June 1866 he was bankrupt. This was William Turton's opportunity. How did it happen?

By 1865 Atkinson had expanded his Hunslet–Sheepscar line and opened a route to New Leeds a little further north, and as late as 26 February 1866 a Leeds–Kirkstall service. He had over-extended himself and his resources. There was uncomfortable competition on some of these routes, not like the friendly co-operation he had enjoyed with Littlewood. He was still paying the unpopular turnpike tolls. There were toll roads in all directions out of Leeds. The toll was £1 per day per vehicle, a considerable amount. The bus proprietors were never content with this. In 1851 the Atkinsons joined with others to object to this rate and requested a composition of £100 per annum. The rate was reduced to 10s per day per vehicle.

Atkinson was 74 years old, and still living modestly with his wife, no servants and apparently no children in a house next to his livery stables in Harrison Street. Calamity struck in June 1866. His creditors foreclosed. One of the largest was William Turton who had supplied fodder. Turton saved William Atkinson a shameful public hearing and bought into the firm. He recapitalised it and formed a partnership with Atkinson to continue the business. Atkinson must have been relieved and grateful. It is highly likely they had been on good terms for some years before this. In any case, after a year of partnership, at the age of 75, William Atkinson was bought out completely by Turton, now aged 42. Turton was in a position to learn and benefit from forty years of Atkinson's experience of Leeds transport. So started a major new phase in William Turton's life. From now on it was 'Turton's Buses' of Harrison Street. 'The name Turton dominated Leeds transport and the transport of many other towns for the next thirty years.'

Turton's sense of timing was sharp. He had his eye on current political and economic developments. At the time he went into partnership with Atkinson he was already involved in local politics. It is possible that he had some prior knowledge of the council's strategies for transport embodied in the new Leeds Improvement Act that was passed on 28 June 1866. This coincided exactly with the Atkinson bankruptcy. This Act enabled the council to negotiate with the owners and toll franchise holders for the purchase of toll roads. Gradually all of these were purchased and all turnpike charges abolished. The first was in January 1867 when the Leeds–Harrogate toll was lifted. Many roads followed in that year including Chapeltown and Meanwood. By February 1872 all roads were toll free. The municipalisation of the roads was complete. This gave the bus proprietors a great advantage. The public's hope for a lowering of fares was not, however, satisfied. In fact some fares increased. Turton had entered this market at a good moment indeed. He also had the benefit of inheriting the name and goodwill of the Atkinson brand that had been so well known, and for so many years, on the streets of Leeds.

Leeds Town Hall now controlled the roads. There began a round of new regulation of the transport system. This was no doubt of benefit to the passengers. Drivers had to be licensed. They had to be over eighteen and demonstrate their competence. Conductors were similarly licensed and the days of child conductors, who were susceptible to severe punishment if caught short-changing the owner, were over. One effect of this was the introduction of new patent ticket machines. By the end of 1869 there were forty-four licensed buses and fifty-nine licensed drivers. The rather small numbers indicate the restricted nature of the bus system.

The Hackney Carriage Committee of the Leeds municipal authority was the primary instrument of the new regulation. It was a new antagonist as far as the owners were concerned. And in March 1866 the RSPCA had appointed its first officer for Leeds. The rights and welfare of the horses were being monitored and protected as never before.

The *Yorkshire Post* of 22 February 1869 has the following report, one of two cases both brought by 'the local officers to the Royal Society for the Prevention of Cruelty to Animals':

Cruelty to animals at Leeds

At the Town Hall on Saturday, Wm Holdsworth a driver in the employment of Mr. Turton, omnibus proprietor, was fined 10s and costs for working a mare on the 12 inst which had raw wounds on its shoulder and neck; and John Nelson, horsekeeper, was fined 20s and costs for sending out Holdsworth with the mare.

It is noteworthy that in another case of mistreating a horse, reported on 15 May 1871, a proprietor and his driver were each fined £5. There were many more serious forms of mistreatment of horses, some of which led to prison sentences with hard labour.

Traffic accidents, then as now, took their toll. One frequent cause was that of passengers getting off a moving bus. Children were especially as risk. This report of 1 November 1876:

Police van, late nineteenth century.

Another fatal accident in Leeds

At noon on Monday, Thomas Summer, aged nine years, of Holbeck Street, New Wortley, was killed by the horses of one of Mr. Turton's omnibuses. The lad had been following a vehicle which afterwards was drawn up by the roadside, and he was leading a dog by a string. The animal pulled him into the middle of the road, and before the driver of an approaching bus could see him, he was trampled upon by the horses. At an inquest held yesterday the jury entirely acquitted the driver from blame, and agreed that the boy had met his death accidentally.

The police kept an eye on the buses. The police had been recently built up by a new chief constable in the wake of Fenian activities (the Irish Republican Brotherhood, a fore-runner of Sinn Fein/IRA).

A caution to omnibus men

At the Leeds Borough Police Court yesterday before Mr. Bruce stipendiary magistrate- J. Graves, the driver and R. Mellor the conductor of one of Mr. Turton's omnibuses, plying on the Hunslet Road, were summoned for suffering an omnibus constructed to carry 20 persons inside, to carry a greater number. The case was proved by Police Constable Mackay who stated that he found the 'bus carrying 24 passengers and four children inside. The 'bus was marked and registered to carry 20 passengers inside with the same number out. The defendant Graves urged that he had nothing to do with the number of passengers carried, while Mellor pleaded that he only got payment for 20 passengers inside while he was taking the fares on top, and consequently was not in a position to prevent them. Mr. Bruce held both the defendants liable and fined each of them in the minimum penalty of £1 / 5s and costs.

However, not all the news was bad, and it seems that Turton's buses and their staff had a generally good reputation, and better than some rivals. Perhaps he paid the fines of his staff in some cases. In the *Yorkshire Post* of 15 May 1871, immediately after the entry on mistreatment resulting in a £5 fine mentioned earlier, there is this:

Presentation to an omnibus driver

A number of gentlemen who have experienced the courtesy of Paul James omnibus driver in the employ of Mr. Wm. Turton, assembled at Mr. Thos. Beecroft's Danzic Inn, and presented him with an excellent silver-mounted driving whip, which bore on the stock a suitable inscription. The presentation made by Mr. A. Bartlet, Mr. James expressed his grateful sense of the gift in appropriate terms. This is the second tribute of respect which Mr. James has received within a few weeks.

The newspapers carried paid advertisements for new and revised bus services. Turton's buses put in notices when it moved offices, for the sale of horse manure and for special events, for example on 17 September 1872:

NOTICE – TURTON'S OMNIBUSES

will leave the 'bus office, Briggate, at 9 on Thursday night Sept 19th to walk round the town during the illuminations. Fares 6d each.

This was just one of doubtless many such excursions and special services that the entrepreneurial proprietor laid on. One notable excuse for such an outing was the arrival of a whale in a lock gate at Goole, about 25 miles from Leeds. It was a female sei whale that had swum up the Humber and broken through the lock gate, where it died in the restricted space. It was lifted out with great difficulty, breaking a crane in the process. The news of this travelled fast. It was exhibited for a few days and visited by many thousands of people from far and wide. It was then cut up and the meat sold. The skeleton was sold by the Aire and Calder Navigation to the Natural History Museum in London, where it is still used for research purposes.

Leeds transport could not cope with exceptionally large-scale events. The movement of large numbers of people across the country for big events was now possible by railway. Annual shows were a great favourite. When the Royal Agricultural Show was held in Leeds in July 1861, 95,000 passengers were delivered to Leeds by train. How were they to get to the show? Our entrepreneurial friend from Manchester, John Greenwood, laid on the extra, and apparently rather superior buses. Over the four days he carried 21,976 passengers.

A good service to passengers was the notice of lost property, including on one occasion 'a black leather bag containing surgical instruments'. On another occasion there is a remarkable notice of some of Turton's own property that had gone missing:

Hired from Wm. Turton's Livery Stable to a gentleman on Tuesday September 27 to go to Harrogate a BROWN MARE and a GREEN STANHOPE G10 spindle-backed and extra elliptic springs supposed to have been left at some hotel. The above will be glad to hear from anyone having the same. (1 October 1870)

As always the bus system relied on the great inns, or hotels as they were increasingly called, for their termini and various other forms of support and publicity. In about 1860 there were fifteen bus routes operating from nineteen inns. A recitation of their names gives a feeling for the localities:

Briggate: The Fleece Inn, The Old George, The Bull and Mouth, The Royal Hotel, The Saddle, The Ship Inn
Kirkgate: The Bradford Hotel, The Golden Cock
Chapeltown Road: The Mexborough Arms, The Queen Inn
North Street: The Black Swan
Commercial Street: The Horse and Jockey
Vicar Lane: The Beehive Inn
Upper Head Row: The Nag's Head

LEEDS TRAMWAYS TIME TABLE.

CHAPELTOWN.—Cars leave Briggate every fifteen minutes from 8.45 a.m. till 12 noon; every ten minutes after 12 till 8 p.m., after then every quarter till 10.30. Extra Cars on Saturdays till 11 p.m.
Sundays.—Every half-hour from 10.30 a.m. till 12 noon, after then every fifteen minutes till 10 p.m.
HEADINGLEY.—Cars leave Boar Lane every fifteen minutes from 8.45 a.m. till 12 noon; every ten minutes after 12 till 8 p.m., after then every quarter till 10.30. Extra Cars on Saturdays till 11 p.m.
Sundays.—Every half-hour from 10.30 a.m. till 12 noon, after then every fifteen minutes till 10 p.m.
HUNSLET.—Cars leave Boar Lane every ten minutes from 8.40 a.m. till 10.30 p.m. Extra Cars on Saturdays till 11 p.m.
Sundays.—Every half-hour from 10.30 a.m. till 12 noon, then every fifteen minutes till 10 p.m.
KIRKSTALL.—Cars leave Boar Lane every ten minutes from 8.40 a.m. till 10.30 p.m. Extra Cars on Saturdays till 11 p.m.
Sundays.—Every half-hour from 10.30 a.m. till 12 noon, then every fifteen minutes till 10 p.m.
YORK ROAD.—Cars leave Duncan Street every fifteen minutes from 8.45 a.m. till 10.30 p.m. Extra Cars on Saturdays till 11 p.m.
Sundays.—Every half-hour from 10.30 a.m. till 12 noon, then every fifteen minutes till 10 p.m.

TURTON'S OMNIBUSES.

ARMLEY.—Leaves (Royal Hotel) Briggate for Armley every hour from 9 a.m. to 8 p.m. Returning from Armley every hour from 9.30 a.m. to 8.30 p.m. Extra on Saturdays to Armley, 9 and 10 p.m. Returning 9.30 and 10.30 p.m.
CHURWELL ROAD.—A 'Bus leaves (Royal Hotel) Briggate, Leeds, to New Peacock Inn, Churwell Road, every hour from 8.30 a.m. to 8.30 p.m. Returning from New Peacock Inn every hour from 9 a.m. to 9 p.m. Extra on Saturdays up to 10.30 p.m.
DEWSBURY ROAD.—Leaves (Royal Hotel) Briggate, for New Inn, Dewsbury Road, 8.15, 8.30 a.m., and every half-hour afterwards till 9 p.m. Extra on Saturdays, 9.30, 10, 10.30, 11 p.m. Returning from New Inn, Dewsbury Road, at 8.40 and 9.10 a.m., and every following half-hour until 9.40 p.m. Extra on Saturdays until 11.20 p.m.
WOODHOUSE CARR.—Leaves (Royal Hotel) Briggate for the Junction Inn, Meanwood Road, at 9 a.m., and every following half-hour till 9.30 p.m. Extra on Saturdays, 10 to 11 p.m. Returning from the Junction Inn at 8.45 a.m., and every following half-hour until 9.45 p.m. Extra on Saturdays, 10.15 to 11.15 p.m.
WORTLEY.—Leaves (Royal Hotel) Briggate, to Wortley and back every half-hour from 9 a.m. to 8.30 p.m. Extra on Saturdays up to 10.30 p.m. The hour 'Bus runs by way of Water Lane to Crown Inn and Queen Inn, Oldfield Lane, Wortley. The 'Bus at half-past the hour by Wellington Road to Star Inn, Tong Road, Upper Wortley.

COATES'S OMNIBUSES.

BURMANTOFTS, BRIGGATE, AND BEESTON HILL.—Leaves Beeston Hill for Briggate, 8.45 a.m., and every following hour to 7.45 p.m. Extra on Saturdays, 5.45 p.m., and every half-hour till 10.45 p.m. *Sundays*—8.30 a.m., 1.30 and 9 p.m. Commercial Street for Beeston Hill, 10, 11 a.m., 12.5, 1, 1.30, 2, 3, 3.15, 4, 5, 6, 6.30, 7, 8, 9 p.m. Saturday nights 6 p.m., and every half-hour till 11 p.m. *Sundays*—8.30, 9.30 p.m. From Commercial Street to Burmantofts, every hour from 9 a.m. to 8 p.m. Extra on Saturday night, 9 p.m. Burmantofts for Beeston Hill every hour from 9.40 a.m. to 8.40 p.m. Extra on Saturday night, 9.15 p.m.
HALTON AND WHITKIRK.—Leaves Whitkirk (Week-days), 9 a.m. and 2 p.m. Returning from Horse and Jockey, Commercial Street, 1 and 5 p.m. Saturday—Leaves Whitkirk at 6 p.m. for Briggate. *Sundays*—Leaves Beeston Hill for Briggate at 1.30 p.m.; Briggate for Garforth at 2 p.m. Returning from Garforth at 7 p.m.; Briggate for Beeston Hill, 8.30 p.m.; Beeston Hill for Briggate, 9 p.m. Returning to Beeston Hill, 9.30 p.m.

OMNIBUSES, &c.

ABERFORD.—Leaves Black Swan, North Street, Tuesdays, Thursdays, and Saturdays, at 4 p.m.
ABERFORD AND BARWICK.—Leaves New Inn, Vicar Lane, Tuesdays, Thursdays, and Saturdays, at 4 p.m. Leaves Aberford at 8.45 a.m.; Barwick at 9.15 a.m.
BOSTON SPA, BRAMHAM, AND CLIFFORD.—Leaves Brunswick Hotel, Vicar Lane, Tuesdays, Thursdays, and Saturdays, at 4 p.m. Leaves Bramham at 7 a.m.; Boston Spa 8 a.m.; Saturdays at 1.30 p.m. Returning from Boston Spa at 8 p.m. *Sundays*—Leaves Leeds at 8.30 a.m., returning from Boston Spa at 6 p.m.
HALTON AND WHITKIRK.—Leaves Black Swan, North Street, Daily (Sundays excepted), at 12.45 and 4.45 p.m. Saturdays, extra, 9.45 p.m. Leaves Whitkirk at 8.50 a.m. and 2.10 p.m. Leaves Halton at 9 a.m. and 2.20 p.m.
KIPPAX.—Leaves Beehive Inn, Vicar Lane, Daily (Sundays excepted), at 4 p.m. Leaves Kippax at 8.30 a.m.
KIRKBY OVERBLOW.—Leaves Black Swan Inn, North Street, on Saturdays, at 4 p.m.
LITTLE LONDON TO BECKETT ARMS, KIRKSTALL ROAD, calling at Horse and Jockey Hotel, Commercial Street.—Leaves Horse and Jockey, Commercial Street, at 8.30 a.m., and every half-hour to 8 p.m.
SCARCROFT, SHADWELL, MOORTOWN, AND CHAPELTOWN.—Richard Machan leaves Brunswick Hotel, Vicar Lane, Daily (Sundays excepted), at 5 p.m.
SEACROFT.—Leaves Seacroft on Mondays at 8.30 a.m. and 2 p.m.; Tuesdays at 10 a.m. and 2 p.m.; Wednesdays, Thursdays, and Fridays at 8.30 a.m. and 2 p.m.; Saturdays at 10 a.m. and 6 p.m.; *Sundays* at 7.30 p.m. Returning from Beehive Inn, Vicar Lane, on Mondays, Tuesdays, Wednesdays, Thursdays, and Fridays, at 12.30 and 5 p.m.; Saturdays at 3 and 10 p.m.; *Sundays* at 8.30 p.m.
SHADWELL.—A 'Bus leaves Shadwell Daily (Sundays excepted), at 8 a.m., returning from Black Swan, Vicar Lane, at 5 p.m.; Saturdays at 2.30 and 10 p.m.
THORNER.—Leaves Thorner on Tuesdays and Saturdays at 9 a.m., returning from New Inn, Vicar Lane, at 4 p.m.
WETHERBY.—Leaves Angel Hotel, Wetherby, on Tuesdays and Saturdays, at 8 a.m., returning from Black Swan, North Street, at 4 p.m.

Urban transport timetable, 1878.

Upper Albion Street: The Commercial Inn
Headingley: The New Inn, The Three Horse Shoes
Hunslet: The Elephant and Castle
Seacroft: The New Inn

William Turton was on familiar terms with many of the landlords of these establishments. It is not surprising that one of his sons, John, should have married the daughter of one such landlord, Joseph Robertshaw of The Horse and Jockey at No.46 Commercial Street.

This John Turton was the father of my grandfather. The third child of five and the second son, he seems to have been the liveliest and most independent. He left home and married in 1879 aged 26. He started his own branch of the family corn and hay firm at No.153 North Street. He specialised in supplying the army barracks close by and joined the Yorkshire Volunteers, which had a base in the barracks. He was a good horseman and won a silver tankard for 'best horse and turnout' presented to Private Turton by the officers of the Leeds Troop of the Yorkshire Hussars. In the same month, May 1875, he won a contract from the Borough Council as chief 'scavenger', namely the refuse collection or recycling contract. He tried to push his luck by suggesting that instead of regularly putting out to tender the council might like to give him a long-term contract but this was voted down. This was a business venture entirely of his own making.

Walker's Reginald Terrace bus overturns, horses startled by a steam tram; the shop on the left is of John Turton at No. 153 North Street. (Sketch by Jim Soper)

John Turton also ran a bus company, even in competition with the Leeds Tramways Company that was his father's special concern at the time. This was short lived however. On 23 May 1887 he was granted a license to start a service of eight 'Jubilee' buses (this was the year of Queen Victoria's fiftieth, Golden Jubilee). He ran a ten-minute service on a route between Spencer Place, just near his home address, South Gothic Villa, on Chapeltown Road, and Roundhay Road and Dewsbury Road. He had stables in Roundhay Road at Grant Row and Beaufort Place. These Leeds-built buses, which later became popular in London, were drawn by a single horse and carried 14 passengers inside and two either side of the driver outside. It was a short-lived initiative. He died less than a year later on 3 March 1888. His bus venture was not incorporated into his father's business but sold on to a notorious character, one John Newton Sharp. Sharp by name and sharp by practice it seems. He had a bad reputation for jerry built premises and badly kept horses and so may serve as a comparison with what was generally the best practice observed by the Turton family. He was charged in 1893 with cruelly treating sixteen horses and keeping his stables in a crowded and disgusting condition. Many horses were lame, sick and plagued by flies. Their food was hardly edible, the heat unbearable. He was imprisoned for one month with hard labour. His firm ceased trading.

The Atkinsons had already sensed that there might be a future for buses on rails – trams. They had applied for a license to construct some tracks at about the time Turton joined them. Turton was at first strongly opposed to competition from trams even when they were just a possibility. It is important to bear in mind that in tandem with his growing involvement with the tram he was to remain a major bus operator. He expanded the omnibus business. In that same year he also took over James Farnell's bus route to Hyde Park (Leeds), and by the early 1870s the Meanwood Road route as well. He sold some routes to the Leeds Tramways Company, as we shall see, but continued running buses until 1888. His reputation was honoured when people widely expressed the view that 'buses had been better in Turton's day'.

The popularity of the horse-drawn omnibus is captured in this florid piece of anonymous verse published in 1865, 'a satire on life seen from an omnibus roof' as H.C. Moore put it:

The Omnibus

August Four wheeler! Rolling Paradise!
Thou Juggernaut to dawdling men and mice!
Thou blissful refuge to the footsore cit!
Thou boast of science and inventive wit!
To thee, in pride careering o'er the stones,
The homeward labourer drags his weary bones.
The burdened porter, staggering on the road,
Climbs up thy hulk and there forgets his load.
For thee the merchant his dull desk forsakes,
And leaves Cornhill to night and thieves, and rakes.

The lover finds thee pensioner of bliss, –
By thee he speeds to reap the promised kiss.
On thy 'outside', no muff can plead his qualms.
And us forbid to colour our meerschaums;
And there unchallenged smoke the pipe of peace.
All hail! Thou kindest gift of human sense!
Thou envy of the wretch – who lacks three-pence!
All hail! Thou huge, earth-born leviathan!
Thou rattling, rambling, two-horse caravan!
Thou dry-land ship, breasting in scorn the waves
Of traffic's whirlpool that round Cheapside raves.
Behind thee, competition lies,
And jealousy but breathes a curse and dies.
Poor Francis Train just hissed at thee in spite,
Then, with his 'Tramways' sank in endless night:
And jobbing railways, near thy presence found,
Smitten with shame, hide, fuming 'Under-ground'.
Though trampled curs may curse thee with a bark,
And godless cabmen call thee – 'Noah's Ark';
Majestic vehicle! Much slandered friend,
To lowest Tophet we their libels send,
And chant thy praises to the City's end.
An eighth world-wonder thine arrival bodes,
Thou greatest, best, Colossus of our roads.

Turton's buses were extremely popular and comprised more than half the town's bus services. The *Leeds Mercury* of 29 October 1881 refers to 'William Turton whose omnibuses now traverse nearly every main artery of the town, whose vehicles, horses and servants are not equalled by any other proprietor.'

Horse-drawn buses maintained their importance on cross-city routes, and in serving the tram termini and linking areas not directly served by the trams. The increase in the population of Leeds and its exceptionally dispersed urban area actually saw a surge in the number of daily journeys by horse buses compared with the increasing tram services. This was especially marked in the period 1885–1900. This was all good news for the corn and hay merchant. You might say it was a win-win situation for Turton. But it was not necessarily assured. There were risks and some bus proprietors went under or lost personal reputation. William had to steer a cautious and prudent course as well as an ambitious and entrepreneurial course.

William Turton's sons helped him with his livery stables and cab services. In 1873 he patented an invention by an employee, a Mr Rogers, for a newly designed two-wheeled side-door hansom cab. This was submitted to the Society of Arts in London. As a corn merchant he would have helped to fuel many kinds of vehicle. Over time he probably owned and hired most of them. A list of some current types, in various conditions no doubt, is given in the *Yorkshire Post* in May 1895. By this time the Dunlop pneumatic tyre had been introduced. American Buggy, American trotting 'sulky (9 guineas), Brougham, Curricle, Gig (30 guineas), Hansom Cab (from £25), Lurry [*sic*] 2 ton, Phaeton, Shooting Cart (£13 10*s*), Tandem Dog-Cart (£50), Victorian, Waggonette, Wherry (for coal). (Prices where known are shown in brackets.)

PART III

SOCIETY
AND
POLITICS

1860–1900

8

A RESURGENT BOROUGH

The period of world history 1845–75 has been termed 'the age of capital' (Hobsbawm, 1975). It follows the electoral enfranchisement of the bourgeoisie in 1832. This period coincides exactly with William Turton's personal progress as a businessman from the age of nineteen when he started with little or no capital, achieving early wealth by the age of 35 and being established ten years later in all his fields of interest.

Hobsbawm refers to the city and the railway as the most striking outward symbols of the industrial world. London, with Paris, Berlin and Vienna, were the only cities with populations more than a million. Three of the next six with populations over 500,000 were in Britain: Glasgow, Liverpool and Manchester. Leeds, which was physically more extensive than any other provincial town in the country, was among several British cities in the next tier of 200,000 and more. In 1851 the urban population of Britain began to exceed that of rural dwellers.

The railways linked the cities with the ports. In global terms, the railway, the steam-ship and the telegraph were an integrated transport and communications system. Leeds saw rapid railway development in the 1840s and by 1848 was connected directly with London. From then on the national and worldwide expansion of mainly British produced railroad and railway engines and carriages, took off at an extraordinary pace and rate.

Railway and steamship construction globally 1846–76		
	Railways	Steamships
	Kilometre of track	No. of vessels
1846	17,424	139,973
1876	309,641	3,293,073

When it became possible to go 'round the world in eighty days' in 1872, this was almost entirely under steam power. The aptly named American railway magnate and tramway pioneer George Francis Train made the journey twice and is held to be the model for Phileas Fogg in Jules Verne's novel, published in 1873. The USA, Europe and India could be crossed from east to west, sea to sea by rail. Mr Pullman had introduced his luxury cars in 1865 to make it more comfortable for the well-to-do. The Suez Canal opened in 1868 and made it faster for international freight and passengers. In 1871 the Derby horse racing results were received in Calcutta from London by telegraph in five minutes. This was thanks to the early work of the Siemens brothers. It is extraordinary to think that this was the first year in which the citizens of Leeds could ride in a horse-drawn tram. Not all inventions moved at the same speed.

This 'age of capital' was an age of urban renaissance or resurgence for Leeds. Every year some new and splendid institution or facility was inaugurated: schools and hospitals, bridges and railway stations, theatres and music halls, churches, chapels and synagogues, hotels, a stock exchange and a Corn Exchange. Leeds became an even more important 'inland port' with keels and sloops of up to 150 tons reaching Leeds docks. There was gradual municipalisation of public utilities: water in 1852, roads in 1866, gas in 1869, and trams much later, by 1895. By the end of the century Leeds had become a city of wide international renown. Eleven consulates were set up including those of Brazil, France, Germany, Russia, Spain and the USA.

LEEDS TOWN HALL

Leeds Town Hall built by Cuthbert Broderick, soon after opening in 1858 by Queen Victoria.

The crowning pride and glory was the new Town Hall. The architect was the young Cuthbert Broderick. It was built on the northern edge of the old town centre on a site costing £9,000. It was conceived in 1851 after a public consultation in July 1850, started in 1852 and took four years to complete. It had a maximum height of 225ft, and the Victoria Hall was 161ft by 72ft and 75ft high. Inside the entrance the mayor, Peter Fairbairn, who was knighted by the queen at the opening, had erected a white marble statue of the queen, 8ft 6in high. He paid the £1,000 cost out of his own pocket. The other principal statues were in bronze, of the Duke of Wellington and the recently deceased local hero Edward Baines.

Reception held for Prince Arthur by Mayor John Barran to celebrate the opening of Roundhay Park; Councillor William Turton would have attended.

The cost of Leeds Town Hall was raised from the rates. It was massively over budget, not I suspect because of inflation or inefficiency in planning or execution but out of a sheer desire to make it ever grander. As Tristram Hunt says in *Building Jerusalem: the rise and fall of the Victorian city*:

Today it is hard to get a sense of the provincial autonomy in that era that produced the intense civic pride and rivalry that saw Birmingham Town Hall trumped by Liverpool's St George's Hall, whose glory was stolen by Bradford's St George's Hall, which was in turn trumped by the Leeds Town Hall.

The building was a powerhouse of municipal authority, containing both police headquarters and law courts. Two years after its completion it was opened by Queen Victoria on 7 September 1858. William Turton and his family would have been among the vast numbers of Leeds people, more than half the population, who witnessed the events. In a few years time he was to be elected a councillor and would get to know the place from the inside, attending not only council meetings but balls, dinners and receptions, occasionally accompanied by his wife. The building and the ceremony were one of those 'giant new rituals of self-congratulation', such as the 1851 Crystal Palace Exhibition had been. At this 14,000 firms exhibited, and in the Great Exhibition of 1862 there were 29,000.

The mottos that adorn the dome of the main hall are wonderfully evocative of the municipal ethos, pious, utilitarian, patriotic, and even democratic:

Honesty is the Best Policy
In Union there is Strength
Weave Truth with Trust
Forward
Good Will Towards Man
Magna Carta
Deo Regni Patria
Industry overcomes all things
God in the Highest
Labor Omnia Vincit
Trial by Jury
Auspicium Melioris Aevi

Except the Lord Keep the City the Watchman waketh but in vain

The event of the opening by Queen Victoria, accompanied by the Prince Consort, Prince Albert, was a highpoint of the century for Leeds. It inevitably touches so many of our themes and strikes so many chords, that a little digression is warranted.

The royal party arrived, by train of course, on 6 September. On that day the town was already in full regalia. Buildings and streets were illuminated until midnight; arcades of flowers abounded. The flags of the Union, the Royal Standard, America, France and Prussia flew. On that day already some 150–200,000 people thronged the streets of central Leeds. People came by train and other means from all over Yorkshire. 200,000 attended on the second day, when all mills closed for the day.

The royal procession went on a 4-mile progress in their carriages and on horse through the central parts of Leeds and even a little further out. On the edge of Woodhouse Moor alone some 60–70,000 people gathered on a natural amphitheatre to watch and cheer. Choirs of 32,000 Sunday school children sang, cheered and kept silent to strict conducting. Nothing had been seen like this since the fall of Sebastopol. The London police were drafted in to help and were reported as coping admirably, even though the wooden barriers broke. Contemporary accounts speak of:

> ... the great mass of human beings who, shouting and cheering, pushing and throwing their hats and handkerchiefs into the air, as if they were demented, thronged up the streets, half wild with exultation and delight.

Inside the Town Hall 8,000 'people of rank and fashion' were gathered. The local aristocracy, some with royal connections, the nobility and the military were mobilised to the fullest extent. After the singing of the national anthem, the town clerk, Mr Ikin, read a 'Loyal Address' to Her Majesty. It included both an apology and a plug for the magnificence of the new building:

> For the mere purpose of municipal government a less spacious and costly building might have sufficed. But in our architectural plans we have borne in mind the probability that at no very distant time civil and criminal justice may be dispensed to an extensive region in this town, the real capital of the West Riding. We were also desirous to provide a place where large assemblies might meet in comfort to exercise their constitutional right of discussing public questions, to listen to instruction on literary and philosophical subjects, or to engage in innocent amusements.

Queen Victoria responded, briefly and less rhetorically, and said that she found 'this noble hall a work well worthy of your active industry and enterprising spirit'.

'The Hallelujah Chorus' followed. For the next week a music festival was held in the hall, the first of a long series that continues to this day.

THE CORN EXCHANGE

After the Town Hall, the new Corn Exchange, now a Grade I listed building, was the grandest expression of commercial pride. The old one, built in 1824, had become too small and obstructed the highway in Briggate. The new one opened in 1862. The architect Cuthbert Broderick (1821–1905) had designed the Town Hall ten years earlier and later designed the Grand Hotel in Scarborough (1867). The imposing and highly practical Corn Exchange allowed grain to be brought into the city centre to the huge basement where it could be sampled and selected for display on the stalls on the ground floor. The beautiful steel and glass dome covered the trading floor, which had up to 200 stalls and 59 offices surrounding. One of the stalls was for William Turton whose family traded here for nearly sixty years.

The Corn Exchange rented out stalls for corn dealers, and offices. People who needed some form of presence could also rent lockers, letterboxes, cardholders and advertisements. Office tenants included Yorkshire farmers, millers and other such groups like the National Farmers Union, the Town Council, the Salvation Army and the Inland Revenue.

Three generations of the Turton family had stalls from the opening in 1862 until about 1920. Philip Campbell, who began to take over the management of the firm, had a stall from 1917, a practice maintained by the successor company trading under Turton's name.

The primacy of the Corn Exchange underlines my emphasis on the context of increasing demand for animal transport and so animal feed in the Leeds economy. It now overshadowed the old cloth markets and took its place besides other large-scale constructions such as the new mills, warehouses and railway stations.

Railways brought the first hotels, the Midland Hotel (1862) and the Great Northern Hotel (1865–69), which were great social meeting places. In the non-commercial sector Leeds saw the construction of a new Royal Infirmary, the Leeds Union Workhouse, the Moral and Industrial Training School, and the Yorkshire College of Science (1874, which became Leeds University in 1904) among other institutions.

DIVERSIFICATION OF THE LEEDS ECONOMY

Leeds began to diversify by about 1851 and this continued until the end of the century. Bradford became predominant in woollen manufactures, though these were still an important part of the Leeds mixed economy. Leeds also continued to grow its flax industry, having 37 flax mills employing 10,000 workers in 1855. Some old industries developed and new ones emerged: engineering, light and heavy (e.g. Clarke, Ford, Green and Kitson); coach building; book printing and other specialist printing (e.g. John Waddington's playing cards); and also leather, pottery and brick making. A neighbour of William Turton at Crown Point was the family firm of Waddington who were the town's chief dyers and dyewood cutters that boasted of supplying dyes and dyestuffs to Queen Victoria, the British Army, the Shah of Persia and the Emperor of China. Needless to say, blue, scarlet and khaki were the most used colours.

From being a town that traded in wool, and then in woollen cloth and the dyeing of cloth and combining wool with flax, Leeds became the centre of the clothing industry, so-called 'ready-made' clothing. In 1851 Isaac Singer, an American, patented his new sewing machine and soon began production in Glasgow. The Leeds clothier John Barran quickly put it to use and other famous Leeds names followed: Marks and Spencer, Montagu Burton and Hepworths amongst them.

Most businesses were owned by an individual or a family. William Turton's business conformed to this norm. It is easy to see from the foregoing sketches that exceptional opportunities existed and were expanding in the sectors he traded in. The railways and international trade needed the capillary system of horse-drawn transport for the movement of goods out of Leeds to international markets. The growing city needed more wholesalers and retailers to supply the population. The scale of urban expansion entailed a corresponding need for passenger transport.

Following the period of accumulation of his initial capital, approximately 1865–75, was a new plateau of wealth for Turton. In 1870 the Liberal politician T.H. Green spoke of a 'general riot of luxury in which nearly all classes had their share'. As leader of the opposition in Parliament Disraeli called it 'a convulsion of prosperity'. In 1874 income tax was an extraordinary low sum of 3d in the pound or 1.25 per cent. Gladstone wanted to abolish it. For Turton's business and his overall portfolio of investments the good times seem to have continued until the end of the century. However, nationally and internationally the period 1873–96 is known as 'The Great Depression', though it was never as severe as the 1929–34 downturn. In the 'age of capital', in the special sense we are using, from 1845–75, Britain had a near monopoly in many areas. In 1870 Hobsbawm writes 'A businessman, looking around the world ... could therefore exude confidence, not to say complacency. But was it justified?' The inherent instability of the capitalist system of production was to make one of its many appearances.

The age of capital had begun with important 'deregulation' (repeal of the corn laws, abolition of various employment laws) all aimed at an ever 'freer market'. The 'age of imperialism' was to see more and new interventions by government and municipal authorities. These were to have a restrictive influence on Turton's tramway enterprises.

Queen Victoria Hall, Leeds Town Hall.

Leeds Union Workhouse, later St James Hospital; Turton was an overseer.

John Barran's ready-made clothing factory.

Moral and Industrial Training School.

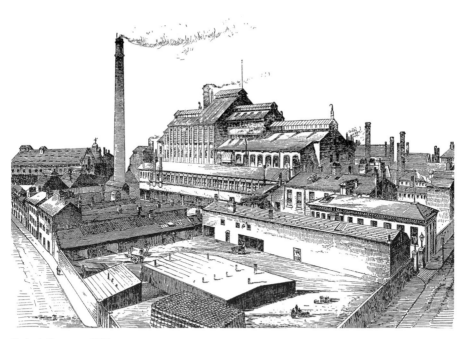

Tetley's Brewery, 1893.

View of Park Row from the east.

9

HAYFIELD HOUSE

A GRAND VILLA

In 1860 William was a young paterfamilias of 35 years old. He and Sarah, also 35, had five healthy children. The family was growing up and the money was coming in. They had outgrown their terraced cottage at No.31 East Street.

By 1860 at the latest the family had moved from East Street to No.114 North Street. This was on the east side, on the corner of Skinner Lane, next to St Stephen's church. North Street is more or less a continuation of New Briggate on a line north from Leeds Bridge to Harrogate. It is at the northern edge of central Leeds. William also bought Nos 149, 151 and 153 North Street on the northern side, which he combined to make his second main corn business outlet. This was well situated to receive and distribute goods. It was also next to the main military camp and barracks, which his corn business supplied. All these buildings have been demolished. William continued to own No.31 East Street and other houses in that street, and Crown Point at The Calls was still his main trading base.

The children in 1860 were two girls, aged 8 and 6, and three boys aged 11, 7 and 3. The family probably wanted three bedrooms at least, one for parents, one for girls and one for boys, and maybe one for baby and nursemaid. They had a resident female servant aged 20. This suggests a six-room house on two or three storeys, perhaps in a fairly newly built terrace.

William wanted the best for his family who had not always had it easy. He also had some social standing to live up to. He was beginning to move in well-to-do and influential circles. He needed to entertain guests. Unlike 'Old Willie Atkinson', William was not a frugal man and he enjoyed a little style and comfort. So with the family growing up and business going from strength to strength he decided to make his final domestic move, his strongest social statement yet. This was to build Hayfield House.

At the time of the 1871 Census we know that they were living at Hayfield House. I shall return to consider when he might have started this project and when he might have moved in. It is interesting because it tells us much about his fortunes and aspira-

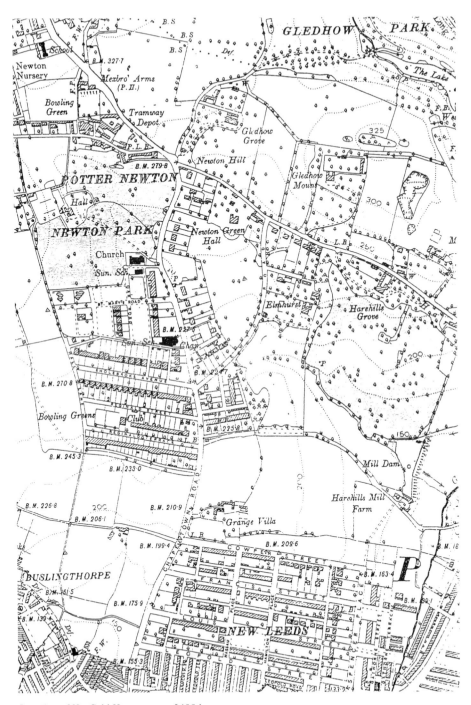

Location of Hayfield House, map of 1894.

tions at the time. But first I need to give a physical description of the locality and the house itself.

The site of Hayfield House is about one mile north of North Street on the western side of Chapeltown Road. This is the road to Harrogate, which rises gradually to higher ground as it leaves the centre of Leeds. At the time it was outside the centre of Leeds. It is not, for instance, included on Brierley's 1866 *Map of Leeds Town and its Vicinity*. This map stops just short of Cowper Street, part of the then incomplete suburb called, rather pretentiously, New Leeds. On this map there are no houses to the west of Chapeltown Road at this level. Chapel Allerton and Potternewton were known as agricultural townships. The relative size of population in Chapel Allerton and Potternewton over the years of William's life there shows the way the suburbs grew:

Population in Chapel Allerton and Potternewton 1871–1900			
Year	Population of Chapel Allerton	Population of Potternewton	Total
1871	3,847	5,107	8,954
1901	5,841	25,987	31,828

The area around Hayfield House was open ground before you reached the old village of Chapel Allerton. There were a few grand estates or lands belonging to gentry and aristocracy. There were plantations of rhubarb ('tusker' in the vernacular) and there was grazing for milk cows. Rhubarb pie and custard anyone?

'Detached villas' such as Hayfield House were rare in Leeds, and its size put it into an even smaller number of large houses. A detailed study of speculative housing in the neighbouring and comparable suburb of Headingley in 1886–1914 emphasises this status difference:

Types of house built in Headingley 1886–1914		
Type of house	houses completed	per cent
Detached villa	44	0.95
Semi-detached villa	1,246	2.79
Through terraces	16,027	34.46
Back-to-back	28,789	61.90

Almost all of the succeeding Turton generations who are part of our story lived in villas of one sort or another. They were thus in the top four percentage point of the housing market.

The house had no street number, and it was not for some twenty years that houses began to be built around it. It is quite possible that William had bought some of the land around his house and later contributed to the development of the immediate area of Reginald Terrace to the south and Reginald Street to the north. The Earl of Mexborough also owned much land in the area and his name survives in the names of a pub and several streets. By the end of the century it could be described as 'a model middle-class suburb', 'a sort of garden suburb' with 'villas of a superior type'. By 1905 the whole area around on both sides of Chapeltown Road was developed and there was a high quality arcade of shops almost opposite Hayfield House. Reginald Terrace became a major bus and tram stop and terminus. How convenient, how very practical to be able to go from semi-rural comfort directly to Leeds Corn Exchange on one's own bus, and later tram.

There is something very practical and even quite modest about Hayfield House itself. I am sure his friends said, 'You've a grand house William', but there was nothing grandiose about it, no frills. Nonetheless it was the largest house for some distance, yielding only to the really grand halls, lodges and parks of the true merchant princes. It was situated quite close to the main road, with space for little more than the double driveway and two gates with large stone-capped pillars and a row of greenery. In its early years the house may have had more extensive gardens on either side and to the rear, before Reginald Terrace and Reginald Street were built. But although at the Chapeltown Road end, Hayfield House always spanned the entire width between these streets, which were built up on both sides to the rear, up to an old bowling green and clubhouse at the rear boundary of the house

Interior of No. 43 Reginald Terrace, late nineteenth century; these were 'genteel villas' that might have one to two servants, more modest than Hayfield House (see colour section).

and garden. Thus the rear garden was not extensive and any garden to the sides quite narrow. The ensemble was imposing enough but the house was not much decorated on the outside.

Based partly on photographs, I would describe the house as follows in a sort of pastiche estate agent style (see colour section).

> Hayfield House is a substantial residence for a Gentleman and his Family, conveniently located some two miles north of Briggate on the Harrogate Road south of Chapel Allerton in a delightful and healthy open area on an eminence with fine aspect and salubrious air. It is a three-storey, double-fronted villa of imposing proportions and considerable depth, having a double-pitched roof. There are basement and attic rooms. In the grounds there is a stable and coach-house with accommodation for a coachman and family. An imposing entrance leads to a generous hall with cloakroom etc. There are two large reception rooms, one dining room, a drawing room and a study. In the basement are kitchens, scullery, storerooms, larders and a cellar, together with quarters for domestic staff, and also in the attic. There are six principal bedrooms on first and second floors, together with two bathrooms. There is running water and WCs.

We do not know what Hayfield House cost. It is highly probable that Turton did not need a mortgage for it. Information from the end of the eighteenth and turn of the nineteenth centuries shows that a rich merchant might spend £1,000 and more, and up to £5,000 on a really grand house. A difference in the earlier years was that merchants usually had their business premises as part of the domestic space, rather like a Roman villa. One of the grandest of all must have been John Marshall's Headingley House, which he bought for £7,500 with 450 acres of land in 1818. This cost about £3,000 per annum to run. It had eight reception rooms, including library, billiard room, school room and smoking room; twelve principal bedrooms, six servant's bedrooms and others.

Another of the grandest houses was Denison Hall, built by John Denison. Denison is an old Leeds family, prominent already in the seventeenth century. Turton was to buy some of his land at Crown Point from them later. Denison reportedly insured his house for £2,600, his business premises for £500 and the contents for a relatively massive £3,000. This valuation of contents, albeit for insurance (and so perhaps higher), can be compared with the total value of the household contents, professionally for probate (and so perhaps lower), of John Hebblethwaite a 'top of the range Leeds gentleman merchant', at £629. A house in Park Square early in the late eighteenth century might be about £1,500. In 1841 William Hey II's inner-city property, mainly shops and small houses, ranged in value from about £25–80 (in an overall range of £18–104). A small warehouse cost £175. A workman's cottage might cost about £50 new. Even as late as 1907 the average cost of a new house in England, outside London, was £250. We could perhaps multiply this by a thousand today.

Deciding when they moved in to Hayfield House takes a bit of reconstruction. We know for sure, from the census, that they were there in early 1871 and therefore 1870 would be the very latest date. It is clear that the money required to undertake this project was derived from the corn and coal trade. It had nothing to do with buses, which he started in 1866, let alone trams. He had been trading successfully for twenty years. William was only 38 when he decided to stand for election to the Leeds Town Council in 1863. The building of Hayfield House implies a degree of self-confidence and social ambition, and wealth sufficient to back his bid to enter local politics. He was elected in 1866, so it is possible that by then he began to think of this project. He bought the land in 1868. William was decisive and tolerated no delay so we may assume that the process of planning the building scheme, and then commissioning an architect, was not too protracted. The actual building works might have required a year or so. We may therefore estimate that they occupied Hayfield House in 1869 or by 1870 at the very latest.

William Turton named his new house 'Hayfield House'. It was a name to acquire iconic status for better and for worse for the next 140 years. His family were to live there for some fifty-five years. His oldest son, George, and his wife, Annie, continued to live in the house until George died in 1920. Annie retired to Harrogate. She moved, interestingly enough, into a house on the edge of the park, No. 8 Leeds Road, at the northern end of the same Leeds–Harrogate road as Chapeltown Road, now the A60. She named it 'Hayfield House' and the name, carved in stone, and the house still stand as solid as ever.

'Hayfield' connotes one of the main sources of his wealth; after all he started as a 'hay dealer' not yet a 'corn and hay dealer', let alone coal merchant. I have in my possession a small and pretty oil painting in a thick, black, original frame. The picture size is just 16in by 10in. The title is 'The Hayfield' and it is by G.E. Hicks (George Elgar Hicks 1824–1914), a well-known painter of the day (see colour section). It is dated 1864. The painting depicts a hay field at harvest time (see colour section). It is picturesquely situated on Hengistbury Head near Bournemouth and has The Needles and Isle of Wight in the background with some boats on the Solent. In the field there are ten harvesters, seven women and three men and a small child. There are four horses, a wagon and haystacks. This was another allusion to hay, that fine, profitable and fragrant commodity. It was given to me by my grandmother Felicia Turton in her old age – she died in 1972 at the age of 95. It was inherited by my grandfather in 1900.

My grandfather seems to have perpetuated the playful use of house names: in 1900 he named his new house 'Bankfield', in 1912 his new house in Scarborough 'Wheatcroft Towers', and in 1923 his Bournemouth house 'Fayremead'.

THE TURTON HOUSEHOLD

If we take 1868 as the date of taking up residency in Hayfield House, the Turton children were then aged 11–19 and still dependent. George would have just started to work with his father. Sarah Ann would have been much occupied with their upbringing and education. Sarah was to die tragically early in 1877 at the age of fifty-two. She had worked hard with William from the early days when life must have been quite a struggle. But she lived to enjoy most of the high moments of his career. At every stage of his progress William shared his wealth with his family and gave them a high priority. She enjoyed several years of life at Hayfield House. She was hostess to receptions given there and accompanied William to various municipal and other events, no doubt a few banquets and balls in the Town Hall, which were truly spectacular and legendary. She was witness to his becoming an omnibus proprietor, a town councillor and director and chairman of Leeds Tramways Company. When she died her children were all grown up – though none yet married – and a credit to her. William built a suitably large tomb for her remains in the churchyard of St Mathew's in Chapel Allerton, not far from Hayfield House. It became the family tomb for the next fifty years but for many years it was for her alone. He did not remarry until his sixties.

For many years before her early death Sarah Ann was mistress, manager, of a large household. She was responsible for the welfare, payment and oversight of her staff. The employment of domestic servants in Britain reached a peak in the year 1871. Already by 1851 the census recorded 1 million female domestic servants. This represented about 10 per cent of the female population (21 million) and a higher proportion of town populations. On the demand side there was an expanding middle class. Their needs, or perceived needs, for added domestic labour included larger families, born in quite rapid succession, a dirty and labour intensive form of heating and cooking, simple methods of laundry and clothes care and more labour intensive forms of food processing. There were none of those 'labour saving devices' that depend on electricity.

What were they paid? Figures from earlier in the century show that a well-to-do family with an income of £500 per annum might spend about 4 per cent on servants' wages. A really rich household might spend up to about 15 per cent. This would certainly include a butler, coachman, cook and several maids. A contemporary rule of thumb that has survived in folklore was that a wealthy merchant had to have an annual income of at least £1,000. By the late 1860s Turton would have exceeded this threshold by a substantial amount.

Sample wages of household servants c.1870	
Sample wages (annual, *approximate*)	
Household servants	
Butler	£40–100
Cook	£18–50
Maids, nurses etc.	£10–30

Comparisons	
Tramway driver	£60–75
School Board teacher	£75
Artisan	£75
Clerks	£50–100
Farm labourer	£29
Shop assistants	£20–50

On the supply side of the market for domestic workers there was the decline in the agricultural labour force, general urban poverty and the availability of young children, whose labour was so necessary to supplement the household income of the poor. The workhouse supplied some of the lowest paid. About one-third of servants lived in, so this was likely to include most of those who came from the countryside. Almost all servants employed by members of the Turton family were born in rural areas, most of them girls of 16 and above. This accounted for quite a regular turnover in staff as women left to get married. The average age at marriage of women at the time was 25. Few of the servants were older than this.

The value of the board and lodging, and perhaps clothing, given to resident servants, was an important benefit. They probably had rather greater personal security and even comfort than they might have at home or in factories. At best they might receive some elementary training in domestic matters that might help them find a husband or in later employment. A male labourer of the same age might spend about 3s a week for a room and up to about 5s or so a week on food and non-alcoholic beverages. A factory canteen provided breakfast for its workers at 1½d to 2d and dinner for 4d ha'penny; to this we might add 2d for tea to reach our estimate. The accommodation and goods in kind in a large household would not cost this in cash terms, but the measure of 8s a week in kind compares well with the 4s a week wage represented by a maid's annual income of £10.

The Turtons employed a coachman who lived with his family in a separate stable and coach house. In 1881 the coachman was Thomas Green, aged 29, with his wife and four children, aged 1–7. The older two are listed as being at school. The address of the coach house was then in Reginald Street. The 1871 census records two resident servants: Elizabeth Booker, aged 21, cook, and Sarah Francis, aged 17, housekeeper. In 1881 the resident servants were Martha Painter, aged 24, and Elizabeth Paterson, both given as 'general domestic servants'. All female servants were unmarried. So including the coachman and his wife there were four resident staff. There were about three other regular staff, one outside, one downstairs and one upstairs, so to say. They would be younger people who came in daily. Most staff were de facto either inside or outside staff and maybe 'clean' and 'dirty', partly corresponding with upstairs and downstairs. Special occasions might call for more servants. So on ordinary days the cook might, without guests, have ten or more people to cater for. What was life like in this house? Let us start downstairs in the basement.

The kitchen would have a cast iron range with several ovens and several warming cupboards and shelves. A lot of cooking was done in the oven, roasting, baking and stewing. These days we have all seen examples of Victorian kitchens preserved or reconstructed as they were when in use. There would be a lot of work required that we no longer need to do, such as cleaning and sharpening non stainless steel knives, polishing silver, copper and brass, blacking iron stoves and so on.

As for main meals, we can expect roast beef and Yorkshire pudding to have had pride of place. One of my chief sources of information, apart from cookbooks and menus of the period, is my grandmother Felicia. She was born in 1877 and knew life at Hayfield, both before she married in 1899 and for many years afterwards. She learnt to cook on these old ranges and in the Yorkshire style. In the 1920s she was still using an old range in her new house in Bournemouth. This was still there when I was a child, when we used it for all sorts of storage. We continued to polish it and blacken it. My grandmother Felicia was also one of nature's good cooks. She much influenced my mother's cooking, and I suppose to some extent my own. One set of prints in the dining room was 'The Fallowfield Hunt', which has a scene of 'Breakfast', no less, in which large joints of roast beef are prepared for the huntsmen who are about to set off. The Yorkshire pudding, which our family still makes better than anyone I know – who wouldn't say that – was eaten as a first course with the 'blood gravy'. If this was intended to reduce the consumption of beef, I never noticed it in the family.

From the census it appears that the cooks did not stay long after their mid-twenties. This was most likely to be in order to get married rather than from any falling out. We cannot tell if there were any cases of disputes between 'upstairs' and 'downstairs', but the children obviously loved living at home. At least there was not serious conflict as instanced in the case of the Leeds Dripping Riots of February 1865. I am grateful to David Thornton for permission to cite his text in full. It is a thoroughly English story but it has special Yorkshire flavour and context:

> The catalyst which provoked [working class bitterness] ... was not some political ideology or religious dogma but a small amount of dripping. Eliza Stafford was the cook at Henry Chorley's house in Park Square. It was general practice that when a cook had roasted a joint the dripping produced was hers to use or sell as she pleased. Chorley, a local surgeon and magistrate, took exception to the practice and had Eliza arrested for theft.
>
> She was sentenced to a month in Armley jail but incensed working class demonstrators set out to embarrass Chorley as much as they could. Graffiti was scrawled on walls, abusive letters were sent to his home and doggerel ballads sung:

Now all you cooks and servant girls wot's very fond of 'tipping'
Don't take your master's scraps of fat and boil them down for dripping:
For if you do bear this in mind, the magistrates won't fail
To try you in a private court and send you off to gaol.

Because a large demonstration was envisaged on the day she completed her sentence, Eliza was released an hour early and smuggled away by train to her daughter's house in Scarborough. When it was realised what had happened a mob marched down to Chorley's home in Park Square. Missiles were thrown and the Leeds Police turned out in force. In the ensuing fracas George Hudson, a potter, was killed, the Chief Constable, William Bell, fell and broke his arm and another officer received a serious head wound. The mayor called for help from Bradford Police and for two troops of cavalry from York. A crowd of 2,000 then gathered outside the Town Hall but eventually was peacefully dispersed. Only five men were arrested and the magistrate, sensing the injustice which had precipitated the event, took a lenient line. (Thornton, 2002, pp.152–3)

I retell this with thoughts of my grandma who used to send beef dripping by post to me at boarding school, in used but unwashed Bovril jars.

Returning to the menu of fare: mutton and boiling fowl were then more popular than now and there was a wide range of poultry and game in season. Tripe is a Yorkshire favourite. Fish was delivered fresh daily to Leeds from the Yorkshire coast. Puddings and pies of all sorts, savoury and sweet, made of flour and beef suet, were boiled or baked.

R. Boston and Sons, Boar Lane c.1900: the Turton family would have bought game, fowl, fish and oysters. Boston was a councillor for twelve years.

Steak and kidney pie, rabbit pie, rhubarb pie and apple pie, eaten with cheese, maybe Wensleydale or neighbouring Derby or Leicester. For tea there was cold meat with Yorkshire Relish. Goodhall and Backhouse of Leeds made over 6 million bottles a year and exported worldwide; empty bottles are regularly dug up on the Western Front. All sorts of homemade pickles and preserves would be on the table. There was fruitcake sliced and buttered, toasted teacakes (a sort of light currant bun), pikelets (crumpets) and Yorkshire parkin made with treacle and ginger. Breakfast was no doubt substantial with bacon and eggs, kidneys, kippers, blood pudding and so on – not necessarily all at once!

Beverages, apart from coffee and tea – maybe Yorkshire tea to suit the water – included Tetley's beers and stout. Wines included German white wines, generally known as Hock, and French reds such as Clarets (Bordeaux, Médoc and St Emilion) and Burgundies. These are the wines most commonly advertised in the newspapers of the time. William specifically left his wife his cellar of wines. Wine was relatively expensive, even the ordinary sorts, due to tax; a hundred years later I recall paying only about five times as much for the equivalent. Then there would be sherry, Madeira, brandy and whisky. Mr Hebblethwaite's cellar was valued at 22 per cent of the total value of household contents.

Due to the isolated location we cannot say for certain what the services were like. It would have had gas lighting and running water. Main drain sewage came later. By the end of the century it could have had electric light, but I recall that my grandparents in Bournemouth did not have electricity until the 1950s, relying on gas and candlelight. The living rooms and bedrooms were heated by coal fires. This was a labour intensive and dirty form of heating, as I also know well from my childhood chores.

SOCIAL STANDING

We can learn from contemporary photographs of the interiors of middle-class houses in Leeds – there is one even from Reginald Terrace – that rooms were comprehensively furnished with heavy carpets and curtains, and cloth covers on tables and chair backs. The walls were well covered with prints and paintings. The mantelpiece and shelves were well endowed with decorative objects and no doubt a few photographs of the family. It was fashionable to have studio portraits taken in town and multiple copies made in the form of postcards or *cartes de visite*. In 1876 there were twenty-five single occupied houses in Reginald Terrace whose households included merchants and manufacturers (nine), reverends (three), cashiers (two), a butcher, a stockbroker and three female heads of household.

William liked to collect contemporary English paintings. I feel sure that many of the paintings and engravings owned by my grandfather at the time of his bankruptcy sale in 1923 had been bought by William Turton for Hayfield House. The painters, with dates of the painting when known, included:

J. Atkinson Grimshaw

Frank Brangwyn

T. Sydney Cooper ARA (1860)

G.E. Hicks (1864)

H. Townley Green RI (1864)

J.F. Marshall (1865)

John Brett (1883)

Edgar Bundy (1892)

Arthur Severn RI

George Wright

R. Hillingford

E. Ladell

James Peel

J.C. Park

Benjamin Barker

Walter Pasmore

He commissioned furniture, including dining chairs that bore his initials on leather. Silverware was the other element of ostentatious display, especially tableware, which bore the initials 'W.T.' and some of it his chosen family 'crest'.

We know he kept a dog or more than one. Pets may not have been allowed in the house, however. Even my grandfather who was a keen breeder of dogs and other animals, birds and fish, would never allow dogs in the house. Caged songbirds were an exception.

How did the family amuse and entertain themselves while 'Dad' – or was it 'Papa' or 'Father'? – was at work, which was much of the time and in the evenings, on Sundays and at holiday times? The girls, the young ladies as they were becoming, sewed and embroidered. They sang and perhaps played the piano and other instruments. Turton's will refers to 'musical instruments'. There was of course no telephone or gramophone yet, though these were installed later. The business offices of William Turton had telegraphic and telephone services just as soon as these media became available.

They read books and were members of the Leeds Library, founded by Joseph Priestley in 1768 and later moved to its elegant building on Commercial Street. The Turton family could borrow books to read at home. Membership was available only to shareholders, or proprietors, who were limited to a maximum of 500. So it was quite an élite club. There was also an annual subscription. Members of the Turton family owned shares for many years as is still evident from the records. Members included William Turton, Robert Turton, Elizabeth Turton (later Mrs J.B. Pegler), George William Turton, Mrs Mary Ann Turton (widow of William Turton) and George Fillingham (husband of Mary Turton). When the girls were older it seems they had a friend or companion whose name appears on their library ticket. Members of the Leeds Library were likely to visit the museum and attend lectures at the Leeds Philosophical and

Ramsden's pianos, advertisement from an almanac; Turton's will referred to 'musical instruments'.

Literary Society close by. The two bodies occasionally organised joint events. In 1878 there was a *Conversazione* for which it was reported that:

> The Lecture Hall was illuminated at intervals during the evening by the electric light, Siemens patent being used and an explanation of its principles given ... Messrs. John Fowler & Co. generously furnished a steam engine to provide motive power [for the electricity].

On another occasion (1880) Professor Graham Bell explained his invention of a 'photophone'; on another (1881) Professor W.E. Ayrton FRS gave a lecture on 'Electric Railways'. Although I have not traced membership of the Philosophical and Literary Society, it is virtually impossible that the Turtons were not members, with a membership at the time of about 700 (compared with Leeds Library 500 and Thoresby Society 300) and with very similar core membership, so there is an *a fortiori* case at least.

When the Thoresby Society, a historical and antiquarian society, was founded in 1889 William Turton soon joined as did his sons George and Robert and his two sons-in-law, some of them life members. Membership of these societies overlapped and members of the Thoresby Society, seldom more than about 300, were from the same recognisable Leeds élite that were preponderant in many other social and public institutions. In 1902 members included three earls, five MPs, three knights and a judge. There were thirty-seven who had postgraduate university degrees and a similar number of fellows of learned societies.

William Turton himself had little time for leisure. We do not know what tastes he and his family may have had in music, theatre or other arts and entertainments. There was a wide range of such attractions. Leeds was already famous for its music and many international stars performed there. I suspect the Music Hall was also a favourite. Perhaps the ladies of the family took themselves to more highbrow events. There was a new museum, an art gallery and, towards the end of the century, a growing array of fine shops, arcades and galleries.

One form of socialising in a relaxed surrounding was the use of public baths. These catered for all classes of people at all prices. There were several stylish new baths of a more exclusive sort, though even these had a large clientele. They were various named spas, Turkish baths, even an electro-chemical bath. The grandest was the Turkish or Oriental and General in Cookridge Street. They were built by Cuthbert Broderick, architect of the Town Hall, at a cost of £12,000. A contemporary description states:

> They are in the Oriental style, presenting a very pleasing appearance, and for completeness and extent unequalled by any similar institution in the kingdom.

Market day in Boar Lane 1872, artist's impression from the Graphic, *2 September 1872, rich in detail; elegant ladies are shopping or hiring servants; the boy is selling the* Leeds Mercury; *horse bus or tram on right and Trinity church.*

Oriental and General Baths.

Grand Theatre 1878, built partly on land sold by William Turton.

Thornton's Arcade, built 1878.

Women were allowed exclusive use of the baths on Wednesdays. Sarah Ann almost certainly accompanied William to a few grand events in the Town Hall, which was famous for its splendid balls and banquets on the occasion of visits by British and foreign royalty. It could seat 400 people at a banquet and the hall accommodated some 8,000 people at its opening in 1858.

In the immediate vicinity of the house there were excursions on foot to Woodhouse Moor where just about everything you can imagine happening in a central urban space did happen: athletics and archery, horseracing and football, cricket, circuses, boxing, political gatherings, balloon ascents, celebrations and galas. Further afield, from about 1872, was the newly acquired municipal asset of Roundhay Park, still the largest of Leeds' open spaces. Roundhay and other excursion destinations just outside Leeds would have been suitable for visits using the family's own carriage.

Seaside holidays became a new fashion for the comfortable classes following the extension of the railway network. The Yorkshire coast offered many well-appointed resorts including Whitby, Scarborough, Filey and Bridlington which provided the equivalent of domestic comfort – or for some a higher standard – and the healthy pleasures of the seaside and the countryside around.

The children lived at home until they were quite adult. The daughters married late and Robert never married. They seem to have been deeply and lovingly attached to their parents. We get a sense of their affection from some of the many gifts they made in their wills. Robert, who died on 2 January 1825, had endowed a hospital cot for £1,000 in memory of his mother soon after her death and his sister Elizabeth was to do the same. Robert also left, among other legacies, £100 to Thomas Gaines, 'formerly clerk to his father', £100 to William Whalley, 'formerly manager to his late brother George' and £100 to Mrs Elizabeth Muscroft, 'formerly servant to his father'. His brother's widow, Annie, had also endowed a cot in memory of her husband. She left considerable sums to a variety of charities for women, children and the sick.

Hayfield House was the home base from which William launched his subsequent career and which provided him with a secure and it seems happy family life. He was well supported by his wife and children. They entertained guests. The 1881 census found a Mr H.C.C. van Hasselt staying and marked as 'Visitor' with his occupation and address given as 'Brick maker/manufacturer, Kampen, Holland'. Often the notables and business colleagues of Turton's acquaintance would hold dinners in the fine new hotels, such as the Great Northern Hotel, that had followed the development of the railways and were often close to the main stations. But Turton hosted some grand events at Hayfield House itself. One such was on 11 November 1874 following the official opening of a new tram service and more passing places on the Chapeltown route. The *Leeds Mercury* records that 'guests were entertained at Councillor Turton's imposing residence, Hayfield House, a large villa ...' Several aldermen and councillors were present including the mayor, Alderman Marsden, and the directors and secretary of the Leeds Tramways Company.

William Turton was aware of the status of Turton as a Yorkshire name of long-standing. At about the time he started to live in Hayfield House he decided to adopt a Turton 'crest' and 'motto'. A crest is that part of a coat of arms that was a detachable sign used on the banners and clothing of a knight. William's crest is a precise copy of the one on the official Turton coat of arms borne by those who claim noble or gentry ancestry. It is a forearm and hand extending from a castellated turret made up of layered brick or stone, holding a short spear horizontally, point to the right, which has a small rectangular flag hanging from its end, with a spearhead extending beyond it. Although not in the original green, silver and gold, the shape and design of the turret, the clothing and cuff on the arm, the gripping hand, the spear and the horizontally divided flag are faithful to the original. This was a deliberate and careful reproduction. William Turton apparently cared about such things.

The crest is to be found only on four small items of silverware, of no great value, which are in my possession. There is a set of three items of tableware: a pair of identical little dishes with Bristol glass linings, tiny silver spoons for salt and mustard, and a pepper pot for finely ground white pepper. The other item, the only one to bear the motto, is a silver box with a double hinge – known in the family as a 'sandwich tin' though it could have been for small cigars. This also has his name and, rather unusually I think, his address, 'Hayfield House Leeds'. The motto is *formosaque honesta*, which is the Latin for 'beautiful and honest'. It bears a Sheffield silver hallmark of 1866–67. It is unlikely that these were the only items bearing these signs of some armorial pretension, but only these have survived. We know that the Victorian age was quite promiscuous with armorial emblems. It might even be that silver merchants recommended their use and did the required research, which would need some care. In any case the fashion was well established and not hard to fall in line with. It was nonetheless another sign of Turton wishing to raise the social status of his family.

10

'TURTON AND VICTORY'

One of the delights for a researcher is coming upon little details that put one in direct touch with an ancestor or event and tell a story in themselves. Right at the start of my enquiries, on my first visit to Leeds ever, I went of course to the Thoresby Society Library. This had been founded in 1889 at the height of William Turton's career but after he had relinquished town politics. It was in a box labelled 'political pamphlets', which contained political ephemera such as leaflets announcing a speech in Leeds by William Gladstone. To my great delight there was a mid-blue card about two and a half by three inches. On it, on one side only, is printed in simple bold lettering, 'Turton and Victory'.

He was a proud and optimistic man. There is no way of knowing in what year this was used (one of 1864, 1869, 1872 or 1878), but I imagine that at each election the cards were handed round in a great many pubs in the ward.

The burgesses had managed Leeds since the thirteenth century. In the eighteenth century it has been said that Leeds was governed by an oligarchy of twenty-eight families in one generation after another. By the middle of the nineteenth century they had become a large, articulate and fully enfranchised bourgeoisie within a capitalist economy. Some of them had become a kind of 'bourgeois aristocracy', boasting of wealthy dynasties of officeholders and knighthoods. Politics was largely 'a struggle for supremacy within the urban middle-class'.

Prior to 1835 the dominant tendency in Leeds Borough politics had been Tory and Anglican, the establishment. The 1830s saw the beginning of many political changes in Britain. In 1835 a new tendency manifested itself that was to prevail for most of the century. In Leeds there were fifty-one Liberal councillors and thirteen Tory. The Tory seats are good indicators of wealth and class of voters, who were in any case a small percentage of the adult male population: Mill Hill, still the old 'West End' – nine seats; Headingley, semi-rural, salubrious residences – three seats; Kirkgate, old town centre notables – one seat.

There were only two political parties of any electoral significance: Liberals (incorporating old Whigs and newer radicals) and Conservatives (Tories, who also had a more radical wing). Both parties and their representatives on the borough council included the wealthiest manufacturers and merchants. The Leeds Conservatives were seldom rural landed Tories. Both parties had to represent themselves as socially inclusive as more adult males were given the right to vote. Both parties were patriotic. Both were fiercely proud of Leeds' independence and its standards of urban management.

The Liberal party was more or less identified with religious non-conformism and the Tories with Anglicanism. Liberals were also the party for radicals to join, such as some former Chartists and Owenites. It was, as the Labour party later liked to call itself, politically 'broad church', a party of all shades. I doubt if any Conservative councillor had any sympathy with the Liberal member who called for a square to be named after Cromwell rather than Victoria; even if people did tend to get fed up with so many things being called Victoria this or Albert the other. But both parties received the votes of richer and poorer alike. The richer constituencies returned a similar proportion of Tory votes as the poorest. However, during the period of Turton's involvement in borough politics, 1863–78, the Tories' share of the vote ranged between just under a quarter to just under a half. There was one exceptional year when they got 58 per cent, twenty-eight seats out of forty-eight.

In the first part of the century several public functions were the responsibility of elected boards. They included the Poor Law, Waterworks and Highways. These were used by political parties or political tendencies used them as arenas for political control. For example, the Highways Board was dominated by radicals. Robert Meek Carter, the Chartist, and later a councillor serving with Turton, began his political career on this board. Fraser (1976) writes that 'In Leeds Tories used the Poor Law as a compensation for loss of municipal office'. From 1844–68 the Tories had a majority on the board in all except three years. In all these years they were in a minority on the Borough Council. The Poor Law guardians who supervised the Leeds Union (workhouse) were elected from a wider territory than the wards and were based on the old parish structures. This board was the only one of significance to survive well into the twentieth century.

THE WARDS

The Borough of Leeds, which did not then contain all the outer townships, had twelve wards, or electoral constituencies. The total population in each ward varied widely from about 3,000 to about 26,000. Their electorates ranged widely from over 8,000 in Hunslet to under 1,000 in Kirkgate. East Ward had a population of 18,945 and an electorate of 3,937. The number of councillors in each ward varied slightly according to number of voters: two, three and four are the most frequent sizes.

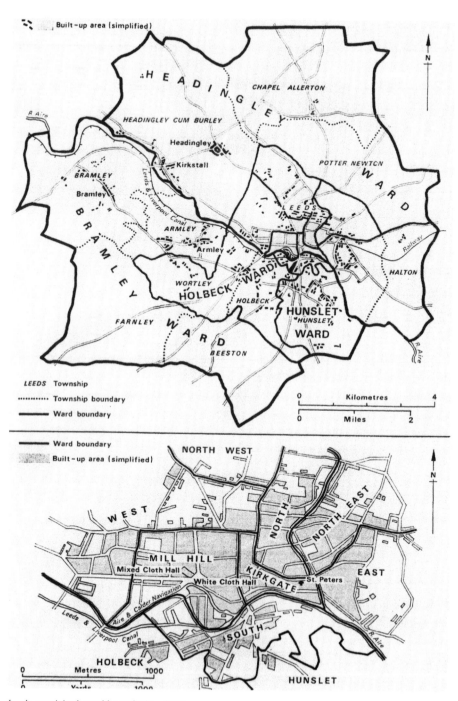

Leeds municipal ward boundaries, 1835.

Leeds ward boundaries 1874			
Wards	Electorate 1874	Turnout 1874	Per cent (1872)
Kirkgate	788	79	(70)
South	1,320	77	(57)
Mill Hill	1,777	60	(39)
North	2,440	70	(48)
East	3,937	64	(40)
Headingley	4,407	54	(39)
North West	5,191	66	(54)
Bramley	5,311	69	(56)
West	6,438	59	(44)
North East	6,474	82	(37)
Holbeck	7,889	58	(52)
Hunslet	8,317	53	(40)

We can see that over the twelve wards there was a wide range of size of electorate and fluctuation in turnout. It seems to have been likely that corruption tended to be higher in smaller constituencies. We shall come back to this.

Despite its size, wealth and position at the forefront of urban and industrial development, Leeds was by no means a city-state, much as its burgesses might have liked it to be. Leeds was not even a city. This status and the accompanying office of lord mayor were not to be granted until 1895. So in Turton's time it was a borough with a town council and a simple mayor, not a lord mayor. The state, in the form of Parliament, had to be petitioned and special Acts and Orders passed in order to enable all sorts of 'improvements' and to authorise borrowing to pay for them. The council had a Parliamentary committee that dealt with these strategic local issues in Parliament. This committee also expressed its opinions on matters of wider national and foreign issues. These were then conveyed by the local MPs to Parliament. It is of interest that William Turton sat on this committee only very briefly, whereas it seems that many of the more politically ambitious and senior councillors took it more seriously. Possibly it had a higher proportion of Liberals on it, but one cannot avoid concluding that Turton was more of a regional man.

COUNCILLORS

In his encomium 'The Story of the Marsden Mayoralty' (1875) J.S. Curtis observes:

> ... a member of the Leeds Town Council is seldom returned on the simple grounds
> of personal fitness; he must be pronounced and definite in his party views and
> sympathies to be acceptable to the ratepayer and so the struggles which are gone
> through each November are fought under the rival flags, sometimes with a bit-
> terness and always with an intensity of effort ...

Hennock, in his important book *Fit and Proper Persons: Ideal and Reality in Nineteenth-
century Urban Government* (1973), writes:

> If corporations were to be great undertakings, providing services on a scale
> comparable with those of the most adventurous entrepreneur, raising loans and
> assuming the disbursement of great sums, then service on their chief commit-
> tees demanded skills normally to be looked for in a successful businessman.
>   'Economists' might object to municipal ambition, but even they could not avoid the
> need to dispose of sewage and of floodwater, to straighten thoroughfares for the grow-
> ing number of horse-drawn vehicles, to pave and scavenge, and to enlarge the gaol.
>   Success in such undertakings demands boldness as well as caution, a willing-
> ness to think big as well as shrewd attention to detail.

This is almost a rationale for Turton's involvement in local politics, a job description
and a record of some of the principal things he did in office.

The men who were elected councillor during the century somewhat declined – if
that is the right word – from those of a more professional and educated background to
a more humble level of middling capitalist. Here are some indices of this (Hennock):

Occupations of Leeds councillors 1862–76			
Selected occupations of councillors (accounting for at least 75 per cent of all councillors)	1862	1872	1876
Lawyer	3	-	-
Doctor	3	-	-
Textile merchant	8	4	3
Metal industries	10	9	9
Leather industries	3	5	6
Dyeing industries	4	2	1
Retail trade	7	17	17
	38	37	36

Councillors also members of the Leeds Philosophical & Literary Society		
1842	1862	1892
27	17	6
(40 per cent+)	(25 per cent+)	(<10 per cent)

TURTON STANDS FOR ELECTION

By the age of 38, in 1863, William Turton decided he would enter politics by standing for election as a town councillor. It is of great interest that he was first nominated as a Liberal candidate, in 1863. He was unsuccessful and thereafter stood only as a Conservative. This might possibly suggest that his first concern was to become a councillor, rather than to support some pre-existing political principles. But then why did he switch to a party with very little likelihood of forming a majority, and then stand against a sitting Liberal. Maybe it was the only nomination he could secure. But why did he stand?

We know that by this time he was a young man of some wealth and social standing. His social status was such that he been both a borough and a Parliamentary elector from quite an early age. But none of his children were yet adult and able to help with his business, as all his sons were to do later. He had not yet bought into the omnibus business nor built his mansion, let alone thought about trams. He was ambitious. He was personally quite a 'popular' man. So he had the basic prerequisites for political success at that time: intelligence, wealth, strength and health. He was also an Anglican, a member of the established Church of England, and the congregation of its flagship church St Peter's, then still known as the 'Parish Church of Leeds'. When he moved to Chapeltown Road he joined the congregation of St Martin's in Potternewton. It was here that his funeral would be held. Yet he left money in his will to St Peter's Sunday school, which he had attended. In January 1876 an appeal to contribute to the Leeds Church Extension Fund and Hook Memorial Fund reached the considerable sum of £50,000. There was one exceptional contribution of £500. About ten people gave £100–£400 including William Turton (£100). The rest was in sums of £5, £25 and £50, with 500 donating £1. It is highly likely that his religious affiliation was a major factor in determining his choice of political allegiance. It used to be said that the Church of England was 'the Conservative Party at prayer'. At the time the Church of England had about one-third of the places of worship and religious congregations in Leeds, a proportion not too dissimilar to the Tory share of the vote. Non-conformist churches and sects made up most of the rest. They were predominantly Methodists or Wesleyans of various sorts, with a few Quakers, Unitarians and Independents. Roman Catholics and Jews made up no more than one per cent combined, though their numbers were to increase.

After an initial term as member for North East Ward, Turton represented East Ward. He was well known in the area and he knew it well. His business was on its border. He owned property here and some of his employees lived here. It was the ward least well endowed with decent housing and infrastructure, and it contained an above average proportion of the Irish immigrants who had come to Leeds in quite large numbers since the 1840s. After the 1867 Reform Act some might have had the vote. On balance a Catholic Irishman might prefer an Anglican to a non-conformist candidate. And Irishmen almost certainly preferred a Tory to a Liberal at the national level on account of the Irish question, Home Rule. Later in the century the Leeds Irish may have held the balance politically on this issue. Inevitably the role of Roman Catholic clergy was critical. On at least one occasion a priest was accused of having directed and assisted his parishioners to vote Conservative.

Turton was not a dyed-in-the-wool Tory from the Shires. I doubt that political theory or dogma interested him greatly. Nonetheless he remained a Conservative for the rest of his life. Motives for entering local politics in these times were no doubt similar to those today. On the altruistic side William Turton clearly knew about the appalling living conditions of so many of the people in his constituency – none of them voters. We shall see later some of his concerns and interventions. The fact that he accepted to be on the 'cellar dwellings sub-committee' suggests that he had a full knowledge of these issues and cared enough to be willing to try to improve things. On the other hand, it is difficult to avoid the supposition that, along with a modicum of self-esteem and concern for civic status, the major motive for Turton entering town politics was to further his own business interests. We shall have to assess this later.

After his first election in 1864 he served for three years and was not returned at the following election. An opportunity arose again in 1869 when he stood successfully against J. Roth with 1,253 votes to 946. He won again, a smaller majority, in 1872 against Thomas Horsfall, an estate agent in Park Row. The *Leeds Mercury* reported the meeting on 3 October 1872 at which Turton was re-nominated:

Municipal Elections, East Ward

A numerously attended meeting was held last night at the house of Mr. Edwin Mosley, the Hope Inn, York-road, when the following resolution was carried unanimously, the motion of Mr. George Giles, seconded by Mr. Jeremiah Butler, and supported by Mr. Wm Ward:– "That the best thanks of the meeting and of the East Ward be now and hereby presented to Mr. Councillor Turton, for the very able manner in which for the past three years he has represented this Ward in the deliberations of the Town Council, believing that no member of that council has more earnestly, assiduously or devotedly attended to his duties and the interest of the constituency than our retiring member, Mr. Councillor Turton." It was also resolved, on the motion of Mr. James Wm Grayson, seconded by Mr. Giles and supported by Mr. Wm Henry Naylor:– "That the general interests of the East Ward and of the borough of Leeds will be most securely promoted by the re-election of Mr. William Turton".

In 1875 he was returned unopposed after the Liberal candidate, Elliot Hinchcliffe, withdrew. By this time Turton was extremely well known from his tramway and bus work and a very experienced councillor. It is tempting to surmise that the Liberals decided not to contest. He stood again in 1878; victory would have made him a very long-standing councillor indeed, and he clearly wanted to continue. But in the event he was defeated by the Liberal candidate. He did not stand again. The area became a safe Labour seat in 1905. The former Deputy Prime Minister Denis Healey was MP for East Leeds for thirty-seven years.

Another glimpse of the political milieu at ward level is revealed by this entry in the *Yorkshire Post* for 15 October 1871, just two or three weeks before the election. Turton did not have to stand again that year:

Municipal Elections, Leeds

A crowded meeting of the burgesses of the East Ward was held last night at the Sussex Tavern, Cavalier Hill. Councillor Turton was unanimously elected to the Chair. After a few opening remarks by the Chairman, and a formal vote of thanks to the retiring Councillor, the burgesses were asked to nominate a candidate as a fit and proper person to serve as Councillor for the East Ward for the ensuing three years, the most neglected ward in the borough. A vote of thanks to the Chairman concluded the proceedings. The meeting was crowded to overflowing.

BRIBERY AND CORRUPTION

Looked at comparatively, Parliamentary government by elected representatives organised on party lines – I avoid the term democracy – always seems to attract the bad behaviour that is generically known as 'bribery and corruption'. Leeds at this time was no exception.

The Reform Act of 1832 removed some shameful excesses from the British Parliamentary system. There had been early but unfulfilled hopes of getting rid of at least some of the temptations that created a venal electorate and corrupt politicians. The 1867 Reform Act extended the franchise and thereby increased the difficulty of winning votes. The Ballot Act of 1872 introduced the secret ballot. Until then the voting preferences of all those voting was recorded and published annually. Election laws were finally to be given sufficient strength and penalties in the Corrupt and Illegal Prevention Act of 1883. By bribery we understand both negative forms such as withdrawal of favour, intimidation and undue influence, and the more common positive forms of giving money, treating to food and drink, reducing debts and so on. In addition there was fraudulent voter registration, personation and all sorts of other tricks. These forms of 'bribery and corruption' were practised, if not by everyone then by candidates of both parties and in a fairly endemic way. Yet the malpractices, the illegalities were not on the same scale as those I have witnessed and researched in Thailand in the 1960s and to date. I have also served as an electoral observer in a presidential election in Indonesia. In many countries of the world, newspapers sum up electoral behaviour in terms of the numbers fatalities among election agents and such like. There was nothing like this in Leeds. But I suspect the banks may have noticed a run on silver shilling coins at election time. The prevalence of electoral malpractice is related to the perceived benefits of electoral victory, both for candidate and party. This begs the question whether, and if so how, it was worth incurring the expense and risking prosecution.

Turton's career as a councillor started with his involvement in a major election scandal. His election was exceptional in another sense in that it seems he had to stand twice in the same month, on 1st and 28th November 1864, due to the resignation of a councillor who had been made an alderman.

In February the next year, 1865, several cases of 'bribery arising out of the recent Municipal Election' were heard in the County Court, in the Leeds Town Hall. The Liberals brought the charges, at a cost of £200, against Conservative candidates and their agents. Two men were convicted, Wray and Seth Joy. Wray was cleared by a High Court decision and returned to the council. Wray was an influential businessman who sat on some committees with Turton. A few weeks later on 6 March 1865 the Conservatives in turn brought charges before the County Court Judge against Liberal candidates and their agents. The case was complicated from the start by the fact that there had been two elections. Sixteen people were summoned but ten cases were withdrawn. The hearing, which lasted from 10.00 a.m. until 7.15 p.m., was reported in seventy three and a half column inches in the *Leeds Mercury*, nearly a full broadsheet spread. It was a big story in Leeds and rather entertaining at times.

The cases were against various men who had been party agents or canvassers. Addresses show that they came from the crowded area between East Street and Marsh Lane, very close to William Turton's area of business operations. The charges were that various sums of money had been offered or accepted as bribes to secure votes for the Liberal candidate, Harley. The most common sum offered for a vote was 4s, in a range from an exceptionally small amount of 1s and 6d to 'five shillings and a glass of brandy'. Sums of £1 5s or so seem to have been offered against a promise to secure several votes. One or two week's rent was the currency used by one agent who was a local rent collector. The practice of 'treating' – giving food and drink to secure a vote – was improper but not part of the charges in this case. I suppose the evidence would not stand up. One witness said he had breakfast, together with fifty other men, at the Forester's Arms, 'I do not know who paid for my breakfast.' 'I did not see any of these people pay for their breakfast.' A 'few whiskies' in the Black Lion, East Street, seems to have been the small change of bribery or vote buying.

The practice of transporting people to the polling station if they agree to vote for you is common and nowadays is mostly done by party volunteers. It can lead to bad practice as when, say, an army officer takes truckloads of his soldiers to vote en bloc. Cabs were hired at £1 4s per day to bring in the faithful. This seems not to have attracted any reproof. We can be pretty sure that Turton would have a good supply of his own vehicles at the ready on Election Day.

The scenes in the courtroom were pretty chaotic. Witnesses would contradict them-selves, other witnesses and their counsel. His Honour the judge had a hard time and often expressed his exasperation, referring to 'flagrantly contradictory statements, and such gross perjury on one side and the other'. Many witnesses failed to appear or turned up drunk. 'David Gaukrodger appeared in answer to the call, and entered the box in a hopeless state of intoxication. He was asked by his Honour where he had been drinking, and answered in a husky voice, but with much good humour "Nowhere" (Laughter).' His Honour ordered the witness to pay a fine of £5 or to be imprisoned for seven days.

In the course of cross-examination several references were made to bribes being offered by Turton's side; all such suggestions were denied and none were proven. Overall it seems that 4s, a very good day's wage, and a few drinks in the pub, was widely regarded as the price of a vote. Other minor inducements included a 6d beer ticket and a 1s ticket for 'soup'. Voters were sometimes offered less and bargained their way up, suggesting that this was a norm. One 'canvasser' said he had asked 'for a few day's pay' for voting. 'The witness made use of the word "voting" inadvertently, and on being questioned with regard to it by his Honour, stated that he meant "day's work" (Laughter).'

The following month the issue of corrupt electioneering was raised in a meeting of the town council, attended by Turton, on 25 April and again on 11 May. At the latter, grim reference was made to a Chief Justice in eighteenth-century Leeds who had been hanged for corruption in office, and to a former tariff of a £50 fine, coupled with disbar-ment from voting or office holding for life. But the 1859 Act on the matter prescribed a 40s fine and six years' suspension. Councillor Tatham proposed a modest tightening up of the law, saying that 40s was no deterrent, for example in the recent East Ward case. The report in the *Leeds Mercury* continued, 'Mr. Turton had great pleasure in seconding the resolution. If the example of bribery had not been shown, they [the Conservatives] would never have had occasion to follow suit' (Laughter).'

Councillor Addyman, ignoring Turton's irony – and his bold candour – said:

> ... he thought Mr. Turton had made a mistake seconding the resolution, and in giving a tacit acknowledgement that his party had committed bribery. (Mr. Wray [the very same] 'I would withdraw it.') Every right-minded man must detest brib-ery and intimidation in any form, and he believed that a great step would be taken in doing away with these offences at municipal elections if the meetings of the candidates ceased to be held in public houses (Hear, hear).

Councillor Price (Conservative) said that he had never spent more than £20 on election expenses in three elections. The usual reply to such declarations of innocence was likely to be, 'Well, your friends paid for you.' Councillor Nichols thought it disgraceful that 'nearly half of the members of Council were returned, either directly or indirectly, by means anything but honourable (Hear, hear).' Another member said that after his first attempt 'he was sent a longish bill, then a middling and at the third that he was elected

Council Chamber, Leeds Town Hall; this accommodated 64 councillors and 300 other people.

free of charge (Hear, hear; applause).' Mr. Yewdell (Conservative) hoped that both parties would dispense with using *coaches* at elections. Another councillor referred darkly
to a councillor who had said that he would rather spend £500 than lose an election.
(Name, name) 'Mr. Yewdell' was duly named and duly denied the accusation.

In the end Turton and Yewdell were among the thirty-three councillors who voted
for the resolution to campaign to increase the penalties for electoral malpractice. None
of the other thirteen or so voted against or recorded an abstention, a most unusual
instance. It was agreed to send the petition to Parliament via Edmund Baines, MP.

The *Leeds Mercury* had an editorial comment the following day. It referred to a
Conservative member (not by name but implying William Turton) and his comment
reported above:

> We know nothing about who set the example or who followed it, but this distinct
> admission that bribery is regularly practised by the Conservatives in municipal
> contests, shows how familiarly the vile thing is regarded as a weapon of party
> warfare ... Bribery is the regularly organised means of warfare used by the two
> great parties in the town ... It shows a moral condition of which a community of
> Hottentots might be ashamed.

Curtis (1875), in his Marsden memorial, writes of the situation in North Ward ten years later. Nothing much seems to have changed:

> [Of] North Ward it is unpleasant to write. That Ward during many years, was debauched and demoralised by unprincipled men. The poverty of many of the voters, the low standard of morality, which prevailed amongst them, and the mixed character of the constituency, afforded opportunities for bribery and corruption of every sort, and they had been abundantly used. There is no need to heap infamy on the graves of the dead, but it is a fact which cannot be contradicted, and which is a matter of history, that for years only the rascality, ignorance and weakness of the Ward was represented in the Town Council.
>
> I do not affirm that either party could claim immunity from evil habits. In fact, it appears as if downright honesty and purity in the conduct of elections was remote from the minds of the Ward managers. Bribery had existed, did exist, and appeared to be recognised as perfectly correct, as quite justifiable, and as needing no excuse. The most scathing denunciation of the system appeared to produce no change. Threats of exposure were so many idle words uttered to the wind. In no Ward in the entire borough had corruption run riot, almost with impunity, to the same extent as in the North Ward. Truly the Liberals had tried to alter that state of things, but, up to 1874, the snake had merely been wounded.

After the November 1874 election there had been an official borough enquiry into North Ward election, which was declared void. This revealed the fullest set of malpractices in a single case that I have come across, 'treating and undue influence', 'did personate and falsely assume to vote in the name of others', 'voting by non-electors', 'miscounting of votes', 'wrongly discarding ballots'.

The *Leeds Mercury*, as so often, summed up this episode in ringing tones:

> If either of the great political parties in this borough has yet left in it a particle of self-respect ... if they are not banded together in a disgraceful conspiracy to debauch the character of the working classes ... each will render hearty thanks to its opponent for unmasking the corruption which lurks and works unknown to the honourable men on both sides, in the lowest substrate of party managers and electioneering busybodies. (8 March 1865)

Turton had his baptism of fire in this party warfare of 1865. He had maybe learned a lesson. He was frank, fearless and also a cautious man. In any case, his wealth and public status increased greatly over the intervening years, buses, trams, Hayfield House and all. He could stand on his record.

MAYORS

The electorate chose the councilors, the councillors chose the aldermen and the aldermen chose the mayor. This political milieu was of the greatest consequence for William Turton's overall activities. Some members of the council were his co-directors, or shareholders. Some were on council committees that took important decisions affecting his affairs. All were responsible for creating, developing and maintaining the infrastructure that benefited his business. A few were personal friends and were occasionally guests at Hayfield House.

Mayors were elected for one year at a time. In the second half of the century only one mayor served a three-year period of office; nine had two years, not necessarily consecutive; the rest only one year each. The list of mayors includes a great many names of famous families. Two families, the Fairbairns and Kitsons, had mayors in successive generations. Several names are of people whom William Turton knew quite well and personally: Luccock, Nussey, Barran, Marsden, Tetley and others. Two of these, Barran and Marsden, were among the most distinguished of the century and were in office while Turton was a councillor. Both were extremely wealthy men. Wealth was more or less a de facto requirement for holding the office. Personal munificence was expected. Even so these two were exceptional in their municipal largesse. There are so many ways in which the stories of these men interweave with that of William Turton that I shall relate them briefly.

JOHN BARRAN

John Barran (1821–1905), a Baptist, was one of the first and largest ready-made clothing manufacturers in Leeds. He adopted Singer's sewing machine in the year it was invented, 1851. He developed other machinery for cutting several layers of cloth simultaneously. He served as councillor in the 1860s and in November 1870 was elected mayor; he was re-elected the following year and completed his term of office in October 1872. He was mayor when all the crucial decisions were taken to authorise the Leeds Tramways Company. He was a Liberal MP 1870–71 and received a knighthood.

Barran's greatest claim to fame in Leeds was his purchase of Roundhay Park. This is now a 373 acre park, formerly part of a 700-acre aristocratic estate. It is rather larger than Hyde Park in London and about half the size of Hampstead Heath, which began to be municipalised at the same time. The descendants of the medieval family sold in 1803 to Nichols, a Leeds merchant who rebuilt, landscaped and made it into fine gardens and parkland. A death without heirs in 1871 put the property on the market suddenly. John Barran, as mayor, was passionately keen that the park should be bought for the people of Leeds. It was actually a little outside the borough proper, and this, together with the need for him to persuade his colleagues and raise the money, led him and a few associates to buy the park with their own money and hold it in trust.

Within a year or so they sold it on to the borough at cost, £139,000, an enormous sum, plus interest. Parliament had authorised expenditure up to £150,000. The vote in the council was not unanimous; there was some strong opposition. Turton is on record as having voted for the purchase. Roundhay Park was opened on 20 September 1872 by Prince Arthur. A crowd of about 100,000 attended the opening, more than one-third of the total population. We can be sure that Turton and his family would have driven in their carriage from Hayfield House to take part in the ceremonies.

On the 1 January 1874, a special meeting of the council was held at which the urgent 'Roundhay Park Fox Question' was discussed. The minutes of the Properties Committee show that a document concerning the park was agreed with the omission of a clause that called for the elimination of foxes in the park. Barran, who by this time was no longer mayor, said that fox hunting was 'the most democratic sport allowed by law'. He was a foxhunting man. He was afraid that the clause 'might engender a bitter feeling between the gentry in the country and those of the town'. The motion was carried. The hunters had it. Turton was one of the thirty-three to thirteen who voted to permit fox hunting with hounds in a suburban area.

Roundhay Park was to play a special part in the transport history of Leeds. There had been massive public support for the purchase, but the park was distant from the town centre and the majority of people could not afford the fares to visit it, or not often. The population of Roundhay village was only 583; quite a few of the families had their own carriages, so there was not a great demand to develop a regular transport service. Even by 1879 it was sometimes referred to as 'Barran's Folly'. Not until 1887 was there serious discussion of a transport service to Roundhay. Leeds Tramways Company had not thought it profitable. An overhead railway was entertained. In 1891 the council decided to construct its own tramway, which opened the following year. Two years later they adopted the electric tram that had been trialled and tested. It opened on 29 October 1891, the first electric tram with overhead wires in Britain.

So not until about 1889 did Roundhay Park start to become a truly mass attraction and for the next twenty-five years it was enjoyed by many millions of people. Activities and attractions included the flower gardens, woods, landscapes, follies and grottoes; horticultural and other shows were held and military tattoos. There was cricket and football, cycling and skating; on the lake there was boating, swimming and fishing. William Turton and family were regular visitors. His grandson, my grandfather, bought a house on the northwestern edge of the park in 1900, where my father was born. I am sure he had memories of playing in Roundhay Park as a little boy, even though he left Leeds at the age of six.

In 1876 Barran became a Liberal Member of Parliament for Leeds, which he remained until 1885, after which he continued as an MP for another constituency. He was later knighted. He died in 1905. A century after his death a Leeds Civic Trust Blue Plaque was erected to commemorate his contributions to Leeds. This was placed on St Paul's House, which occupies half of the south side of Georgian style Park Square. This very large rectangular building was completed for Barran in 1878. It has variously been described as Hispano-Moorish and Moorish-Venetian and is likely to have been influenced by drawings of the Alhambra in Spain. It is built of pink and red bricks with terra cotta and polychrome tile decoration. It has minaret-like turrets on all four corners of the roof. It looks more like the Doge's Palace than a ready-made clothing factory, the purpose for which it was built, full of Singer Sewing Machines. It is one of the author's favourite buildings in Leeds, even if only the shell of the original building survives, finely restored.

HENRY ROWLAND MARSDEN

Henry Marsden (1823–76) was, like Barran, a close contemporary in age to William Turton. Marsden's time in office is the subject of an encomium by J. Sydney Curtis written to celebrate his two years of office as mayor at the end of 1875. By the age of ten he was working in Marshall's Mill. He must have benefited from Marshall's education policy, for he became an apprentice engineer with W. King Wesley, Engineering Tools. In his twenties he went to America where he is said to have 'amassed considerable wealth'. He returned to Leeds in 1862, aged 39, and in 1866 was elected councillor, becoming an alderman in 1872. He was elected mayor in November 1873 and left office in October 1875. He was considered by many to have been the most popular mayor of Leeds.

The author of the adulatory book on the Marsden Mayoralty is confident in his judgement that Marsden was the most generous of any mayor of Leeds. His private benefactions over many years were never less than £2,000 per annum. Two quite small instances of his generous spirit may be cited.

By 1874 the two-day Roundhay Regatta on Waterloo Lake had become a special attraction. Competitions included rowing, canoeing and swimming; walking [*sic*] the greasy pole, a 'duck hunt' and a tub race. There were lots of gold and silver medals to be won, and the Roundhay Park Challenge Cup with a value of £50, on the first day. Not to be outdone, Marsden presented his Marsden Grand Challenge Cup, value £80, on the second day.

Another anecdote is instructive in various ways. A servant girl had found a ring in the street. Her parents recognised it as a diamond ring that could not belong to her. They took it to the police station. It belonged to Henry Marsden. He was so impressed by the family's honesty that he gave the girl a £10 reward, which was a great sum for her, maybe equivalent to a year's wages.

In the middle of Marsden's second year of office, on 18 May 1875, the Duke of Edinburgh visited Leeds to open Edinburgh Hall. The procession at the Town Hall is described thus, 'A long double line of Town Councillors, with one exception, in purple robes, and of Aldermen, in scarlet and fur, entered first.' This is the only pen picture of Turton in his ceremonial purple robes. The one exception is likely to have been a Quaker or other strict non-conformist who often avoided civic functions, if not office-holding altogether, for dislike of frequent 'toasting' at dinners and other practices.

ALDERMEN

Aldermen – a feature of local government in Britain until the 1960s – were a sort of upper house or senate, chosen from within the council. They were usually senior, experienced and respected or maybe just influential councillors. They tended to occupy the chair of important committees. Conservatives complained that aldermen were always, de facto, Liberals. Liberals responded artfully that they did not wish to overturn the original Tory law whereby the elected majority in council should elect Aldermen. In the case of Leeds this had meant Liberal aldermen for decades.

Turton himself nonetheless stood for election as Alderman. He received only the Tory votes among the councillors of course and so was not elected. At a special meeting of the council on 22 April 1876 Turton spoke honorifically of a deceased councillor and mentioned a Conservative councillor who had recently narrowly missed being elected alderman. Turton said, 'it was unkind of the Liberal Party and the council now to discard that gentleman [a Mr Nettleton], who, after long service, had been so nearly elected at the last occasion.' This might suggest that some Liberals might vote for a good Conservative councillor to be an alderman.

Turton served for many years as a councillor (1864–67, 1869–78) and worked hard on the committees, as we shall see in the next chapter. With that and his wealth and status, he was unquestionably 'alderman material'. Under different political circumstances it is highly probable that Turton would have become an alderman and even possibly a mayor of Leeds.

VOTERS

Turton began to think about becoming a councillor at an interesting time. Throughout the early 1860s Councillor Edward Baines had been campaigning for a Parliamentary Bill to extend the franchise. His basic demand was to reduce the householder's wealth qualification from £10 to £6 per annum. This was high enough to keep out 'unskilled' working men and of course the 'feckless and criminal poor'. His campaign encouraged the setting up of a Liberal 'Leeds Working Men's Parliamentary Reform Association'. The Conservatives responded on 17 November 1862 with the 'Leeds Working Men's Conservative Association' (LWMCA). This was particularly active in North East Ward, where Turton stood for his first term. Turton was to remain Treasurer of the LWMCA into the 1880s. The period of Turton's political activity coincided exactly with this surge in the development of local party organisations, both Liberal and Conservative. There is not much record of these but they had a paid officer, a secretary or agent, who might receive an annual salary of £150. They accumulated funds; for example the Leeds Liberal Club had £430 in 1881. In the same year the paid membership of the two main clubs was as follows:

Political club membership 1881		
1881	Leeds Liberal Club	Leeds & Country Conservative Club
Life member	92	102
Town member	745	724
Country member	126	488

As can readily be seen, membership in the first two categories was nearly equal. The Conservatives outstripped the Liberals only in the countryside as one might expect.

In the event it was the Tories, under Disraeli, who introduced their Reform Act in 1867. Despite Disraeli's publicly declared 'abhorrence of democracy' the reforms were as strong as the Liberals might have wished. All male urban householders were now enfranchised. The number of adult males able to vote had doubled. But this enfranchised no more than 40 per cent of all adult males over the age of twenty, and no women. It did, however, increase pressure of popular demands on Parliament, and it helped to reduce electoral corruption.

Hitherto the limited franchise had meant that the electorate consisted of 'gentlemen', professionals, traders and businessmen, property owners, skilled artisans and so on. Those more likely to vote Conservative included doctors and lawyers, and the large number of people connected with trade in alcohol and entertainment, in hotels, inns, taverns, alehouses etc., the latter rather useful at election time. Voters at the lower income-earning end were more likely to be susceptible to rigging of the electoral role. In some cases the right to vote was just the de facto presence of a name on a roll, regardless of how it got there.

Under the new franchise, suddenly the majority of voters might be called working class. It is of interest to consider who among these would vote conservative and thus for William Turton, if not for the local party in power. One excellent source for this is *Angels in Marble: Working Class Conservatives in Urban Europe* (McKenzie et al., 1968).

The authors do not stress the Anglican/dissenter and catholic divide. One notable feature is that the Tories were the party of drinking and friends of the brewers and innkeepers. They probably received few votes from the temperance lobby. At times the majority of Liberal councillors were members of the Leeds Temperance Society, fifteen in 1868, twenty-one in 1882. Some members were not necessarily strict teetotallers and tolerated the sale of beer but not spirits. In 1884, however, with support from the *Leeds Mercury* they passed a resolution not to renew the licence for any intoxicating drinks for Roundhay House in the Park; it was overturned a month later.

Working-class Conservatives clearly included those who were close to and reliant on the good will of their employers for patronage, such as foremen and other such supervisors. These were the sort of employees for whom William Turton would provide free or low cost housing. Certain 'traditional emotions' and habits of deference to the élite are also cited as likely to lead to working class Toryism. Turton was patently wealthy, well dressed and confident, but he would probably not have come across as a 'toff' or flaunter of status. And he spoke the local language! And of course, almost by definition, those members of the working class who wanted to be considered, or already regarded themselves as, 'middle-class' were more likely to vote Conservative. Among these would be the better off and the older.

11

COUNCILLOR TURTON

THE COUNCIL

William Turton became a councillor only some fifteen years after the palatial new Town Hall had been opened by Queen Victoria. It had scarcely had time to blacken. It housed the council chamber and all the usual meeting rooms for committees, caucuses and so on, and of course the magnificent Victoria Hall with its monumental organ. It also housed the county court and the central police station. It was the very hub of local authority.

The council met monthly and held special meetings ad hoc in between, usually something like four a year. Council business, whether in committees or offices, was conducted throughout the year with no long breaks. The busiest month was November, following the annual elections early in that month. Since there were always elections for some seats each year, this provided an opportunity to change the membership of committees. November was also Turton's best month for attendance at committees of all sorts, with an average of about 80 per cent attendance compared with his lowest months, July and August, when the average was little more than 55 per cent. Councillors' attendance records were occasionally published in the newspapers and serious defaulters duly shamed.

Minutes of full council and all committee meetings are preserved in the West Yorkshire Archive. They are written in various styles of often beautiful and always clear to read copperplate handwriting (*see* p.180). Sometimes a clerk has embellished the record with initial letters in gold and blue like a medieval manuscript. Highlights of meetings were reported in the *Leeds Mercury* and the *Yorkshire Post*. Occasional reports about the activities of councils in Bradford, Manchester and Liverpool ensured that members were up-to-date on regional affairs. There was an element of competition between these municipal fiefdoms. Of course Turton often visited all these towns and many others in order to run his tramway interests. He sometimes went to them on Leeds Council business.

Turton spoke in council on a wide variety of subjects. He seems to have spoken briefly and straightforwardly and not in a contentious or quarrelsome manner. For example in 1875 he supported the extension of the Kirkgate Market, saying that it was a favourable opportunity for utilizing land which had been taken in order to clear away old dwellings which were unfit for habitation (2 January). On 2 May there was a proposal to raise the salary of the stipendiary magistrate from £1,000 to £1,250. Turton asked whether Mr Bruce received any income other than that of stipendiary magistrate and also if he was required to devote the whole of his time to the duties this office. This seems quite a sophisticated 'Parliamentary' approach, implying that Mr Bruce earned well in fees from his private practice. The motion was defeated by a large majority. Turton voted on several occasions against increase in the salaries of higher paid officials, though he did back an increase for staff in the Sanitation Department, and he argued eloquently for a carriage to be provided for the Medical Officer of Health, who had been using public cabs at some inconvenience. The sum of £180 was voted to cover the cost of buying a horse, carriage and harness, stable rent and provender, and the coachman's wages. He seconded the proposal to build a police station at Sheepscar, a working-class area downhill from his home on Chapeltown Road, at a cost of £900, with a new branch library added for only £200. He said it was 'a step in the right direction (Hear, hear)'.

Out of 125 resolutions for which I have noted Turton's voting records, he voted for a successful resolution in 52 per cent of votes, against a successful resolution in 8 per cent of votes. He abstained from voting in close to 40 per cent of votes. This seems surprisingly high. The overall pattern might suggest that he tended to vote in a quite independent way. This would be in keeping with his general character.

For all of his time in office Turton was an omnibus owner, supplier of coal to the Leeds Union Workhouse, and for most of the time a tramway director. He avoided any charges of conflict of interest and rarely spoke on transport matters. He displayed his detailed knowledge in one instance when a complaint was presented to the Watch Committee about a 40s fine for a carter who had got in the way of a tramline. Turton said that in the case referred to the carter would not leave the tram rails even when he had an opportunity and on being requested to do so, he had used abusive language. Turton was present when decisions were taken to purchase the first steamroller and the first steam fire engine, which cost £1,000, rather more than the estimate. He was in favour of public open spaces. He voted against a motion, in the event defeated, to sell off part of Woodhouse Moor, the most popular of common land parks on the edge of the town centre. He voted for the purchase of Roundhay Park, a motion that was carried, with a substantial vote against.

These and other instances show that councillors did not always vote in party blocs. On the issue of aldermen, Turton was adamant. On 8 April 1876 he spoke against a monopoly by 'a certain section of the Council' in appointing aldermen. Two weeks later he made a short speech in honour of a deceased councillor and followed up by his remarks already quoted about the 'unkindness of discarding' a Tory councillor who had come close to election as an alderman. There must have been some wider politics in the air, for in May, and again in June 1876, we find Turton opposing a petition to Parliament from the Leeds Council against a Parliamentary proposal, the aim of which was to alter the rules for election of aldermen and end the 'monopoly' situation. This must have been a Conservative three-line whip vote. Alas, he showed himself to be less democratically minded when he voted against another Leeds Council petition to Parliament to remove electoral disabilities for women. This could not have been a party vote only since the motion was carried with thirty-two votes for and twenty-one against.

As I mentioned, the council was not shy in making its opinions on wider national foreign issues known during the time of Turton's office holding. Deaths of notable figures were reported at council meetings: Richard Cobden, President Lincoln. It discussed the 'Eastern Question', of course. On 2 January 1878 it sent a memorial to Parliament 'expressing pleasure that Turkey had asked for British assistance in defence against Russia [for which help Turkey was to cede Cyprus to Britain] but appealed that the Government does not enter into a war'.

An intriguing instance of a kind of 'cross-party' solidarity was the occasion of a memorial fund and dinner in honour of Edward Baines' 80th birthday in 1880. The fund raised £3,000 for scholarships at the Yorkshire College of Science. William Turton was a subscriber at 5 guineas. He was one of 521 who contributed. These seem to have included all the great and the good of the Leeds élite. Headed by the Archbishop of York, the Bishop of Ripon, Lord Halifax and Lord Cavendish, they included names which have become part of a litany of the Leeds élite: Barran, Tetley, Waddington, Hepworth, Kitson, Thomas Green, Lupton, Nussey, Eddison, Firth and Baxter. Baines showed his appreciation of the event in his speech of response:

> It was particularly gratifying for me to observe from the newspaper that among the gentlemen who met in the Mayor's Rooms to devise a tribute of respect, there were not only many of my lifelong and faithful friends, but also respected and generous men who had frequently differed from me on political or religious questions [including notably William Turton]. I cannot think of these gentlemen as opponents because the points on which we agree as Englishmen and as Christians are incomparably more important than those on which we differ (Hear, hear!) But the fact of our belonging to parties which are often opposed to each other gives their conduct on this occasion the character of a special kindness, and I therefore feel that it demands my special acknowledgement.

In his last months as a councillor – though he did not know then that he would not be re-elected – Turton was a member of a senior sub-committee to consider inviting the Yorkshire Agricultural Society to hold their annual show in Leeds. The idea was adopted and the show was held in August the following year. Turton was then no longer councillor, but we can imagine that he would have sat with the dignitaries at the opening and the dinner. As one of the largest corn and hay merchants in the West Riding he would have been well known to many of those from the countryside who attended.

COUNCIL COMMITTEES

Most of the work of the town council, then as now, was done in its committees. The committee structure was fairly consistent in this period, though there a few changes in designation or function; for instance the Scavenging and Nuisance Committee became the Sanitary Committee (SC). The largest number of committee titles was twenty-two. In October 1878 the inevitable committee to review committees was set up, one aim being to see if the nineteen committees could be reduced to twelve. Nothing was changed.

All elected members of council sat on committees, several at a time. Turton never sat on fewer than four or more than eight at a time; maybe about five or six was the norm. Aldermen were more likely to be chairmen. Though Turton was never an alderman, as we have seen, he was elected to be chairman of the strategic Sanitary Committee. The mayor sometimes chaired important meetings or the first meeting of the year. Committee membership was reviewed each year after the November election, but there was considerable continuity of membership and some very long service on some committees. Total membership of committees and frequency of meeting varied according to the workload. The Highways Committee was one of the busier and more strategic. In 1883 it had a meeting at which the chair was taken by the mayor with five aldermen and sixteen councillors present. Exceptionally, a minor committee such as the Printing Committee might meet once every two months. The Highway Committee might meet on twenty occasions in a year, probably ten to fifteen times was close to the norm. Meetings tended to start at 2.15 p.m., so most likely after lunch, and last about two hours, sometimes longer.

Committees would set up sub-committees to audit, to provide teams to make site visits, consider special purchases and other tasks. The committees would require various council officers to attend and occasionally there would be attendance by other citizens to make their requests, complaints and proposals, and sometimes to explain or exculpate themselves. After he had ceased to be a councillor, this would include Turton and others from the Leeds Tramways Company.

During his twelve years as a councillor, Turton would have spent at the very least an average of two days a week attending meetings of the council, its committees and sub-committees. Then there were the party caucus meetings and ward meetings. For much of the time he was a councillor he was also attending meetings of directors and shareholders in several tramway companies. There were occasional meetings of other bodies that he was involved with, notably the Leeds Union. Maybe three days a week included a formal meeting of some sort. And he was running an omnibus business, a corn and hay business and a coal business. He was a busy man. His age at the time of his council involvement was from 39 to 53.

Turton sat on thirteen out of twenty-two committees over time. It is instructive to examine which ones he served on and which he may have tried to avoid.

The following shows, in summary form, which committees he sat on, for approximately how many years, and what his approximate attendance rates were:

William Turton's committee membership 1866-78		
Committee	No. of years served	Attendance rate
Full Council Meeting	11	85 per cent
Sanitary Committee	11	80 per cent
[with Scavenging & Nuisance]		[83 per cent]
Markets Committee	9	70 per cent
Purchase of Property Committee	9	62.5 per cent
Highways Committee	5	88 per cent
Gas Committee	5	54 per cent
Water Committee	4	56 per cent
Becks Committee	4	66 per cent
Finance Committee	4	44 per cent
Streets and Sewage Committee	3	3 per cent
Parliamentary Committee	2	73 per cent
Printing Committee	2	92 per cent
Committees on which he did not serve were the following:		
Watch Committee (supervising judiciary service and police)		
Hackney Carriage, and Omnibus and Street Traffic Committee		
Corporation Property Committee		
Building Clauses Committee		
Public Library Committee		
Reformatory Schools Committee		
Lamps Committee		
Burial Grounds Committee		
Cattle Diseases Committee		

The Watch Committee was the one strategic committee Turton never sat on. The possibility of conflict of interest presented by the Hackney Carriage Committee did not prevent him serving on other committees where a similar objection might have been raised.

Given the importance of the Sanitary Committee (together with other health related committees), I have devoted a chapter to it. The important Highways Committee is so much involved in his business interests that it occurs in many chapters of Part IV.

The **Finance Committee**, surprisingly, seems not to have been the powerhouse one might have expected. It held few meetings and the minutes are brief. There are few issues of great importance recorded. The **Parliamentary Committee** attracted the more politically ambitious councillors and was dominated by the presence of the town clerk.

Turton's interests were more local and regional. The **Printing Committee** was of minor importance and closed down soon after Turton left it. The **Gas Committee** and the **Water Committee** would have held some interest for Turton but his attendance suggests that these were ones that he might sacrifice in order to balance and prioritise his activities. Nonetheless work on these committees gave him opportunities to engage with engineering firms he already had dealings with (Kitsons, Green and Son). As an extensive town centre property owner who had already experienced an expensive warehouse fire, he would sympathise with the needs of citizens to have good water pressure in case of serious fires. A fatal fire in Briggate, near one of his offices, when water pressure had been inadequate, had occurred on his watch on the Water Committee.

His interest in public health also gave a strong motivation to help regulate and maintain the council owned waterworks, reservoirs, pumping stations and distribution systems

The **Gas Committee** minutes are full of references to retorts and boilers, condensers and scrubbers, meters and governors, and gasholders. The link here with coal would have fired his interest. Some fifteen coal firms supplied the fuel for gas production but it seems that his was not one of them.

There were many markets owned and managed by the borough, which came within the remit of the **Markets Committee**:

Corn Exchange
Wool Market
Farmers' Market
Fat Cattle Market
Pig Market
Egg and Butter Market
Open Market
Covered Market
North Street Market
Kirkgate Market
Central Market

Turton remained on this committee for nine years. In each year he also served on the **Weights and Measures Sub-committee** that carried out site inspections and had oversight of the public weighbridge.

Several tasks overlapped with other committees, some of which Turton sat on. Land had to be purchased, even from the egregious Mr Wray (Conservative councillor for Kirkgate). Foot and Mouth disease in the cattle market would concern the **Cattle Disease Committee**. 'Sweepings' at the Corn Exchange were sold for 1s a stone.

John Barran, chairman in 1869, proposed a vote of thanks to the General Post Office for installing the first telegraph at the Corn Exchange, a crucial new international link that was of great advantage to William Turton and other corn merchants. The same Corn Exchange also presented problems. It held bazaars at night and had become a venue for undesirable social behaviour. There was vandalism and graffiti by 'boys'. The steps at the rear were used as 'a nightly resort for prostitutes'. This was the **Watch Committee**'s concern.

The markets were a good source of revenue for the borough. In 1874 the Covered Market, Open Market, Fat Cattle and Pig Markets accounted for £497 in February alone. In 1877 the total revenue for a month reached £1,000.

These valuable properties needed insurance, which was a booming business. The following report on just some of the borough's properties in 1877 gives some idea of the scale:

Insured value of markets 1887		
Insured value of markets and related property		
Property covered	Insurance company	Amount insured
Covered Market	The Royal	£5,500
Smithfield Hotel	The Mutual	£1,000
Central Market twenty-two shops	The Mutual	£8,000
Egg & Butter Market	The Mutual	
Nos 3, 4, 5 York Street	The Mutual	£2,500
Block of six shops	The Mutual	£800
Corn Exchange	London & Southern	£8,000
Corn Exchange	The Mutual	£4,000

Turton served on the **Purchase of Property Committee** for nine years. This committee attracted senior political figures on the council, among them Barran, Meek Carter, Luccock and Wray. It had dealings with all the main landowners including the Railway Companies and the Aire and Calder Navigation Company. The committee must have presented possibilities for conflict of interest. The purchase of Councillor Wray's land, in his constituency, to extend the Kirkgate Market would have been referred to this committee, of which he was a member. We can note that the Maude family, into which Turton's eldest daughter was to marry, sold property in East Street, Turton's early home, for the large sum of £7,700 for street improvement.

Key areas of this committee's work were to the purchase of land for roads and road extensions, new markets and market extensions, new cemeteries and, in turn, their extensions, theatres and so on. In 1871 they voted £15–16,000 for a new Leeds bridge.

HIGHWAYS COMMITTEE

Turton was on the Highways Committee at a critical moment. He was there when the Busbys put forward their first bid to construct a tramway in 1870. With the mayor in the chair, they voted not to accept the bid. Later in the year Turton was a member of the sub-committee to re-examine Busby's plans and the draft agreement, employ an engineer and produce a report. The sub-committee recommended that the council request the Board of Trade in London to modify the fare structure, in effect reducing the highest fare. The Board of Trade turned this down and the committee decided not to appeal. In December 1871 Turton supported the committee's decision to oppose Busby's petition for a Leeds Tramways Bill, which the Parliamentary Committee over-turned in May 1872. As we know, three months later he was a director of the successor company, the Leeds Tramways Company (LTC).

Turton attended meetings of the Highways Committee more assiduously than any other, although he was on it for only five years. What is of particular note is the extent to which his membership overlapped with his other transport responsibilities and financial interests. Of the eighty-six meetings he attended that I have noted, the overlap was as follows:

Overlap in William Turton's business interests and Highway Committee meetings	
While an omnibus proprietor	13 meetings
While an omnibus proprietor and during early tramway discussions	37 meetings
While an omnibus proprietor and while he was a director of LTC	23 meetings
While an omnibus proprietor and chairman of LTC	13 meetings

Turton was so well known that he must hardly have had to 'declare his interest' in so many items discussed in the Highways Committee. Employees of his omnibus company and of the LTC, and possibly his election agents, were occasionally charged and at times convicted of fairly minor offences. Turton was himself once or twice the victim of crime. A fellow director on LTC had to resign in the face of criticism for 'insider dealing'. When Turton was selling some of his omnibus interests to the LTC while he was chairman, he resigned for the best part of a year. He sold and exchanged land with the council during his tenure of office. But Turton seems always to have stayed well on the right side of the law and to have maintained a good reputation for honesty and integrity.

The Highways Committee was of course primarily concerned with keeping existing roads in repair. This was a task shared with the LTC and, as we shall see, led to all sorts of conflicts. They also widened roads and built new ones. They had responsibility for other aspects of the streetscape (street furniture and advertisement) and public behaviour (traffic regulation and safety). They were frequently in touch with other related committees: Watch Committee (police enforcement), Sanitary Committee (road works for sewers etc.), Lamps, Becks, Purchase of Property, Hackney Carriages etc.

Turton was appointed to the influential Audit Sub-committee of the Highways Committee and to a Visiting Committee. He attended when the first complaint was received about the poor state of the Headingley line, being run by the Busby firm at the time. Turton was absent when an interesting issue was discussed: the purchase of the first steamroller, manufactured by Thomas Green and Son, a firm in which he was a major shareholder. He was there when the committee received the first bid to start a steam tram service in 1875. The committee said it regretted it had no powers but decided to include a discretionary clause in the next Leeds Improvement Bill. He was also present in 1878 when LTC received a serious reprimand and demand to repair defective lines in seven days. It was at about this time that Turton ceased being a councillor.

After his retirement from borough politics in 1878 Turton, usually accompanied by his manager William Wharam, appeared before the committee on several occasions, both at their request and his. Turton and Wharam were invariably polite and though firm in their stance, were accommodating and prompt in their responses. In later years the committee came up with barrages of complaints and demands of the LTC. These chiefly concerned repair of the tracks and related issues of customer satisfaction. Special services and fares for working people were other issues. And the committee, on the back of considerable public concern, later raised matters of the working conditions and remuneration of LTC employees. These will be looked at in detail in the chapter on Municipalisation.

COUNCIL OFFICIALS

Turton had to deal with numerous council employees, both as a councillor and as a businessman. These included all types and levels of workers from the street sweepers, clerks and inspectors to the more senior professionals, the borough engineer, borough surveyor and most especially the town clerk, invariably a lawyer. He would have become familiar with several of these, if they held office for an extended period, such as Town Clerk Capel A. Curwood, who served for an exceptional twenty-five years. Nowadays it is customary to question the large salaries of Town Hall officials. These are probably higher than most elected councillors. This was not the case in the nineteenth-century. I give below a list of annual salaries or wages of various Leeds borough employees in order of magnitude, with other salaries for comparison in brackets.

Salaries of Leeds Borough employees
£1,000+ Town Clerk
£1,000 Stipendiary Magistrate
(£1,000 Senior Inspector of Railways)
£800 Borough Engineer

£500 Medical Officer of Health
(£450 William Wharam, Secretary and Manager Leeds Tramways Co.)
£400 Borough Treasurer
£400 Governor, Borough Gaol
£300 Borough Surveyor
£300 Chief Constable
£300 Borough Librarian
£300 Assistant Supervisor, Leeds Union
(£300 LTC director's fee)
(£300 Mayor's base fee, Cardiff 1880)
£250 Superintendent of Sanitary Department
(£250 Managing Superintendent, engineering works)
£180 Inspector of Nuisances
£150 Chief Clerk, Rates Office
£136 Police Superintendent
£125 Chief Clerk, Highways Department
£120 Clerk, Night Soil and Scavenging, Crown Point
£120 Inspector of Paving and Flagging Works
£117 Inspector of the Construction of Sewers
£114 Police Inspector, first class
£110 Counter Clerk, gas office
£104 Police Inspector, second class
£90 Collector of water rates
£80 Rate collector
(£60 Wesleyan College Resident Steward)
£50 Junior clerks

This gives us a 'wage differential' of 1:30. This might be roughly compared, in twenty-first-century terms, as the difference between, say a clerical assistant on £12,000 and a chief executive on £360,000. Salaried posts, or 'positions', no doubt gave greater security of tenure and perhaps better working conditions and shorter working hours than manual or artisan labour, which offered annual incomes of from about £30–£100.

Some councillors, including Turton, had annual private incomes of several or many thousands of pounds. Marsden was reckoned to have never given less than £2,000 each year for charitable and philanthropic causes. This puts into perspective the relationship between councillors and the borough employees at this time, even the highest paid.

LEEDS TRADESMEN'S BENEVOLENT INSTITUTION

This was founded in 1843 by Alderman Thomas Sydney of Leeds and London. Its mission statement was 'To give relief to distressed reputable merchants, manufacturers, and tradesmen when in old age and under infirmities and to their widows or dependants.'

There is still a Leeds Tradesmen's Trust, which carries on this tradition. We are used to the idea of State Welfare benefiting anyone in need. In Victorian times it was a particularly shocking anomaly that members of the middle classes should fall on hard times for no fault of theirs. Hence we have societies for 'Distressed Gentlefolk' and for 'The Relief of Clergy'. In this case 'the tradesmen' looked after their own.

This might be the place to raise a question to which I have found no answer. This is whether William Turton was member of any friendly society or similar, such as Freemasonry or the Order of Foresters. All of these of course were conspicuous in their provision of welfare to those they thought fit to help. They are also known for providing networks of friendship that could benefit business and other careers. It was sometimes said that unless a man were Scottish or Jewish, or a Freemason or member of another friendly society or order, then he had better belong to a Livery Company, in order to promote his career or business. Turton may have been none of these. But he was active in the Leeds Tradesmen's Benevolent Institution.

THE WEST RIDING TRADES PROTECTION ASSOCIATION

Here is the only example of an organisation wider than the area of Leeds, other than tramway companies, of which Turton was a committee member. This was founded in 1848 to promote the interests of Yorkshire businessmen, ensure their profitability and prevent them becoming in need of the benevolence of others. By 1858 it had 3,000 subscribing members, so it must have been seen to serve a useful function for businessmen. The association still trades. It states on its website that in 1848 its aims were:

> ... for the mutual assistance of businessmen seeking to recover overdue accounts. Today our aim remains the same, but now our service extends worldwide, helping members not only to recover debts, but also to ensure that those they are doing business with are financially sound.

Of interest for the family side of our story is the connection with George Fillingham. He was to marry, in 1886, Mary Anne (1854–1948), William Turton's second daughter. He was secretary by 1890 at the latest to the West Riding Trades Protection Society, as it was first known. It was later for a time known as the West Riding Bankers', Merchants' and Traders' Association for the Protection of Trade. He had an office at No. 16 East Parade, just a stone's throw from the Town Hall. This is still the address of the association in the twenty-first century. He was an incorporated accountant. This was not his only interest, as he is listed in one year as being also secretary of the Leeds Boot Manufacturers' Association. In 1890 his home address was No. 59 Louis Street, off Chapeltown Road. By 1894 it was 'Ladywood', Roundhay, an altogether smarter address. His brothers, S. and J. Fillingham of No. 14 Butts Court, were also accountants and managed a firm called West Riding Assets, Purchase and Realisation Company. The Fillingham brothers seem to have been fairly comprehensively interested in business opportunities.

THE LEEDS CHAMBER OF COMMERCE AND LEEDS EXCHANGE

This was founded in 1783, an early 'civil society' initiative. It was refounded in 1850. By 1862, the last year in which the occupations of members are listed, there had been only one corn factor. Turton was a member in the 1890s and perhaps earlier. Prominent names of members at that time included Tetley, Waddington, Hepworth and, interestingly, George William Turton as well as his father. Turton was also a member of the Leeds Exchange (along with Barran, Lupton, Kitson, Thomas Green and others). There may well have been yet other bodies in which he was a member, and perhaps even a committee member. Candidates for these might include Sunday schools, parish bodies, the Leeds dispensary, hospital trustees and so on, all of which were to feature in the family wills.

COUNCILLOR TURTON, A SELF-MADE MAN

The anonymous obituary for William Turton in the *Yorkshire Post* of 7 August 1900 emphasises, understandably, Turton's business and especially his tramway activities and commercial interests. It goes on to say, that because of all this:

> Mr. Turton had little time for public life, even if he had cared for it. Many years ago, however, he represented the old East Ward in the Town Council for about eleven years. He was a thoroughgoing Conservative, but did not take a prominent part in political matters.

This view is from a misleadingly short-term perspective in 1900. We have seen that Turton's involvement in 'public life' and 'political matters' shows that he gave a great deal of time to them. It is true that his time as a councillor, twelve years in fact, was well in the past, a generation earlier. And it is true that his tramway interests took up an increasing proportion of his time, as his three sons entered the corn and hay, coal and omnibus businesses. But we have seen plenty of evidence that he was actively involved in a great many organisations and associations until his death.

William Turton liked to combine opportunities for civic and social engagement with his business interests, and his family and social life. He wanted to turn his wealth to increasing his social status, and in turn to benefit from 'networking', as we now say, for his commercial interests. His inside knowledge of procedures and politics in the Leeds Borough Council must have served him well in his many dealings with other local authorities in the North of England.

In the previous chapter we saw municipal corporations likened to 'great undertakings ... comparable with those of the most adventurous entrepreneurs'. 'Self-made man' is almost the nineteenth-century equivalent of our 'entrepreneur'. It did not need Samuel Smiles, a famous Leeds example of the stereotype himself, to encourage them. The self-made man was already a widely appreciated role model and folk hero of the age. Many books were written at this time on the subject and it is interesting to see how many exemplars of the type are germane to our story. The following lists show some examples: Newcomen, Benjamin Franklin, Arkwright, Watt, Wedgwood, George Stephenson, Brunel, Peter Fairbairn ... (Fowler, 1863). John Bunyan, Edward Baines, Hugh Miller, John Kitto ... (Anderson, 1861). Benjamin Franklin, William Cobbet, Sir Titus Salt, Charles Dickens ... (Cochrane, 1879).

The criteria or desiderata are often pious and platitudinous. Anderson for example, whose heroes included Edward Baines, lists the following:

- a deep sense of their native dignity and grandeur;
- high hopes as to the position they will one day occupy;
- a proper appreciation of the value of spare moments;
- a true estimation of the value of odd pence;
- industry;
- perseverance;
- decisive of character, sturdy and stubborn;
- eyesight (powers of observation);
- what they do they do thoroughly.

Most councillors were 'self-made men' or entrepreneurs in both politics and in commerce and industry. William Turton was one of them.

12

CELLARS AND SEWERS

'Public health reform was the most important single item of the agenda of any local authority in the nineteenth century.' (Barber, 1982, p. 67)

Low life expectancy, high infant mortality, diseases and accidents caused by environmental and workplace conditions, epidemics – these were the downside, the self-inflicted cost and penalty of the great capitalist industrial revolution and urbanisation. There was increasing awareness in Leeds as elsewhere that all dwellers in the city were at risk, that none were safe, and that improving conditions for the many would also benefit the few. The worst was very bad and hardly imaginable in early twentieth-first century Europe.

James Hole, Hon. Secretary to the Yorkshire Union of Mechanics Institutes, wrote an excellent essay, which won a prize offered by J.D. Luccock, mayor of Leeds in 1866, entitled: 'Homes of the Working Classes, with Suggestions for Their Improvement'. In it he says:

One naturally thinks that the three cheapest things in this beautiful world, the three things that every one might have as much of as he liked, would be sunlight, pure air and clean water. Yet they are becoming the scarcest luxuries a man could wish for.

In an earlier prize essay: 'Light, More Light! On the Present State of Education Amongst the Working Classes of Leeds and How It Can Best Be Improved' (1860), he wrote:

Few towns are so advantageously situated as Leeds for securing the health of a large population, and in few localities are these advantages so sacrificed.

There were relentless efforts to investigate, analyse and regulate working conditions and practices, diseases and living conditions generally, and to invent means of overcoming or at least mitigating the worst. One can write about these in more or in less optimistic or congratulatory terms. Their efforts never caught up with the scale of the problems. But throughout the century 'sanitation', or public health as we would say, remained a major issue in the local politics of 'improvement'.

Boroughs engaged in more and more areas of responsibility: water, roads, gas, police, street lighting, burial grounds and so on. Education notably was not yet one of them. None of these could compete in priority, in political importance, with public health. The political importance of the Sanitary Committee can be partly judged by the calibre and seniority of those who sat on it. For example during Turton's years it contained J. Barran, H.R. Marsden, J.D. Luccock, R. Meek Carter, Mason and Wray.

Leeds Borough Council had been called to account in a report made by Dr Hunter to the Privy Council's Medical Department in 1865:

To the eyes of an inspector who had just left Newcastle and Sunderland, and who in the same week visited Sheffield, Leeds in August 1865 presented a surprising sight, bringing to remembrance the condition of many English towns of twenty years ago, but finding hardly a standard with which to be compared in the present state of any town.

In the same year there had been an enquiry into the causes of the high death rate in Leeds. For England 1855–62 the rates were:

Mortality rates in Leeds 1855–62		
Locality	crude death rate	death rate from from respiratory diseases and consumption per 1,000
England	21.8	5.7
Chapel Allerton	17	–
Leeds Township	26.7	8.8
Manchester	31.9	9.2

The appointment of a Medical Officer of Health was an immediate consequence. This had been proposed by the radical Meek Thomas and others in 1862 and turned down. Dr Robinson was appointed in 1866 at a salary of £500. In the same year a new post of Borough Chief Sanitary Inspector was advertised in the *Lancet, Medical Times* and *Manchester Guardian* at a salary of £500 per annum. Turton was to have close contacts with several Medical Officers. When Robinson left to take another post at some £300 more in 1872, the council advertised for his replacement at £400. The borough, it seems, had not learned the lesson.

Despite the importance of health issues the majority of the population was excluded from participation in the politics of improvement, in the electoral sense. Those excluded were all people under the age of twenty-one, all women and a majority of adult males, namely those with lower incomes. This included not only the poorest at the furthest margins of social life (whether due to health, unemployment or criminality) or only those in the workhouse, or even just the casual labourers. Most low-paid wage-workers, white and blue collar, were out of the loop.

William Turton served on public health related committees in every year of his time in office. This record was matched only by his membership and attendance at the full council, which was far less onerous. Council records are so susceptible to mini-statistics that we can compute that over one-third of all his total committee attendance was on health-related committees. This in turn was some three times the effort spent on matters relating to highways and transport. It is this unexpected dimension to Turton's overall contribution that warrants this chapter.

He started off in his first year on what was known as the 'Scavenging and Nuisance' Committee. We need to understand that 'scavenging' was then the normal term for 'rubbish collection', 'waste disposal' and included what we would now call recycling. 'Nuisance', another old term, included all sorts of health hazards; it was something like our use of 'pollution' to refer to air, soil or water, and even to noise and unsightliness. Here is a list of some of the forms of nuisance reported to a meeting attended by William in 1865:

Public 'nuisances'	
Dirty, defective privies and ashpits	55 cases
Dwellings over privies	53 cases
Defective drainage	37 cases
Piggeries with swill	8 cases
Want of privy access	6 cases
Offensive urinals	5 cases
Offensive trades	4 cases
Bad pavement flags	3 cases

Turton also served on two other committees that were to be merged with the Sanitary Committee, namely the Streets and Sewage Committee (and its Sewage Utilisation Sub-committee) and the Becks Committee.

In his second, unbroken, term of office from November 1869 to October 1878, he was re-appointed each year to the Sanitary Committee, the overall 'public health and environmental services committee' as we might call it now. He was for all these years simultaneously a member of its Night-Soil Committee (later Night-Soil and Repairs). For a shorter time he was a member of the Cellar Dwellings Committee. As well as committee work at scheduled meetings, there was much work to be done on site: visiting to assess conditions, inspect damage and repairs, trial equipment and appliances, and to discuss with users and contractors. As always Leeds was keen to see what its big neighbours were up to. Turton made several visits on behalf of the Sanitary

313

20 November 1873

That permission be granted to Messrs Nail and Scriven to reopen the Well.

Wm Scott
Chairman

At a Committee Meeting on Thursday the 27.th day of November 1873.

Present

Mr Councillor Turton the Chair

Aldermen

Edmund Stead
John Dainton Luccock

George Tatham

Councillors

James Stables
Joseph Marshall Farnell
Thomas Cogill
Edwin William Batley
William Wray
William Nicholson

Joseph Lucas
John Blakey
John Ingham
William Barker
George Smith

This Meeting was called for the purpose of considering the following Report —

As our expenses of late years have been steadily increasing, we determined to look into the causes of the same, which we can now show result from the following sources:—

1st.—The large increase of the quantities and weights of Removals of Night Soils.

2nd.—Advance in the Price of Labour.

3rd.—Increase of Cost of Freights and Carriage generally.

4th.—Difficulty of Disposing of Manures.

5th.—Increase of the Cost of Horse Hire.

We have felt ourselves compelled to lay before you a full Statement of our income and Expenditure, this we do, comparing the years 1870 and 1873.

In the latter year we shall observe the great increase of costs arising from many causes, as stated above, and specially from an Increase of Work, as shewn from Boxes, &c., in the East Ward and other parts of the Borough.

Then in the Scavenging Department we find some anomalies which we desire the Sanitary Committee to look into.

You will find from the Sheets enclosed that our Gullies and Ventilators cost us £1,525 8s. 0d.,

Sanitary Committee, minute for 20 November 1873.

Committee to places such as Manchester, Liverpool and Salford, with which he was very familiar from his tramway connections.

Borough responsibilities, and hence the various committees set up to handle them, were imposed or at least redefined by Acts of Parliament that affected the whole country. They were subject to periodic inspections from London. The specific Acts that helped determine the work of committees that Turton sat on relate to the field of public health generally (infectious diseases, epidemics, mortuaries, offensive trades, baths and wash houses), housing conditions, environmental services (water, air, streets, waste disposal) and food safety and hygiene (bake-houses, slaughter-houses, quality control, adulteration of drugs, unwholesome meat).

A closer look at some of these activities will give us a greater understanding of the social conditions at the time of Turton's involvement and his contribution to improvement. Let us begin not with the great factories or work places that were the cause of so much of the trouble but with the lives of ordinary families.

HOUSING

We have to recall that Turton grew up and started business in the area of worst housing in Leeds. Poor quality housing thrown up in the early years of the century was already overcrowded and in bad condition. This area, being close to the Aire, was regularly flooded. By mid-century all available space in the centre of town had been filled in with housing: the back streets, courts and alleys, cul-de-sacs, yards and folds. The new housing included galleries of vertically stacked back-to-back rooms on four storeys. Back-to-back does not here mean houses with a backyard and alley between it and the back of the house behind. These were 'blind cottages', of one room per floor depth having a shared back wall with the one in the next street and a door straight onto the street. Thus they had no open spaces at all. The larger houses were run as 'common lodging houses', having two to six rooms, with one or more persons inhabiting a single room.

Most new buildings had cellars. These became the worst kind of accommodation and 'living space' from the start. There is a reconstruction of one of these in an excellent display of old Leeds Streets and dwellings in the Thackray Museum of Medicine in Leeds. The museum occupies what was the old workhouse or Union building. It is a single room about 3 square yards. The ceiling is low, but the occupants would have been about 6in shorter on average than today. There was no window. The only ventilation came from the door and the chimney flue. A small stack of coal was in the corner. The floor was rough stone, brick or earth, no paving, no boards. The only item that could be called furniture was a three-legged stool. Apart from that there were only boxes and ragged pieces of cloth and straw. It was damp and stuffy, and would have smelled bad. In cases of families with children the intimacies of such close co-habitation must have presented all sorts of problems. There would also have been vermin as companions.

So in a perverse way perhaps it was merciful that the occupants spent so little time 'at home', apart from mothers with very small children. They could be working for twelve to sixteen hours a day. Then there was the walk through the streets to get to work. Much of what time was spent in the room would have been in hours of darkness, though perhaps that made no difference.

At William Turton's first meeting as chairman of the Cellar Dwellings Committee of the Sanitary Committee on 13 January 1873 he proposed and it was recorded:

> That the General Committee [of the Sanitary Committee] be recommended to discuss the desirability of closing down the whole of the Cellar Dwellings in the Borough.

In the event the Committee began a long-term programme of inspecting the dwellings and recommending their clearance if necessary. Turton was a member of many ad hoc visiting sub-committees, accompanied by the Medical Officer of Health, even as early as 1871, that visited blocks of as many as ten or twelve streets at time 'to visit Courts and Alleys in the Borough and to recommend those which they deem it advisable to demolish with power to purchase'. Again in 1876 there is an account of Turton seeing to 'the regulation of houses let as lodgings and cellar dwellings, or other buildings deemed unfit for human habitation'. In the following year some 326 houses let as lodgings were inspected. Many visits took him to parts of the ward that he represented on the council. His knowledge of the living conditions of the people of Leeds must have been unparalleled.

NIGHT-SOIL

The disposal of human and household waste is a challenging task in a big town. Compared with today, the poor probably produced very little household waste. Theirs was a hand-to-mouth, day-to-day existence. Little, if anything at all, was stored or accumulated. They used other people's waste and used it until it ended in their fireplace. No food that was at all edible was wasted. But everyone has to dispose of human excrement, or night-soil as it is referred to in the Sanitary Committee. If you look this up in the Oxford Dictionary you find, 'Night-soil, excrementitious matter, removed by night from cesspools etc.'

In order to get a feeling for late nineteenth-century usage I use a four-volume publication that has been in my wife's family since the end of the nineteenth century. It is no less than *The Imperial Dictionary of the English Language: a Complete Encyclopaedic Lexicon, literary, scientific and technical*. The definition here is indeed complete and very practical.

> Night-soil [From its generally being removed in the night.] The contents of privies etc., employed as a manure. This is found to be very powerful manure,

and very liable to decompose. Its value in this respect depends on the salts and ammonia of the faeces, and also in a great measure on the ammoniacal and other salts of the urine.

Very few people at this time had water closets, perhaps between 1,000–2,000. Even other sorts of dry soil privies with boxes were rare. Privy, by the way, in any spelling is hard to find in a dictionary, except in a general sense as a '[private] place of retirement', but this is the term in the minute book. The majority of the people shared outdoor facilities that led into cesspits. These were often referred to as 'nuisances' and 'noisome', and were harder to empty.

The scale of the operation, and also the likelihood that most people were outside the reach or capability of the Sanitary Committee's employees, can be seen in the following fragment of information from a minute for the period 16 August to 19 September 1871, duly minuted in a fine copperplate hand and bound in leather.

Sewage removal 1871, 1877–78				
1871				
Ashpits disinfected		829		
Boxes removed		11,841		
	Middens emptied	Dry Ashpits	Boxes	
1877	3,046	14,803	58,863	
1878	3,519	15,138	57,243	
Date	Night-soil (per cent total)	Dry ash	Rubbish	Total
1877	4,784 (53 per cent)	607	2,591	8,982
1878	5,980 (65 per cent)	928	2,349	9,257

Turton's committee had to deal with all aspects of the administration of this programme, even surprisingly detailed matters. They had to deal with the hire of horses and carts, sub-contractors, purchase of fumigating and disinfecting machines. Their remit included disciplinary action and wage levels. On one occasion the night-soil workers requested an extra penny per ton shifted. They were granted one-halfpenny.

The Sanitary Committee also had to deal with complaints. These were usually about the proximity of night-soil tips to residential areas and their bad smell, which was believed not only to be unpleasant but harmful to health. One of the biggest tips was the borough's 'Sanitation Yard', which was right next door to Turton's warehouse and wharf in The Calls, on the Aire. He exchanged land with the council to enable the waste to be deposited further downstream towards Fearn's Island. One of Turton's tasks was to find suitable sites and locations for new night-soil depots. Land in this area was also purchased by the council from other landowners; the minute of a full council meeting is instructive as to the storage and dispersal of night soil:

> [Proposed] That the sum of £6,300 be granted to the Scavenging and Nuisance Committee [of which Turton was then a member] for the purchase of the premises at Crown Point, Leeds, belonging to the Rt. Hon. J. E. Dennison [sic] Esq., and others, for the purpose of depositing night soil for immediate shipment, but that the Scavenging and Nuisance Committee be instructed not in any case to use the wharfe as a depôt for manure.

Interestingly Turton voted 'No' to the resolution, which was passed twenty-five to eight, suggesting a vote on party lines.

MANURE

Industrially produced 'chemical' fertilisers were not in use at this time. The cost of manure was largely a function of the distance of transporting it. Barges were the best means, hence depots on the river, not only for night-soil but for the products of stables, street sweeping (mainly horse manure) and filtered sewage residue.

We have seen that horse manure was a commodity that even Turton's corn and hay business dealt in. It paid to follow the carts and trams and collect the droppings. In London Mayhew documented the trade of collecting dog faeces for sale as a commodity. The material was known, oddly, as 'pure' and was used in the processing of leather. It would be surprising, given the importance of the leather industry in Leeds, if this were not also a niche occupation there. But it was not within the municipal remit.

Manure of all sorts was a critically important commodity for the agricultural sector. To a significant extent the growing towns and cities helped to meet the needs of the countryside. We might say that Turton's work, in all its dimensions, was part of a virtuous cycle of renewal. The Sanitary Committee took manure seriously. In 1873 they began a series of trials to test the value and cost-effectiveness of different kinds of fertiliser. They were held at the new sewage works at Knostrop in eastern Leeds.

Six sorts of fertiliser were tested, each on a half-acre plot of similar land, then planted to grass. The resulting hay was assessed for weight, amount of leaf to stalk and so on. Labour, transport and other costs were taken into account. The six types of fertiliser were street sweepings, stable manure, Peruvian guano, native manure, native guano and sewage mud.

They all had their merits, even the sewage mud, which was incidentally also used to make a kind of cement. The winner was judged to be the native guano, closely followed by the Peruvian guano. The latter was used up too much in the first year. So it was decided to re-sow and see what happed the following year of application. The full report was noted in printed format in the Sanitary Committee minutes.

The Imperial Dictionary, referred to earlier, defines guano as follows:

Guano [Spanish **guano**, from Peruvian **huanu**, dung] a substance found on many small islands, especially in the southern Ocean and on the coasts of South America and Africa, which are the resort of large flocks of sea-birds, and chiefly composed of their excrements in a decomposed state. It sometimes forms beds from 50 to 60 feet in thickness. It is an excellent manure, and since 1841 has been extensively applied for that purpose. Its active constituent is ammonia, containing much oxalate and urate of ammonia with some phosphates.

OTHER RECYCLABLES AND RUBBISH

Alongside the humans were all the animals they used for food and transport, and not only their excrement but also their carcasses. It was still not unknown for human corpses and remains to be 'recycled'. The gathering and processing of horse and cattle carcasses continued to be important. As we have seen, dead horses were quickly removed to the knacker's yard and hoof, hair, hide, bone and so on all re-used, as were the products of slaughterhouses.

A particularly problematic animal in Leeds was the pig. Everybody – apart from the still small Jewish population – liked a bit of bacon. A great many poor people as well as others kept a pig or two. Some were even kept in living areas. A family living all together in one room was known as 'pigging it'. The widespread keeping of pigs led to complaints and efforts by the authorities to reduce their number. Any attempt at prohibition was met with outrage; a campaign group to save the Leeds pigs was set up. They were regulated. 'Piggeries', or 'pigcotes', namely pigsties, were to be kept at a certain distance from dwellings. No more than two pigs were allowed per household. There were rules for daily cleaning and monthly disinfection or whitewashing.

The bulk of solid waste that was not carried away by water or recycled was used for fuel, no doubt causing further pollution. The remainder was either 'carbonised' or destroyed by means of a 'destructor', presumably a compactor. Much of the rubbish came from the markets. Turton sat on the Markets Committee from 1870–78 and may have been amused at the ways committees passed on financial responsibility to other committees, using other budgets. Thus the Markets Committee would have to pay for the 'scavenging services' provided by the Sanitary Committee.

THE GREAT STINK

In July 1858 there occurred what was known as 'The Great Stink'. The River Thames in London was so foul from the proximity of cesspools and all sorts of waste, that the smell, the great stink, reached into the chamber of the House of Commons. Parliament was suspended.

This episode precipitated an extraordinarily rapid development of the London sewage system, some of which is still in use today. If Leeds Town Hall had been sited on the banks of the Aire, maybe the Sanitary Committee would have acted more vigorously and sooner. Three years earlier in 1855, the 36-year-old Joseph (later Sir Joseph) Bazelgette had been appointed chief engineer to the London Metropolitan Board of Works. In the ten-year period following 'The Great Stink' Bazalgette had built 83 miles of main sewers. This took 400 million gallons a day from London down to past Barking and Plumstead. Even if this was not enough by today's requirements, it was a wonder of the modern world. Once again things had to get really bad before they began to get better. And, as in Leeds, the sources of water supply were removed further upstream from the centre of town.

The old sewage system in Leeds was a combination of existing becks or streams: Sheepscar, Timble Beck, Holbeck, Benyon and others. Over time a few purpose-built underground channels were built. Mainly it was the open sewers that carried storm water and waste alike. The 'covering of the becks' and repairs and re-covering was a constant exercise. These were spectacular undertakings and were much photographed, so there is a good archive. Since they were largely built following the lines of the road, the works frequently disrupted the tram services. Sewers need ventilation. This was a recurring topic in Sanitary Committee meetings; at one point in 1873 there were monthly reports of the number of 'ventilation shafts constructed and gullies ventilated', in one month 5,016, the next month 5,437 and so on.

FOOD SAFETY AND HYGIENE

Regular inspection of common foodstuffs, fresh meat, food additives and beverages was an important duty of the Sanitary Committee. Even the poorest had to buy almost all of what they ate. Given the level of poverty of so many, unscrupulous producers, and especially retailers engaged in the adulteration of food. The Adulteration of Drugs Act of 1872 gave the Sanitary Committee new responsibilities and tasks. Inspectors' reports were placed before it at frequent intervals.

We can be sure that families such as the Turtons bought their provisions from the very best baker, grocer, butcher and vintner in town. The poorest had no choice but to buy cheap and cheap often meant adulterated. Nowadays we tend to think of improper or undesirable additives in terms of chemicals used to preserve, colour or enhance taste. In the nineteenth century adulteration consisted in dilution and bulking up:

water in milk (up to 30 per cent), water in beer, chalk in bread, lime and plaster of Paris in tea and coffee, sand in sugar, low grade flour in mustard and so on. With some products, such as dairy and meat, the issue was the safety of the source and the freshness of the product. There was little or no sense, except nose and eye, of a 'use by date'. There were regular reports on the following: milk and butter; bread, flour and sugar; pepper, mustard and spices; tea, coffee, beer, wine, whisky and gin. Meat was a special concern. The inspectors were usually butchers by trade. Temptations and opportunities to cheat, to sell or condone the sale of tainted meat were strong and commonplace. Conflicts of interest, to say the least, occurred, and the dismissal of inspectors for improper conduct was no rare occurrence.

It is interesting that advertising of industrially produced food in this period, which was beginning to take off on a big scale, emphasised 'purity' as a main attraction. With increasing literacy there was a need to reassure and guarantee the consumer that food was not adulterated. This is similar to the way such terms as 'natural', 'free range' and even 'organic' are used today.

HEALTH AND MEDICINE

The borough had quite limited powers to provide or supervise medical services. They were, however, obliged to take the lead in many related matters of public health, notably infectious and epidemic diseases and the disposal of human remains. The latter was the remit of a Burial Grounds Committee, on which Turton did not sit. The provision of mortuaries, however, was part of the committee's remit. Following the appointment of a Medical Officer of Health, the committee received reports on morbidity and mortality. These gave them background information on which to base their priorities and decisions. The MOH was familiar in turn with the latest scientific work in these fields. He made it clear at the start that poor sewerage was the cause of typhoid fever and waterborne diseases generally: cholera, diarrhoea, gastric fever and so on. Other major infectious and epidemic causes of ill health and death were smallpox, phthisis (consumption, TB), scarlatina (scarlet fever), diphtheria and measles. They were great levellers. Potternewton and Chapel Allerton, home to the Turtons, suffered as did the streets he grew up in. However, people in the latter suffered higher rates and were often blamed for their ignorance, habits and less than deserving poverty.

There was great need of hospital beds during epidemics and for subsequent recovery. Smallpox and cholera were the most demanding. The SC was responsible for a smallpox hospital and a smallpox house of recovery, or more than one. Charitable giving was a critical form of 'noblesse oblige', or rather the obligation of wealth. The Turtons were regular contributors. Some joint ventures were undertaken, as when Darnton Lupton, a Leeds commercial aristocrat and former councillor, donated a large part of his ancestral home and estate to be a convalescent home. The SC contributed £500 to allow adaptation of the buildings.

As always the Sanitary Committee had to deal with the obligations of the employer of a large and varied workforce. One committee minute in April 1872 records that men working in the smallpox hospital were to receive a daily allowance of one ounce of tobacco.

The following tables show the high relative cost of horses in the Sanitary Department's budget:

Cost of horses in the Sanitary Department		
Cost of horses	No. of horses	Cost (£s)
Night-soil	25	1,950
	7	546
	11	1,287
	40	4,680
Scavenging	32	2,246 8s
	30	1,053

Wages & salaries (annual) in the Sanitary Department		
Medical Officer	1	400
Inspectors and clerks	7?	551
Inspector of Nuisances	1	60
Foremen	10?	405 12s
Foremen	2	104
Foreman	1	98 16s
"	1	91
"	1	80
Men	137	8, 192 12s
"	1	91
"	1	62
"	1	52
"	12	624
"	18	889
"	1	52
"	1	49

Summary (approx.)		
Total horses	145	£11,762
Total employees	191	£11,800
Average annual cost per horse (range 60–91)		£81
Average annual cost per employee, excluding Medical Officer (range 49–91)		£49–£91

THE LEEDS UNION

The Sanitary Committee often received delegations bearing memorials or petitions. The Leeds Board of Guardians was the most prominent of public bodies outside the council concerned with health and welfare. They needed to have the ear of the .

For centuries English legislators, including the established Church, had decreed the statutory means to provide some relief for the poor and destitute, the 'deserving poor' that is, or some of them. In addition to statutory provision there were numerous other forms of private and institutional charity. As a wealthy man with social concerns that went beyond family and business, William Turton was involved in both these main types of what we now call 'social welfare'. Turton's first involvement with the Leeds Union, or Poor Law Workhouse, was in the 1860s when he was contracted to supply coal and coke to the workhouse.

A Leeds Civic Trust Blue Plaque commemorates the old workhouse on Beckett Street East Leeds. The building has been magnificently restored to become the Thackray Museum of Medicine. The text on the plaque gives a succinct account:

Opened in 1861 at a cost of £32,000
to accommodate 800 paupers.
In 1944 it became part of St. James Hospital
and in 1995–97 it was splendidly refurbished as the
Thackray Medical Museum.
Architects Parkin & Backham

In 1869 a new Poor Law administration came into being, replacing the old Leeds Guardians. The administrators were still termed guardians however. The Poor Law Union area was larger than Leeds Borough, comprising:

Chapel Allerton (2 guardians)
Headingley-cum-Burley (9 ")
Leeds (18 ")
Potter Newton (2 ")
Roundhay (1 ")
Seacroft (2 ")

Turton was an overseer, not a guardian. The history of the Leeds Union has not been written, but it seems that the position of guardian may have gone with that of councillor, if only de facto. There were thirty-two guardians. They attended the many meetings of the Union to decide on allocations of welfare grants and the standards of welfare of the paupers resident in the Workhouse. The role of overseer is not entirely clear; they do not feature in the voluminous minutes of the guardians. They probably had a senatorial sort of role. In any case they had their own committee of fifteen members, with two elected guardians, an office in South Parade and their own paid committee secretary. There was obviously a responsibility attached to the position and some work. Whether overseers did or were expected to contribute any of their own wealth to the union is not known. Turton's obituary refers to his long-standing work as an overseer over 'a great many years' and to other charitable acts. In 1901 his eldest son George William is listed as an overseer of the Leeds Union and continued for some ten years.

The Leeds Union building was situated on the eastern edge of the town near a municipal cemetery. It was on the border of Turton's constituency. In this case as in other interventions of William Turton for the general good, *pro bono publico*, there is a strong suggestion that whenever he could he favoured his own constituency, East Ward, and the neighbouring areas of his birthplace and centre of his business. We need to ask whether Turton benefited directly in financial terms from any of his connections with the Sanitary Committee and the union. We saw that before he became an overseer he was selling coal and coke to the union. There is no evidence to suggest that he took on any sub-contracts for horses or carts etc., though his son did on at least one occasion. We might say that anything that benefited trades that needed horses and fodder and horse-drawn transport was of some benefit to Turton and other corn merchants. Similarly any improvement in highway provision and maintenance benefited his bus and tram interests. And any improvement in public health, working conditions and household income would enable more people to ride on trams. For Turton at least public service in elected roles, charitable services and donations were part of an integrated way of life. He seized commercial opportunities in the same way he assumed social obligations.

Turton did buy and sell land in exchange with the council in several parts of Leeds, in Harrison Street, Sheepshanks Yard and especially at Crown Point, while he was serving as a councillor. For example he was permitted to buy a small plot of land at Crown Point in 1866 for £15. A larger deal was done in 1875; a minute dated 9 August 1875, with Turton present, reads:

> That the Council be recommended to sell to Mr. William Turton the land with buildings thereon, situate in The Calls, Leeds, at present occupied by the Highways Committee, and to purchase from Mr. Turton the land with the buildings and appurtenances thereon situate at Crown Point Bridge, Leeds, at present used as a Night Soil Tip, the price to be paid by the Council and Mr. Turton

respectively to be fixed by Mr. Thomas Fenwick, Surveyor, of Leeds, and the Council to pay in addition the sum of £800 in lieu of an allowance for compulsory purchase and sale, which the Council would have had to pay to Mr. Turton if they had acquired the land from him under compulsory purchase.

This makes clear that Turton also let land and buildings to the council for sanitary and highway work.

By definition any secret, and therefore probably improper dealings that individuals may have made with council committees or officials, will have left little or no trace. On one occasion the *Yorkshire Post* had an editorial that stated there was 'good reason to fear that the extravagance thus shown [in a public works contract] has been due, in many cases to transactions very closely resembling jobbery'. (Jobbery: providing private advantage in public matters by unfair or underhand means.) Turton's dealings seem to have been above board and well signposted, and to have involved independent assessors.

Turton himself, or at least his companies, were on rare occasions brought to task for lapses in performance. One wonders what mixture of good humour, remorse and chagrin he exhibited when during a meeting of the SC on 8 April 1878 at which he was present, it was:

... resolved that serious complaints having been made of a perpetual nuisance arising from the ashes and other material used upon the Tramways, the Tramways Company [of which Turton was at the time chairman] be informed that unless some steps be at once taken for the abatement of such nuisance, the committee will feel it their duty to take immediate action to put a stop to it, as the use of the materials not only creates a nuisance but renders necessary considerable extra expenditure in keeping the roads in a clean condition.

Panorama of Leeds from the east 1885, from the Graphic, *18 July 1886.*

Leeds Bridge by J. Atkinson Grimshaw, 1880.

The Hayfield by G.E. Hicks, 1864.

Hayfield House, Chapeltown Road, Leeds.

Turton's warehouse at Nos 64–66 The Calls corner.

Turton's warehouse horse and carriage entrance.

Turton's warehouse, east side from Crown Point Bridge.

Turton's wharf on the Aire.

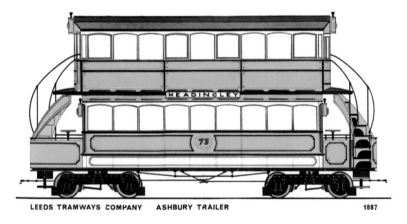

LEEDS TRAMWAYS COMPANY   ASHBURY TRAILER   1887

Leeds Tramways Company double-decker horse tram, 1871–1887.

LEEDS TRAMWAYS COMPANY
SINGLE DECK HORSE CAR   1874-75

Leeds Tramways Company double-decker horse tram, 1871–73.

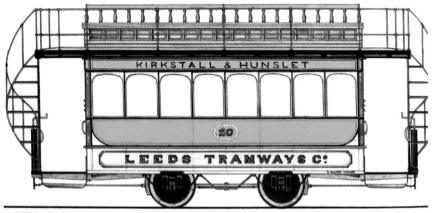

LEEDS TRAMWAYS COMPANY
DOUBLE DECK HORSE CAR   1871-73

Leeds Tramways Company single deck horse tram, 1874–75.

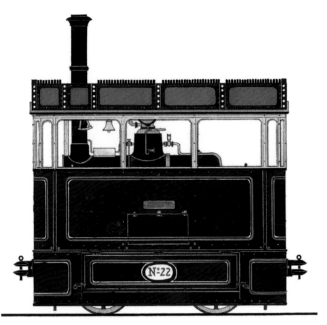

GREEN TRAM ENGINE

Thomas Green steam engine.

KITSON TRAM ENGINE

Kitson steam engine.

Bird's-eye view of Leeds.

TURTON
AND
VICTORY

Political campaign card of William Turton.

Invoice letterhead of William Turton, in use c. 1876–1900.

Turton family arms.

PART IV

TRAMWAYS

1870-1900

13

ENTER THE TRAM

The passenger tram took a long time to arrive. And this was not even rocket science. Horses, carriages, suspension, inner-city road surfaces, urban transport needs and systems had been developed. Metal rail tracks and cars – indeed 'trams' in the earliest sense of small containers on wheels that could be pushed or pulled on rails of whatever material, by humans or other animals – had been in use since the sixteenth century at least. What held up the tram in Britain?

In a broad perspective, the years after 1815 saw the start of an era of peace in Europe and North America that favoured the combined growth of industry, urbanisation, population, and more specifically the urban middle classes. Householders at the top of the scale now had the vote. Over-represented rural counties and 'rotten boroughs' that could be bought and sold were things of the past. By 1832 the middle classes in Britain had achieved a kind of political enfranchisement. They had begun to require a new 'freedom of the city', namely new forms of urban and inter-urban transport.

With the opening of the Stockton to Darlington railway in 1825, and more importantly the adoption of Stephenson's *Rocket* engine in 1829, regular passenger railway services began. In 1827 Paris saw the revival of a regular horse-drawn 'omnibus' system, which was adopted in London by 1829. In the year in between, as if to prove the cliché about waiting for buses that do not come and then having three arriving at once, a horse-tram service started in Baltimore, a port city on the Atlantic coast of the USA. The 'horse-car', or 'streetcar' as the Americans called it, soon spread to New York (1832), New Orleans (1834), Philadelphia and Boston. Most American cities had them by the 1850s.

The definition of a tramcar was a horse-drawn carriage for passengers running on metal rails set in roads in towns, along fixed routes to an advertised schedule. They were for public not private use and did not need to be hired in advance. We will later consider briefly why the steam engine was not adopted as a means of traction for urban transport, whether on road or rail until forty years later, and then only for a brief period.

The tramlines or tracks were the key element. Wooden rails had been in use in coalmines and as connections with canals in 1676. From 1767 these were made of iron.

One-horse tram c.1897.

Iron rails considerably lowered the coefficient of friction. This enabled a horse to pull twice the weight it could pull on an average road surface. A rail made to take a flanged metal wheel may seem a simple thing, but the number of inventions and modifications and patents for their design over the years in many countries is quite extraordinary and complex. Steel tracks were used much later. One sign of the pre-eminence of Leeds in engineering and transport development is that by 1889 Leeds Steel Works became the largest producer of steel tramway tracks in Britain.

One of the things that held back the general adoption of tramways was the earlier use of lines that protruded above the level of the road surface. Though level crossings were possible these lines were in conflict with other road uses. In the 1850s American systems began to use a flush track, but the first lines to be introduced experimentally in Britain had the protruding type. A French engineer, Alphonse Loubat, saw the New York system and introduced something similar to Paris in 1853, which was inaugurated the following year at a World Fair, as such major technological innovations often were.

In turn a London civil engineer, William Joseph Curtis, of Sebbon Street, Islington, was keeping up with developments in Europe and the USA. He began to think of ways of improving the mechanisation and making it more suited to the needs of British towns. He patented his tramway design in 1856, GB patent 1071 of that year. He ran a trial along a long flat road, Liverpool Street (now Liverpool Road) in Islington, but the design was not taken up. However, in 1860 he supplied a tram for use in Liverpool docks. This was for railway goods traffic of the Mersey Dock and Harbour Board, following the existing 'line of docks' passenger bus service. The new goods tram was operated by one of the two bus owners, almost certainly William and Daniel Busby (1814–87), with whom Turton would later work closely. Curtis fell out with the busmen because the board started to charge him for use of their rails, and the service ended within two years. Rather more successful was George Francis Train's tramway service that started on the docks at Birkenhead on 7 May 1860. Train (1829–1905) was primarily a railway entrepreneur, financier and land speculator in the USA, and an early pioneer of tramways

G.F. Train's trams were 'derailable'. The wheels had retractable flanges which allowed the vehicle to be run on both rails and road. Another early hybrid was John Haworth's 'Patent Perambulating Principle'. This will be discussed again in a later chapter. It was basically a horse bus with normal carriage wheels running on flat tracks with a third rail in the middle that took a flanged tram wheel. It was a one-off design

George Francis Train 1829–1904, American railway and tramway pioneer.

but nonetheless was in service for the Greenwood brothers in Salford for ten years leading up to Britain's tramway age proper.

G.F. Train tried to persuade the borough of Leeds of the advantages of his tramway system, still using protruding tracks. In March 1861 he offered to lay a mile of track along Wellington Road, a straight and level road in the town centre. The council referred him to the Highway Surveyor who recommended no further action. To judge from newspaper comments at the time there was a general public antipathy to the idea of tramways, despite a few ardent enthusiasts. This was a common pattern at the introduction of so many major technological initiatives that were successfully adopted. In the same month London saw a trial on a stretch of Bayswater Road extending less than a mile from Marble Arch.

Bear in mind that these tentative experiments took place in Britain over thirty years after the tram had been found attractive in the USA. A number of other European cities had begun the install them. So we may ask again, what held up the tram in Britain?

Was there a market?

– Was there a sufficient urban market of would-be travellers?
– How could trams compete with existing bus services and other transport for hire?
– Who would put up the capital for the infrastructure and the operating service?

Was the technology adequate?

– Could trams provide a new level of efficiency and reliability?
– Could they increase carrying capacity?

– Could they operate on gradients?

– Could they operate on narrow, short streets and on corners?

We have already noted that many early experiments were on short routes along straight and level roads, and often on privately owned land in docks, collieries, tin mines and so on. Passenger transport required a more versatile, flexible and safer system. American cities with their grid-pattern development since the early nineteenth century were well suited, as were some newly constructed continental European boulevards; but old English town centres, with short, narrow and winding streets, much less so. Until the middle of the century it was common for merchants and small manufacturers to have their workshops combined with their domestic residence in the town centre. Factory workers lived within walking distance of their work. It was not uncommon for children to walk several miles each way to school. Who needed the trams?

Lord Rosebery famously said of trams, in his lordly and disdainful manner, that they were 'the inconvenience of the opulent and the luxury of the poor'. He was right. They were ideally suited to a new middle class for whom they were convenient and just about affordable. This was an expanding middle class, with more disposable income and who above all were beginning to live in greater numbers away from the smoke in the outer townships of Leeds. When they came, the Leeds trams were not 'for all', as the omnibus once claimed. The early tram routes in Leeds extended, in spoke-like fashion, to the more prosperous suburbs. When the Leeds Borough took over the toll road system in 1866 and began to lift the tolls, they in effect freed the outer townships from being highly taxed with regard to transport into town. Everything was now in place.

Similar developments were happening in other towns and by late 1869 Parliament had received several applications to build tramways. The Busby brothers proposed a tramway system for Birmingham, where they were already operating an omnibus service. In addition there were two bids from Leeds. Fisher and Parrish and Partners, an American firm, introduced 'The Leeds Tramways Bill' proposing three routes with a 5ft 1in gauge. Solicitors on behalf of Ashworth, Morris and Co. introduced 'The Leeds Street Tramways Bill'. Their proposals were similar to ones being developed in other European cities such as Brussels and Copenhagen. They offered two routes with a gauge of 4ft 8in. The Leeds Town Clerk cited the trouble that Liverpool tramways had experienced when they tried to start on 1 November 1869, despite their use of flush rails. The two Leeds bids were dropped. Nonetheless an experimental demonstration by Messrs Fisher and Parrish, on a track just one hundred yards long in Oxford Street, near the Town Hall, impressed some councillors. The Leeds Town Council was in a strong position. It had almost completed the process that would give them control of all the streets in the town and the roads leading out. The general feeling on the council was that the borough itself should build and run the tramways. The elected council reflected not only a kind of collective municipal interest but also several other private and sectoral interests. Councillor Archibald Marsden, later to become alderman and mayor, had shares in American tramways companies. He was a champion of granting powers to private companies. 'He compared outright opposition to tramways to attitudes thirty-five years earlier when railway construction was opposed on the ground that the smoke from engines would blacken the fleeces of the sheep' (Soper, 1985). All tramway supporters, municipal or private, referred to the benefits of tramways in towns of America and other European countries, and their generally favourable reception there.

On 9 February 1870 the council considered a proposal that the corporation should promote a bill in Parliament to enable it to construct tramways. This was in opposition to the private tramway bills that had already been submitted. The council had won the first round. But there was another lobby, the omnibus proprietors, who by this time included William Turton, a new Conservative member of the political opposition on the council. He began to make his voice heard from the start. He opposed the tramways on the grounds of unnecessary competition with the existing horse buses. Together with John Ramsden, another bus proprietor, he petitioned Parliament, no doubt at some expense, against the Leeds Borough's Transport Bill. This was reported in the *Leeds Mercury* on 24 February 1870 and again at the second reading on 26 February.

The Leeds Council's initiative was in the end capped by a government bill already under consideration covering all aspects of the introduction of tramways. This received Royal Assent on 9 August and was known as the 'Tramways Act 1870' or in full 'An Act to facilitate the construction of and to regulate the workings of Tramways'. The new legislation ended the uncertainty and established the rules of the game for the next twenty years and more. The clauses of the Act placed strenuous restrictions on the would-be tramway entrepreneur:

1 Promoters could apply for a Provisional Order to the Board of Trade instead of promoting a private Bill in Parliament as formerly. Tramway Order Confirmation Acts confirmed the Provision Orders at intervals.

2 The tramway operators were responsible for paving and maintaining the road-way between the tramway tracks and for a distance of eighteen inches on either side to the satisfaction of the local authority.

3 Local authorities had the power of veto if they objected to a line passing through their area and could use this power to impose such terms as they wished upon the promoters.

4 The local authority could purchase the tramway after 21 years from the date of authorisation. The purchase price was to be the 'then value of the tramway and works without any allowance for compulsory purchase, goodwill, prospective profits or other considerations'. (Soper, 1985)

The Busby brothers, William and Daniel, had operated omnibus services in Liverpool, their hometown, from 1834, and had been involved in the early dockland tramway in Birkenhead. Their Liverpool operation currently had 1,340 horses and 146 buses, a huge undertaking. They now moved to submit proposals in Leeds. One of the Busby brothers and their engineer Joseph Kincaid met the Leeds Highways Committee on 12

October 1870. Their proposal was to construct four tramway routes of '4 foot 8 and a half-inch gauge' (four feet, eight and a half inches), which was to become the standard, if not universal gauge all over the country. All four routes departed from Boar Lane off Briggate at either its western or eastern end. They later agreed to build two other routes or extensions.

The Busbys' memorial or submission stated that Parliament was already considering twenty-seven applications for 515 miles of tramway. They compared their trams favourably with New York (reduced accidents) and Copenhagen (4 million passengers in a population of only 100,000). With wheels underneath the body of the carriage these were wider and could accommodate three times as many passengers as the omnibus.

The Highways Committee was not at first in favour, saying that they considered it 'undesirable to give the consent asked for as it was probable street tramways would be superseded by some other invention'. This sounds like a recipe for never doing anything, which was not at all in the spirit of the times. What they had in mind was likely to have been the current trials in Edinburgh of a steam driven omnibus. City authorities and entrepreneurs were very much aware of what other towns and cities were up to.

Ten days later 'at a stormy meeting of the Council' the Highways Committee was criticised for its delay over the past year. The mood was for allowing a private company to construct the tramway, encouraged by Councillor Marsden and a new body of supporters. Interestingly they used the argument – which might well have been put the other way – that private companies would use discretion as to where they built their routes whereas the corporation might build only in areas where it would be remunerative, to which rate payers might object. The matter was referred to a special meeting on 28 October. Other private bids were being submitted, including one, ominously perhaps, from the Edinburgh Steam Omnibus Company. Councillor William Turton and Councillor John Ramsden submitted a proposal that if trams went ahead, the omnibus owners should receive compensation. They were beginning to position themselves for a favourable outcome, whatever decision was taken.

In the event the council had four bids to consider. The Busbys agreed to compensate Turton and Ramsden and also to pay £1,000 to the corporation for the concession. It is not clear whether the council had requested this. The other bidders made rash offers to build additional lines, but were not prepared to pay for a 'concession'. 'At their meeting on 9th November 1870 the Council unanimously gave their consent to Messrs William and Daniel Busby to undertake the construction of the Leeds tramways' (Soper, 1985).

The Busby's, the 'Promoters', were directed and authorised by the Board of Trade Leeds Tramways Order of 22 April 1871. The document is preserved in the West Yorkshire Archive in Sheepscar at the southern end of Chapeltown Road, Leeds. The Order lists in detail the agreed and authorised routes. They all start in Boar Lane just off Briggate:

1 to Headingley (Cardigan Arms) via Wellington Street and Kirkstall Road. (In this as in the following there are various specifications of shorter routes within the main routes. One started in Wellington Road from the 'West Riding Hotel' which still stands there.)

2 to Headingley (Three Horse Shoes) via Cookridge Street, Woodhouse Lane and Otley Road.

3 to Potternewton (Queen's Arms) via Chapeltown Road.

4 to Hunslet (Crooked Billet) via Call Lane and Crown Point Road.

5 to Marsh Lane (Shoulder of Mutton).

Promoters may make, maintain, alter, and remove – such crossings, passing places, sidings, junctions, and other works [a later hand has underlined this on the original] *in addition to those particularly specified in the Order, for the efficient working of the Tramways, or for providing access to any warehouses, stables or carriage houses, or works connected with the undertaking.*

The fares were to be one penny a mile or fraction of a mile. The local authority or any group of twenty ratepayers could petition the Board of Trade if they thought the company was overcharging. A pencil note added later states, 'From Chapeltown to Cowper Street is less than 2 miles. Company charging 3*d*.'

There is a long section on freight charges that suggests early expectations of much greater use of the trams for unaccompanied freight. Perhaps it was just clerical punctiliousness or maybe an adaptation of railways prescriptions.

Freight charges on trams	
28lbs [accompanied] luggage free	
Parcels:	
up to 7lbs	3*d*
7–14lbs	5*d*
14–28lbs	7*d*
28–56lbs	9*d*
56–500lbs	as the Company thinks fit

There are rates for freight up to 4 tons and up to 8 tons, and most surprisingly charges for transport of livestock: pigs and sheep 6*d* each, cows 8*d*, horses 1*s*. The trams played an important role in the delivery of Royal Mail and newspapers.

The Busbys were true pioneers. They moved fast. They first had to draft the Tramways Bill and agree it with the council. They did not wait for this to become law. They contracted a local firm, Messrs A. Speight and Sons of Canal Basin, Leeds, to construct the Headingley line. They began work on 5 June 1871 at the south-eastern side of Woodhouse Moor, moving north-west with a team of thirty men. Other gangs soon started at the Boar Lane and Park Row end. The two-and-a-quarter mile route was completed in three months despite competing gas works in the road and bad weather. Things moved faster. The Busby Tramways Bill passed through Parliament as an unopposed measure and became law on 14 August. Three of the Headingley route tramcars arrived by rail from Birkenhead on 6 September. The next day Captain Tyler the Board of Trade Inspector made his inspection accompanied by Busbys' engineer Joseph Kincaid. The tramway was passed fit for traffic and on Wednesday 13 September 1871 the Highways Committee inspected everything: routes, cars, horses, drivers and conductors. On Saturday 16 September, losing no time at all, the first two-penny and three-penny tickets were sold. The tramcars were decked with flags. The horses were Mr Ramsden's omnibus horses. There was to be no respite for them. The trams ran no fewer than fifty-two departures daily, at first, compared with twenty-four departures by the buses.

There were some early complaints about the trams. At first, surprisingly, there was no manager and despite the improved frequency of service and the continuing addition of routes and extensions, the services were somewhat disorganised, passing points were insufficient in number and the drivers not too well disciplined or co-operative. Some passengers in letters to newspapers signed 'Ratepayer' and the like complained of dangerous driving, swearing by staff and delays. Even four horses were said to have difficulty hauling the cars up the steeper gradients. The carriages of notables together with humbler carts and wagons were damaged by the lines or by the inexorable passage of the cars that could develop considerable momentum. Accounts for payment of damages were submitted and disputed. The macadam road surface developed holes. The council blamed the operators who in turn blamed the council for not accepting their original proposal to use granite setts. The Busbys seem to have come off best, although their farsighted proposal to build a route to Roundhay Park, bought by the council just a few weeks previously, was rejected. Woodhouse Moor, the only other municipally owned public space, was however served by their Headingley route.

By April 1872 a manager, Charles Smith, was finally appointed. He set about promoting the image of the tramway. On May Day 1872 he organised a parade through the town of decorated cars drawn by grey horses and a supporting team of a further twenty-five greys dressed up for the occasion. The guards had fine new uniforms. Such processions were a popular kind of public display and must have made a positive impression. Similar shows were put on for the opening of other lines and extensions in that year.

The Busby brothers decided to take their profits early and applied to Parliament for a bill to enable their undertaking to be transferred to a new company to be known as the 'Leeds Tramways Company'. The 'Leeds Tramways Act 1872' received Royal Assent on 6 August 1872 and the Leeds Tramways Company was incorporated.

The six founding directors of the Leeds Tramways Company (usually LTC hereafter) were William Bower Esq. Ironmaster, from Drighlington south-west of Leeds; William Coghlan Esq. Ironmaster, of Coghlan and Drury Ironmasters, Hunslet, Leeds; William Illingworth Esq. Timber Merchant, of Illingworth, Ingham and Co. timber merchants, Leeds; Alexander McEwan Esq. Lombard House, Lombard Street, London, who seem to have been a banker or financier; William Turton Esq. Omnibus Proprietor, Leeds; and Thomas Wright Esq. Chairman, Liverpool Omnibus and Tramways Co. Ltd [clearly a Busby nominee].

The solicitors were Barr, Nelson, Barr of Leeds. Joseph Kincaid was the engineer; he had worked on the project with the Busbys from the start. Edward Bellamy was company secretary. He was also secretary of the Continental and General Tramway Company of No. 3 Park Row, Leeds and Westminster Chambers, London, which doubtless had a stake in LTC.

We can only imagine what conversations took place between Turton and the Busbys and others over the nearly two-year period from October 1870. He had only begun to make his mark as a bus operator four years before. He probably had few contacts and a limited reputation in towns and cities beyond Leeds. But he was a wealthy man and a town councillor, so he could exercise some political influence. Reading back from his later active association with Daniel Busby it is obvious that he impressed Busby with his style of doing business and the ease of his personal dealings. William Turton was a generation younger than the Busbys, a man for his time.

If we look at the list of directors we note that one is from London, one from Liverpool and the four others from Leeds. Only one of these, Turton, had a strong involvement with urban transport. Of course this included not only running buses, but also providing fodder for the horses, and coal for associated steam machines in the depots and in the manufacturing of carriages in the Thomas Green steel works, which we shall discuss further later.

William Turton was compensated for a few of his prime bus routes that were naturally required for the tramway services. He was to sell various lots of rolling stock, horses, stables and other assets to the LTC over the coming years. But he remained a substantial bus operator as well as having his core business in corn and coal. Turton was not bought out; he did not sell out. Rather he bought in with a substantial investment.

William and Daniel Busby handed over to the LTC all their commitments and undertakings entered into so far, and all their assets in land, stables, plant, rolling stock and horses. In return they were to receive repayment of their outlay and the issue of £13,000 fully paid up shares in the LTC.

The capitalisation of the LTC at its formation was £160,000 divided into 16,000 shares of £10 each. So the Busbys had some 8 per cent of the capital. Other major shareholders included the six directors, Joseph Kincaid and the secretary. No doubt some of the prominent councillors and transport proprietors such as Archibald Marsden subscribed. They had to move quickly, as there was no shortage of interest.

Invitation to subscribe was made on 9 September and the list closed on 3 October. At the first meeting of shareholders on 5 February 1873 William Coghlan took the chair and announced that the total of paid-up shares was £153,350.

The process of transferring the whole undertaking from the Busbys to the Leeds Tramways Company took a few more months of complicated legal wrangling. On 1 March a new manager, William Bulmer, was appointed. He had previously worked with the Busbys in Liverpool. Even more importantly a new secretary was appointed, William Wharam. Wharam was 37 years old and lived with his wife and two young children, William and Samuel, in Headingley-cum-Burley. In the 1871 census his occupation is given as railway clerk; he was cashier in the goods department of the Great Northern Railway Company. His appointment to the LTC seems like a big step up. He did not disappoint and was to remain secretary of the LTC for the whole of its existence and continued in the service of Leeds Council when it took over the tramways. On a frivolous note, one cannot help wondering how everyone coped with all these Williams! I suppose Mr Wharam and Mr Bulmer were commonly used at first, but there were four directors called William and one can only go so far with Will, Willie, Bill and so on.

On 15 May 1873 a partial transfer from the Busbys took place and the first receipts began to be taken by LTC on Whit Sunday 1 June 1873. The Busby brothers received their cheque for £13,000 and a public notice appeared on 8 August, signed by William Wharam, to announce the completion of the transfer. The Leeds Tramways Company was now in sole charge and able to go ahead with the other commitments to provide Leeds with its tramway system.

14

LEEDS TRAMWAYS COMPANY – INFRASTRUCTURE

William Turton has been called a great 'promoter' and 'pioneer' of tramways in the north of England. He specifically denied that he was a promoter of Leeds Tramways Company. He was quite right. It was Daniel and William Busby who set things in motion in 1869 anticipating the Tramways Act of 1870. Turton was, however, a pivotally important pioneer of tramway systems in many English towns and cities, as we shall see in Chapter 18. Arguably neither he nor the Busbys were the truly great pioneers of the tram. The top honours probably go to John Stephenson (not related to the railway pioneer) and George Francis Train. They were engineers and inventors in virgin territory. Their main contribution was in the USA, whose major cities had extensive tramway systems some thirty or forty years ahead of their British counterparts.

From early experiments in Britain until final withdrawal from service, the horse tram system had a life of some thirty, at most forty years. Nonetheless the horse tramways made a big contribution to urban passenger transport at a crucial moment of urban expansion in the UK. Much of the pioneering work on rolling stock, track, routes and so on, served to inform the subsequent sixty years or so of the electric tram.

If the horse tram as a system and the tram horse are relatively neglected, the same cannot be said of the technological aspects of tracks and carriages, routes and ticketing and so on. Even so this is chiefly focused on the electric tram. My intention is to augment the political and economic, the social and personal contexts of the horse tram era. However, this chapter deals with some of the infrastructural issues we need to take into account.

Leeds population increase and the development of urban transport
1771-1901

population	1771	1781	1791	1801	1811	1821	1831	1841	1851	1861	1871	1881	1891	1901	
450,000															
420,000															Leeds Townships
390,000															
360,000															
330,000															
300,000															
270,000															
250,000															
210,000															
180,000															Central Leeds
150,000															
120,000															
90,000															
60,000															
30,000															
							1838 horse omnibuses				1872 horse trams		1891 first electric tram		

Increase in population and the development of transport services 1771–1901.

ROUTES

The first considerations in proposing to construct a tramway system must be what routes to run on, what the likely passenger demand would be, what the likely known costs (carriages, horses) and less known costs (track laying and maintenance for example). All this was in the context of national and local legislation, and the potential role of the corporation in enforcing byelaws on traffic and sharing responsibility for road maintenance.

William Turton was well placed to take part in the early stages of this planning. He was not directly involved until some two years after the Busbys initiated their quest to build tramways in Leeds. They were not Leeds men. Turton was a Leeds man. He knew the city, its people, government and transport probably better than anyone. He certainly knew as much about horses and horse food as anyone in Yorkshire. Moreover, by 1871, he had run horse omnibuses for several years and had a monopoly or near monopoly of several of the key routes of interest to the Busbys. He had experience of introducing new routes and of competition on old routes. He both posed a threat to the introduction of tramways, and was in turn threatened by them. He was soon aboard the tram. Daniel Busby was to find him a perfect partner for this venture and for many others in northern towns over the next few years.

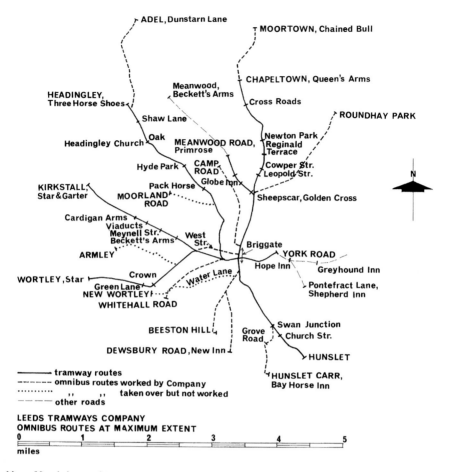

Map of Leeds bus and tram routes.

Daniel Busby proposed five tramway routes in Leeds in 1870. Work started on the first, to Headingley (The Oak) in 1871 (extended to The Three Horse Shoes in 1875) and to Kirkstall in 1872. The others, to Chapeltown (The Queen's Arms), York Road (The Wool Pack) and Hunslet (The Crooked Billet) were all completed by the end of 1874, within the first two years of the Leeds Tramways Company's operation. Two other main routes were added by the LTC: to Meanwood (Buslingthorpe Lane) in 1874, extended 1887; to Wortley (The Crown) in 1879, extended later that year to The Star; and to Roundhay in 1889.

The LTC bought some of Turton's competing bus routes and continued to run some horse buses as extensions of or as feeder routes to the tramway: on the Headingley line (to Adel), Chapeltown (to The Chained Bull, Moortown) and to Hunslet Carr. It ran its own bus service to Roundhay Park, Beeston Hill, Dewsbury Road, Whitehall Road and Camp Road. In addition it bought out other competitive routes and discontinued the services.

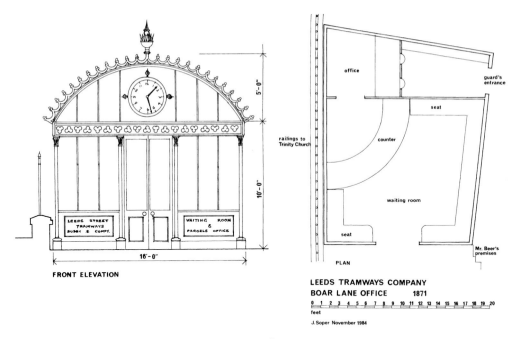

Busby's office in Boar Lane, later Leeds Tramway Company.

By 1874 LTC was running trams on 17 miles of route. By 1890 the approximate lengths of routes were (from Boar Lane):

Leeds Tramway Company Routes 1874	
Routes	Miles of track
Headingley	5
Chapeltown	4.5
Kirkstall	4.5
Hunslet	3.5
Roundhay	3.5
Wortley	3
Meanwood	1
York Road	1

When the LTC was transferred to the borough council in 1895 the total length of routes was 27.5 miles.

The general pattern of services at first, with only minor variations, was that trams ran daily at quarter of an hour intervals from 8.45 a.m. until 10.30 p.m.; 11.00 p.m. on Saturdays.

Compared with the eventual scale of tramways in Leeds in the twentieth century, this may seem a modest undertaking. But by 1877 the total length of tram routes in the UK was only 212 miles of which 135 were in England and Wales. If we add the lengths of tramways in other towns where Turton or Turton and Busby were promoters and/or chairmen and/or directors we can say that Turton was a major investor and influence in over one quarter of the tramways in England at that time, including most of those in the North.

The distribution of tram services and their users in Leeds shows a familiar pattern. The system did not serve the working class on any scale until the late nineteenth century. For some time Hunslet was the only terminus south of the Aire where most of the factories and mills and other sources of employment were situated. Most people continued to walk to work. At best a workman might walk to the nearest stop from which he could get the minimum fare of one penny.

Leeds Tramways Company insignia.

TRACKS

The company's expenses were chiefly for horses, rolling stock and track and track maintenance. Horses and cars were relatively unproblematic to manage. The tracks were to give endless trouble, increasingly so in the final years. The engineer employed by the Busbys was Joseph Kincaid of London, who had worked on the Peckham line in London. He used iron rails laid on timber cross sleepers six inches by four set in a trench seven and a quarter inches on a three inch bed of concrete. Surrounding the rails and sleepers were five inches of stone paving on two-and-a-quarter inch of clinker and ash.

The standard works on tram construction of the time (Clark D. Kinnear 1878, and 1884) show numerous variations and improvements in track construction and laying. Kincaid's own patented 'iron way' – always using the standard four foot eight-and-a-half inch gauge – went through several stages of development. His early designs were used on the Headingley line in October 1872 and in Sheffield for William Turton in October 1873. In 1876 they were superseded by a patent which used more expensive steel rails that gradually replaced the early Leeds tracks. They were also used on Turton's tramways in Leicester, Salford and Newcastle, and in other parts of the UK (including Bristol) and in Australia (Adelaide).

The 1870 Tramways Act gave local authorities latitude as to how much or how little they might invest in the infrastructure before they handed over to the operating company, the lessee. This was also the case with responsibility for track maintenance. It seems that the smoothest relationships between tramway companies and corporations were in those towns where the local authority had built and maintained the track and were therefore in control of the entire road surface. If not, the company was responsible for using granite setts or macadam to a certain distance either side of the rails as well as in between. Mismatch of materials, repair schedules, and intermittent municipal road works, especially the construction of sewers, led to continuing disputes and inefficiencies in the case of Leeds.

The tramway company was required to lay the track, whether single or double, in the middle of the road. Byelaws required other road users not to use this section except for crossing and overtaking. But they did, and often 'strings' of heavy wagons carrying coal and construction material would deliberately use the track, sometimes at night, and occasionally it seems, using wagons that fitted the tram rails. This caused a good deal of the wear and tear of the track, and the company complained that it was unfair that it should have to bear the full cost of repairs. The Highways Committee might or might not agree to share costs. When the company asked the council to enforce the byelaws and police the use of the road more strictly, some members of the public called the LTC 'arrogant' and accused them of abusing their monopoly.

The rising cost of track maintenance, even just over the first four years of operation can be judged from these figures:

Cost of track maintenance 1873–76	
Annual cost of the LTC track maintenance per mile	
1873	£16
1874	£20 5s
1875	£50
1876	£121 7s

Two particular sources of grievance to the public were the irregular heights of some rails, and dust and grit. The latter were caused by the grinding of sand, granite chips and salt that were used to maintain good traction in bad road or weather conditions and prevent 'greasy' rails. Passengers, rate payers, and the occasional shareholder, were known to go about with a one foot ruler measuring – just like the Board of Trade Inspector – just how many inches the lines projected above or had sunk below the road surface. This was clearly a danger to other vehicles. The problem for bicycles was soon to arise.

In August 1879 shopkeepers in central Leeds brought a case against the LTC before the Stipendiary Magistrate. They argued that the dust and debris from the tramlines blew into their shops and were detrimental to trade. The Magistrate, Mr Bruce, conceded that the shopkeepers had a point but was sympathetic to the LTC and the requirements of its operations. He imposed a 'nominal penalty' of 1s with one guinea costs against the LTC.

ROLLING STOCK

When the tramways started their life, there were several engineering firms in Leeds and nearby that specialised in making vehicles for haulage, omnibus and railway. Providers of mechanical traction will be considered later. These firms were quick off the mark to design and manufacture a variety of tramcars or 'horse trailers' to be drawn by horses. In the first year of operation LTC had fifteen cars, all double decker. Double decker omnibuses were already running and continued to run alongside single decker cars for the whole of the horse tram period. By 1874 LTC had forty-one cars.

The single decker cars carried fourteen to twenty-four passengers and the double-deckers thirty-six to forty-eight. A full carriage could weigh about five tons. At first the upper deck, 'on top', was also 'outside', uncovered. The top was used mostly by men, and from photographs almost always wearing hats. The staircase was an outside, spiral steel structure. 'Inside' had plush seats and sometimes cost a penny more. When the Boar Lane to Headingley line opened in September 1871 Busby had just five cars. Four were from Starbucks in Birkenhead at a cost of £180 each. One was imported from John Stephenson, New York, costing £300. By 1887 LTC had seventy-seven tramcars, not all of which would have been in service at any one time.

HORSES

We have already introduced the most important part of the whole system, the horse, in Chapter 6. Compared with the many thousands of horses at work drawing trams in London, the LTC owned relatively few. But they were crucial to the enterprise and by far the costliest element.

Stock of horses, Leeds Tramways Company 1874–93			
Year	Horses	Carriages	Steam engines
1874	184–270	31–41	
1877	279		
1878	312		
1879	334	51	
1880	342		
1881	332		2
1884	357		
1886	274		16
1891	303	69	26
1892	308		
1893	368		

Shareholders, as well as the directors as we shall see, were concerned at the scale of running costs and often made comparisons with tramways in other northern towns. As much as 60 per cent of total working expenditure could be taken up by 'horsing costs', excluding replacement costs. The largest part of the cost was for horse food. These figures show the rising costs of keeping the horses in the first four years, when the number was between 180–270 horses:

1873	£5,016
1874	£10,236
1875	£17,653
1876	£18,384

These figures have to be gleaned from sources that are not systematic or complete, so the sequences are sometimes a little odd. Here is another set of figures that show quite dramatically that LTC tried to reduce horse costs:

Weekly cost of maintenance of LTC horses 1873–91							
	1875	1877	1879	1880	188	1886	1891
Food	16s 4d	13s 2d	11s 5d	9s 8d	10s 5d	14s 10d	10s 5½d
Total	22s 2d	19 9d	16s 11d 1f	15s ½d	15s 3d 3f	14s 5½d	

As a prominent horse fodder merchant William Turton would have exercised all his skills to reduce the cost of fodder to the LTC. He would not have liked shareholders reminding him that some of his other tram operations managed to achieve lower costs than the LTC. It is a wonder that Turton managed to avoid any charge of insider dealing. Some of his infrastructure contracts with tramways companies were done before he became a director. This may also have been true of dealing in fodder. As we shall see, one director was to leave the board following a charge of 'insider dealing' in oats.

DEPOTS

The fixed property of the LTC consisted of its track, an office in Boar Lane and the various 'depôts' – as they were properly spelled – and stables. There were at first no tram stops, shelters or other street furniture, except for a few horse water troughs.

The LTC offices were in Boar Lane near the junction with Briggate. They were at 'Trinity Chambers' in a little alley immediately to the east of Trinity Church, now part of the new 'Trinity Quarter'. It comprised, to begin with, only two rooms, put up by Busby in 1871–2. Later a waiting room was added and a façade of ornamental glass with an imposing clock, a cashier's room where the fare boxes were kept, and store rooms. In 1896, after the corporation had taken over, they were described as 'a stuffy little structure' but were in use for several years afterwards. Next to the office was Samuel Lee's 'Tramway Restaurant' which offered a 'substantial dinner' for 10*d* and 'tea' for 4*d*. Business must have been good, what with all these tram passengers, and it was renamed 'The Silver Grid'. Even cheaper meals, along with wines, beer and sprits were available round the corner at Whitelock's Luncheon Bar, famous to this day:

Soups	2*d*
Sausages and potatoes	3*d*
Hot pies	2*d*
Sandwiches	2*d* (and 4*d*)
Gorgonzola bun	2*d*
Stilton (bun)	2*d*
Rocquefort (bun)	2*d*
Cheshire cheese (bun)	1*d*
Plate of bread	2*d*

The LTC depots were situated at or near the end of the line; the more important at the out of town end. The trams would terminate there at night and be ready for the early morning commuters. This reduced the mileage horses had to haul the cars. Dispersal was also part of the strategy for reducing the effects of infectious horse diseases.

William Turton sold some of his stock along with rights to run buses on certain routes, but he continued to run bus services for many years and had substantial resources. These included omnibus depots, stables, provender stores and so on. Some or parts of these he rented out to the LTC. His omnibus premises in Harrison Street, off New Briggate, provided some stabling for LTC horses from 1873 to 1876 at an annual rent of £71. In 1878, or earlier, he sold the site for the building of the Grand Theatre, which still stands. His stables and provender stores in High Court Lane, off Marsh Lane, was let to LTC from 1 March 1874 for £100 per annum and increased in 1877 to £114. The use of these stables was superseded by 1883 by the North Street depot.

The North Street depot was in Sheepshanks Yard, next to the fine early eighteenth century merchant's house (now demolished), Sheepshanks House. The Yard was close to the junction of Vicar Lane, New Briggate and North Street. There was a cabman's rest hut at the intersection. Turton bought a substantial part of Sheepshanks Yard, 1,724 square yards, at auction in December 1874. In June 1878 he applied for permission to build more stables, workshops and office. This was for his own private business purposes. When in 1882 the LTC acquired Turton's omnibus services he continued to own the site. He charged LTC £300 per annum, increased to £345 in 1888. It was the largest of the LTC's inner-city depots. It had stables for 100 horses, a feedstuff store and was the main base for carriage repair. It remained the only LTC depot for horse trams until their withdrawal on 31 May 1902, when it was still let by the firm of William Turton (Leeds) Corn and Hay Merchants. It was never used as part of the electrified system. When Turton first bought property in the Yard, other residents included, incongruously, two Jewish tailors and a pig dealer. By the time of the 1890 Ordnance Survey, a Jewish Synagogue with 450 seats had been built. For several years after the horse trams departed the depot was used for horse sales. It was demolished to build the Ritz Cinema, later renamed the ABC Cinema. By 1967 all these structures and their rubble, if not quite all their history, lay under the Inner Ring Road, the mighty A64 (M), sacrificed to the internal combustion engine.

After a few years the LTC began building depots to a fairly standard design of their engineer Joseph Kincaid. The Hunslet depot, which opened in October 1875, was built on a green field site next to a farmhouse bought from the Middleton Colliery. By 1889 the area to the north was well built up. The larger depots (Chapeltown, Headingley, North Street) had stables for upwards of 100 horses, and tram sheds. They were built of brick, steel and slate with granite setts. They were well ventilated and lit. There were stalls for sick horses, a blacksmith's shop, paint shop, a room where the lamp boys could clean and fill the lamps and trim the wicks, stores for salt, sand and gravel, a manure pit and close to it a privy.

The Headingley Depot was at the end of the longest and more profitable lines. It was built near The Cardigan Arms, named after the commander of the Charge of the Light Brigade, who was a large local landowner, on 5,587 square yards of land bought from Lord Cardigan in 1873 for £1,267 4s 10d. It was designed by Kincaid and cost £2,000. It opened on 15 May 1875. It sported a tramcar weathervane. As well as the usual sheds, workshops and offices, it had stalls for 124 horses. It was a hilly route that needed a greater number of horses per car. Most depots had some separate accommodation for the foreman, chief horse-keeper and other key staff. At Headingley a new street was built with five cottages for LTC employees at £74 2s per cottage and in April 1887 ten additional houses. Turton also built houses for his senior employees in his corn and coal businesses.

A special report in the Leeds Mercury of 31 May 1878 described the stables at 'The Calls', one of LTC's depots at the time. It was part of William Turton's new buildings at Crown Point, Nos 64–66 The Calls, completed just two years earlier. In the loft were 'gas engines' for chopping and mixing food. Despite its proximity to the Sanitary Yard, which included a night-soil deposit and municipal dung heap and was notorious for its bad smells, the *Leeds Mercury* reporter refers to 'a sweet country smell' of hay! This depot was not particularly large, as it had space for only twenty-eight horses. But it was the main depot for saddlery repairs. The reporter was clearly delighted with what he found. The stables were 'kept in an admirable state of cleanliness' with that 'sweet country smell' and the horse stalls were 'touched up artistically with horizontal designs in sawdust' and glue. He concludes by stressing the 'public satisfaction with the facilities of conveyance'. The LTC did occasionally have good public relations.

15

LEEDS TRAMWAYS COMPANY – STAKEHOLDERS

Some of the key players have already been introduced. We have some idea of the infrastructure of the Leeds tramway system. It is time to turn to the various stakeholders, the directors, staff, shareholders and of course the passengers.

DIRECTORS

Of the original six directors of the Leeds Tramways Company only Turton was to continue until the winding up in 1895. Bower, McEwan and Wright lasted only a year or two. Coghlan, the first chairman, was voted off in 1876 and Illingworth resigned at the same time. Councillor Mason who joined in 1873 left under a cloud in 1876. Interestingly, Daniel Busby soon joined the board. He was the largest shareholder at the time. He was to stay for some eleven years until 1883. Several other directors came and went: Ashcroft, McLure and Walker. The second longest serving director by far was William Baxter who joined in 1879 and remained on the board until the end. At the end, Hargreaves, Sharp and Simpson were also on the board having served for some nine to twelve years respectively. Another director of note is John Eddison who was on the board from 1877–87 and vice-chairman for most of this time. He was voted off the board but remained a vocal shareholder at subsequent meetings.

The directors met ad hoc and at quite frequent intervals during the year in between the twice-yearly shareholders' meetings. They also participated in meetings with the corporation, especially its Highways Committee and later its Tramways Subcommittee. They also met the Watch Committee and individual council officials. They attended trials of equipment and vehicles in Leeds and in many other towns. They attended opening ceremonies and other public events with numerous lunches and dinners. They were all busy people with their own companies to run and other directorships. A few had other transport interests, some of them involving William Turton.

Turton worked closely with William Wharam after his appointment as secretary for the life of the LTC. Wharam prepared the detailed half-yearly reports and other information to brief him when he became chairman, in order to help him answer awkward supplementary questions from shareholders. When Councillor Petty proposed, in February 1887, that the number of directors be reduced to five, he remarked that 'He gave the Chairman [Turton] and Secretary [Wharam] the credit for about nine-tenths of the work.'

After one year of the LTC's existence, the shareholders voted a fee of £300 each to the directors. After a promising few years, in February 1879, this 'remuneration' or 'consideration' as it was also termed, was raised to £500. Directors were expected to work. Shareholders were ready to note the absence of directors from meetings and their overall contribution to the work of the company. One critical intervention at a meet in August 1887 observed that 'one director had received £500 and was not worth 500 pence'. In February 1886, after a downturn, the remuneration was reduced to £300, with an unsupported motion suggesting £200. It was later increased again.

The LTC directors had major legal and other responsibilities, and a hands-on role in the running of the company. Wharam seems never to have had the support of anything like a senior management team. Directors took decisions about routes, track, rolling stock and horses. They had to assess innovations and suppliers. They notably had to deal with shareholders. There was a de facto vice-chairman. He seldom had to deputise for Turton, but spoke after the chairman to second the adoption of the Report. He would add his own comments and encouragement.

The most fraught task of all was dealing with Leeds Corporation. At first Turton was an insider as we have seen, serving on the Highways Committee at some crucial times but coming off it soon after he became chairman. When discussions were under way for the purchase by the LTC of many of his remaining omnibus routes in 1882, he resigned from the board, or stood down temporarily. There must have been a good understanding between him and other directors seeing that he

William Turton, studio portrait, 1870s.

returned in a year or so and resumed his position as chairman immediately. Relations between the LTC and the corporation were often poor to bad. On the council side complaints ran from foot-dragging and hard bargaining to strong criticism of LTC policies and practice regarding track maintenance and staff working conditions. One shareholder, who was also a councillor, said in August 1880 that 'The Highways Committee and the corporation generally, were beginning to show a more kindly spirit towards the Tramways Company (Hear, hear!)'. Relations became strained again from 1892 when the winding up of the LTC began to be considered. This will be dealt with in Chapter 17. Even at this difficult time William Turton showed

WILLIAM WHARAM,
Manager of the City of Leeds Tramways.

William Wharam, General Manager, Leeds Tramways Company.

his customary tact and courteousness, telling shareholders that 'the directors had always dealt with the corporation in a fair spirit and he could say there had been no unpleasantness between the two bodies'.

There was nothing to be gained by getting hot under the well-starched collar. Turton also showed considerable forbearance towards hecklers and troublemakers at meetings. Towards critical correspondents in the *Yorkshire Post*, or more often the *Leeds Mercury* – of whom there were not a few – he affected to show disdain and disregard, especially if they were anonymous. Only once have I come across anything approaching exasperation, when at the February 1885 meeting, he declared that 'Shareholders had little idea of the difficulties of the Directors'.

Some directors left little trace. Only Councillor Mason (1873–77) who shared a tramway interest outside Leeds with Turton, left 'under a cloud' in 1876. It seems it was illegal for directors of a company to trade with it. Mason was suspected of some kind of improper dealing; a rumour that he had sold 'tainted oats' was floated in order to flush him out. Mason finally explained himself. He had bought a quantity of oats speculatively and warehoused them. He had eventually sold them to the LTC at no profit. He claimed other directors had done as much, but he resigned. The first chairman, William Coghlan, was not re-elected at the February 1877 meeting. A large shareholder or broker, Mr Abbot from London, said that Coghlan 'had neither the health, tact nor temper to be Chairman'. William Turton argued for the re-election of both

Mason and Coghlan, but he was in a small majority. He understood the dilemmas, difficulties and perhaps the temptations faced by the two men.

SHAREHOLDERS

LTC meetings were held in the first half of February and August. In some years a special additional meeting was called. Under the first chairman they met in the Great Northern Railway Hotel. When William Turton was chairman they met, all but once, in the Philosophical Hall which was more conveniently located. This was the home of the Leeds Philosophical and Literary Society and housed a museum, library and lecture theatre. It was built by R.D. Chantrell in 1819–22, who had designed the new St Peter's parish church. This grand and prestigious building was damaged by enemy bombing in 1940 and later demolished.

Meetings were well attended. When a 'large attendance' is reported this is usually upwards of 100 people. The company issued its reports a week or more before the meeting and this, or an edited version, was published regularly in the *Yorkshire Post* and usually in the *Leeds Mercury*. The meetings were reported within a day or two; again this was more regular in the conservative *Post*. These are our only accounts of the conduct of the meetings. Turton would open the meeting and present the report at length, adding and emphasising points here and there. Company accounts and operational details were reported in an open manner. The weekly cost of keeping the horses, broken down as to food and the rest, was accounted to the nearest farthing – one 960ieth of a pound. On the whole difficulties and disappointments were treated head on. When receipts and profits were low, the chairman invoked the need to invest in stock and build up reserves. Weather and unfair compensation costs were blamed together with the high cost of corn in the market place and the prevailing economic climate of the town and in the UK. Whenever possible the company was praised in comparison with tramways in other towns, though when shareholders thought they could cite examples elsewhere of more efficient and profitable tramways companies, they were quick to raise the matter. The focus was always on the bottom line, the half-yearly dividend.

Meetings were often quite lively and even enjoyable occasions. There are frequently reported instances of witty or sardonic comments from the floor, cries of 'Hear, Hear', applause and laughter, even 'loud laughter'. The length of meetings is seldom reported. Three hours was the longest and no doubt exceptional, and two hours or so more usual. Meetings normally started at 11.00 a.m. and lasted until about 1.00 or 2.00 p.m. when those attending would disperse for lunch, which was often taken as late as four o'clock in those days. By holding meetings in the Philosophical Hall rather than in hotels previously, the opportunity for shareholders to spend time at the bar was diminished. At the end of each meeting there was a vote of thanks to the chairman. It may be due to the vagaries of newspaper reporting, but it seems only occasionally was the vote proposed to thank both chairman and directors, and once or twice William Wharam.

The company's original capital £160,000 remained constant throughout. Additional loans were raised as necessary for specific initiatives. Shares were in £10 units, so the maximum number of shares was 16,000. It was always well subscribed. It seems there was no lower threshold for holdings, but there was a maximum of one quarter of the total. As part of the original transfer of his undertaking to the LTC Daniel Busby received 8 per cent of the share (1,280) which he had reduced by 1877 to 780 shares. One of the largest shareholders, possibly a stockbroker acting for clients, was Mr Abbot of London, who was knowledgeable about tramway operations in other towns. He claimed to hold 3,000 shares or 18.75 per cent of the total.

Shares were traded and were occasionally manipulated to ensure, for example prior to bids to Parliament and so on, that the company was seen to be fully paid up. The value of shares does not seem to have fluctuated much above about 10 per cent over the period. They were not quoted on the London Stock Exchange. This was said to be too expensive and not in any case necessary. William Turton makes a point of saying at the February 1879 meeting that he was 'very glad that they [the shareholders] chiefly resided in Leeds or the neighbourhood'. This form of 'local capitalism' is an interesting feature I shall return to later.

The current number of shareholders was announced at the start of each meeting. The median range was 720–780 shareholders. It had a low of 712 (in 1880) and a high of 800 (in 1877). There were a few larger shareholders. We can assume that in addition to Busby and Abbot (whose holdings amounted to nearly one quarter of the total) each of the six directors had substantial shareholdings and perhaps some of the senior company staff and advisors (Wharam, Kincaid). Some former directors and other well-known names of councillors and aldermen appear in reports. One might therefore estimate that about half the shares were owned by no more than about twenty persons. This leaves more than 700 shareholders and 8,000 shares. Averaged out this would mean holdings of 10–12 shares, or investments of little more than £100. Some shareholders would have been very small investors indeed, considering that at the final meeting in May 1895 William Turton refers with sympathy to the plight of a 'smaller shareholder' who had 'only 60 shares'. Judging from the attendance at meetings a great many smaller shareholders were keen followers of the LTC.

Shareholders who participated in meetings were generally supportive and good-humoured. A few spoiling motions and amendments to the board's motions were proposed. Often these were for a slightly higher dividend; these were usually lost, with occasionally only a single voice in support. In February 1877 Vice-Chairman Eddison claimed that LTC 'paid the steadiest dividend of any tramway company'. Some shareholders' names crop up repeatedly over a period, such as Mr Hatch (1877–85) and Councillor Petty (1880–87). There are other recurring names: Mr Smyth, Mr Nussey, Mr Busby junior, Alderman Elmsley (1888), Thomas Hammond, Mr Brown (1892). Only one is reported as having been totally out of order. This was a Mr Butterfield who in 1887 repeatedly used abusive language and called William Wharam a liar.

Wharam responded long-sufferingly, and William Turton seems to have calmed things down.

Shareholders were primarily concerned with the size of the annual dividends. We have the figures for most years. The overall mean is 5 per cent per annum. This compares with a steady 6 per cent for the York Tramways Company. The early years 1873–81 were generally good at 4.7–6 per cent per annum. The next five years were poor, 'disappointing' as the chairman said, with a mean of just 3.5 per cent. Things picked up well with the introduction of steam engines on some routes, and in one year, 1889, 6.5 per cent was reached. The original optimistic forecast was for 11 per cent. This became a shibboleth invoked by shareholders over the years but was never in sight. In 1893 when the company had begun running down, a nil dividend was declared and voted through, though this meant a transfer to reserves and was followed by 6 per cent in the first half of the following year.

At the end, the shareholders, if they had stayed the course, had received an average annual income of 5 per cent on their investment in £10 shares. For the present reader it is most important to emphasise that this was tax free, and in a time of generally zero inflation. Given low taxation and inflation, the numbers for interest rates, dividends, return from bonds and consoles etc. were all low. Given the relative stability of share-holding in LTC, the rate must have seemed tolerable, if not thrilling. To anticipate, when the LTC was wound up shareholders were to receive only £5 10s for each of their £10 shares. It had been carefully managed. But it made few people rich.

There is scarcely any evidence of LTC's relations with bankers. There was always a London bank and London based solicitors. Occasionally Turton travelled to London for meetings. He most likely stayed at the new Northern Hotel, King's Cross, or the Midland Hotel at St Pancras.

PASSENGERS

Trams are for passengers of course. There has probably never been a time in this country when people using public transport have been content. The service is not available, is inconvenient or infrequent. The fares are too high. The cars are not comfortable, clean or accessible. Members of staff are not as polite and considerate as they should be. The drivers sometimes act dangerously. There are too many other road users. The company is not interested in modernisation and development.

We have already met some passengers and know of their concerns. The local news-papers regularly published letters from critical and dissatisfied customers. There are many complaints about the behaviour of other passengers, especially for drunkenness and abusive language. One correspondent argues strongly for a first class carriage for 'the better class of passenger who would be willing to pay more'. In the early days the dress and comportment of drivers and conductors comes in for adverse comment, but Wharam's discipline overcame this weakness. The most frequent criticisms are of the

TRAMWAY

DINING ROOMS,

Entrance adjoining Tramway Waiting Rooms.

BOAR LANE,

WHERE YOU CAN OBTAIN

The Best Dinner in Leeds.

LIST OF PRICES.

DINNER FROM THE JOINT, including Vegetables and
Bread   -   -   -   -   -   - **10d.**

CHOP OR STEAK, including Vegetables and Bread   -   **1s.**

TEA, with Muffin or Bread and Butter   -   -   - **4d.**

„   Cold Meat   -   -   -   -   - **10d.**

„   Chop or Steak -   -   -   -   - **1s.**

Broiled Ham and Eggs, Welsh Rarebits, Cheese, Salads, &c.

NOTE THE ADDRESS,

Adjoining Tramway Waiting Rooms

BOAR LANE, LEEDS.

H. HARPER, Proprietor

N.B.--CHOICE CIGARS.

Tramway Dining Rooms menu from an almanac of 1877.

condition of the track. These start very early on and reach a crescendo as the track ages and steam engines and other road users stress the system.

Passengers must have been aware of the possible dangers of riding on trams. Surprisingly there seem to have been no fatalities among passengers during the tenure of the LTC. Shareholders meetings occasionally reported accidents to street users or joy riders. The most serious accident I have come across was in Huddersfield when on 3 July 1883 a tram going too fast down hill left the tracks. three passengers on top were killed and fifteen injured. The driver was held responsible.

Passengers were in close physical contact with drivers and horses. They knew many of them well, men and horses, and affectionately. They could observe their working conditions and chatted with them, sometimes sitting beside them on the slow journey into town. So it is not surprising that there are instances of reproof of the LTC for over-working both staff and horses. Organised groups of ratepayers usually campaigned for their own convenience and comfort. The LTC staff increasingly had the attention of the growing Trade Union movement and other radicals who were working for better pay and working conditions, and shorter hours. They had support from the radical and liberal newspaper the *Leeds Mercury*. The horses had the backing of the very respect-

View of Briggate looking north with trams and other horse-drawn vehicles c. 1880.

able and newly influential Royal Society for the Prevention of Cruelty to Animals, and its many supporters. We shall return to this.

Passengers' experiences on trams soon began to contribute to a sort of humorous folklore of images and anecdotes. Murray's book on the horse trams of York has some cartoon postcards of this genre. One shows a three-horse team being urged uphill by a small boy. There is a sign on the carriage that reads:

Will Ladies remain seated when hill is reached? Gentlemen should get out and wait at the top.

Another is more elaborate. It shows a completely exhausted horse drawing a carriage that bears several mottos; inside it reads, 'To be raffled: 5 tram cars'. On the outside, the first on the top deck, the second on the lower, it reads:

Passengers left behind may get there first.

Passengers desiring to sleep should instruct the conductor at what time they are to be awakened.

People vote with their feet, we say, or by not using their feet. Most people continued to walk to work and recreation. With the expansion of the town into suburbs, mainly still for the middle classes, this became more of a challenge. There was still a penny bus service on many routes, and this became serious competition for LTC. A person might walk and ride to save fares. Within about seven years of operation in 1879, four million passenger journeys were made. This was about fifteen times the population of Leeds. This seems a lot of people, at first sight. However, a rough assessment of the number of people who commuted from outlying areas daily, maybe six return journeys a week for most of the year, suggests that four million journeys could have been made by fewer that 100,000 people, maybe no more than 60,000 or 15 per cent of the population. This was not mass transit. Photographs show a preponderance of male passengers, often wearing hard hats (top hats and bowlers) not the predominantly soft caps of the working classes. In 1885 the number of journeys was reported to be 6,382,200 and there was even a slight decline thereafter. In any case the horse-drawn tram system did not expand much after that date. The great expansion in services, lower fares and increase in number of passengers came in the late 1890s and early twentieth century following municipalisation. This pattern was not invariably found in other towns where Turton and Busby ran trams. Bradford had a half-penny fare for 'workmen' or 'artisans, mechanics and daily labourers' starting at the earlier time of 5.30 a.m.

The walking population seem to have resented the tram passenger as this excerpt from a letter to the *Mercury* of 18 February 1881 about the poor condition of footpaths suggests:

I have been often struck by the smug, complacent, seeming indifference exhibited by the well-shod and warmly-clad occupants of the tram-cars, in witnessing the unfortunate outsiders toiling and moiling through the slush, who are in too may cases, badly shod and thinly clad. Let us hope that the well-to-do will lend their aid to this needful road reform ... [Signed] NOT A SHAREHOLDER IN ANY TRAM-CAR COMPANY

Gordon Stowell in his semi-fictionalised social history of Chapeltown (*Button Hill*) gives an excellent account of the meaning of the tram for its passengers:

It is impossible to overstress the fundamental importance of the trams. The whole history of Button Hill [Chapeltown] from start to finish is closely interwoven with the history of its tram-service. Indeed, it is not too much to say that, without the tram Button hill would have had no history. For social evolution depends largely on the history of transport, and it was the invention of the road-tramway which made practicable the idea of the modern residential middle-middle-class suburb. The essence of such a suburb is that it shall be, as Button Hill was, at once clear of slums and soot and noise, and yet not so far as to render the daily journey to town tiresome or expensive. And in the nineteenth century you could only fulfil these conditions exactly with the aid of trams. Whenever a town gave birth to a new suburb, the umbilical cord was a tramline.

The trams of Button Hill were, of course, horse-drawn vehicles. The extent of a suburban builder's activity was rigidly conditioned by that fact. That is why no one had yet built to the north of the Bentham Arms [The Queen's Arms]. Button Hill was essentially a horse-power suburb.

MANAGER

The first manager of the LTC was William Bulmer, who had been mentioned as a potential director. He left on 3 March 1877 to take up a post as Chief of the Manchester and Salford Tramways Company, another Turton and Busby concern. In 1878 he was involved with Turton in promoting trams in Liverpool. There were 700 applicants for his job. Mathias Smith was appointed but remained only about six months before being replaced by William Wharam as secretary and manager. This coincides exactly with the start of Turton's long tenure as chairman. Turton said at the time 'The Directors were not sorry of the change they had made'.

William Wharam is a major contributor to the history of Leeds Tramways and not just the LTC. The 1871 census gives him as head of household aged 36 in Headingley, with his wife Rebecca (28) and sons William (5) and Samuel (3) and an elderly boarder. He was a railway clerk, presumably quite a senior one. In his youth he was reckoned to be a respectable athlete and skater. He had relevant management experience in the railway system, and must have been familiar with many of the kinds of operational issues that affected the tramways: rolling stock, routes, timetables, staff, ticketing and so on. Although a single shareholder once criticised him in the early days for not knowing enough about horses – which was possibly true at the time – he is said to have developed a good knowledge of them, no doubt tutored by Turton. His obituary in the *Yorkshire Post* says that he was a strong disciplinarian but that in private life he was 'the personification of geniality and he counted his friends by the score'. He accompanied Turton on many of his tours of inspection outside Leeds.

William Wharam moved in the 1880s to live at No. 41 Sholebrooke Avenue, off Chapeltown Road in Potternewton, just north of Hayfield House. This was a newly built street of comfortable middle to 'upper-middle' class houses, many of which had mews coach houses. This made him a close neighbour of William Turton and soon of other members of the family, as we shall see. In the 1891 census, his sons William (25) and Samuel (23) were still unmarried and they had one resident servant. Samuel provided veterinary services for LTC, and in 1901 he is still listed as a veterinary surgeon, unmarried and living with his parents.

Wharam remained secretary and manager of LTC until the corporation takeover. The newly municipalised company kept him on as manager until his resignation on 20 January 1902, at the age of 67. He successfully managed the transition of the Leeds tramway system to electric traction. But his management style began to come under criticism for not being up-to-date by the late 1890s. The first strike by Leeds tramway workers took place on his watch, for which he received some blame. His salary at the LTC was £450 per annum. It is hard for a reader in the twenty-first century to understand that this remained his salary until he resigned on 20 July 1902. This was in spite of the fact that he had successfully managed the introduction of electric trams. His successor J.B. Hamilton received a salary of £900 as 'Leeds Traffic Manager'. He was to hold the post from 1902–25 and was awarded a CBE.

Wharam was reluctant to resign even at the end and he had bluntly refused to do so a few years before. His letter of resignation recognised that apart from his age – though he still felt vigorous – there were new developments that might call for a new hand on the tiller. Just over a year after his resignation, aged 68, he left home early on 24 February 1903 to catch the 7.30 a.m. tram from Reginald Terrace. He had a heart attack on the tram and died soon after reaching Louis Street on Chapeltown Road.

OFFICE AND DEPOT STAFF

We hear very little of Wharam's office staff. There seems to have been no significant other senior management figures. There were of course a chief cashier and bookkeepers, clerks and other staff in the small LTC offices in Boar Lane, and in some of the depots.

The depots would each have a depot manager, inspector, foreman, chief horse-keeper, blacksmith and other craftsmen: saddlers, shoe smiths or farriers, coachbuilders, carpenters, painters and others. Some of them were concentrated in certain depots that specialised for instance in saddlery or coachwork. They in turn might have assistants, perhaps apprentices learning a trade. These are sometimes referred to as 'boys' and would include the stable boys; the lamp boys who prepared the lamps carried fore and aft by each tram; the sand, salt and gravel boys; the point shifters; and then there were the general labourers: sweepers, cleaners and humpers of grain and other provender.

DRIVERS AND CONDUCTORS

Those members of staff who have pride of place in the LTC story are the drivers and conductors, or guards as the latter tended to be called at first. Soper pays tribute to horse tram and horse bus drivers:

> The horse bus driver, like the stagecoach driver before him, was a highly respected person. To drive a three-horse bus required a great deal of skill and the passengers who came down with the driver each morning and returned each night sought a seat alongside him, especially if there was a 'funny' [or awkward] horse in the team.

There were a few complaints about the behaviour of drivers and conductors. This was mainly in the early years before stricter codes of conduct had been devised or enforced. Offences were not grave: impoliteness, refusing to stop when hailed, allowing over-crowding and so on. There are quite isolated cases of speeding, illegal parking, and mistreatment of horses. The latter includes a case in which Wharam, a driver and a horse-keeper were summoned for allowing a sick horse to be used. The charge against Wharam was dropped and the others received a £5 fine each.

Claims for compensation arising from accidents involving trams are referred to in shareholders meetings. In a given year it might be noted that there had been no claims or liabilities. In other years compensation might reach £600 or more and have an effect on dividends. A few claims came to court, where either side might win. Most accidents and injuries were found not to be the responsibility of LTC. The company blamed the police for not enforcing byelaws, and for not dealing with the problem of young children jumping on and off moving trams, causing injury to themselves.

The main issues were to do with pay and conditions of work. There were scales of wages in a range of from 5s 4d for a senior driver to 2s for an assistant in a depot per working day. Wages were not paid or reckoned by the hour, so the length of the working day was of crucial concern. The highest wage went to the steam tram drivers, who commanded a slight premium over the horse tram driver. Drivers received more than conductors. Inexperienced drivers and conductors might receive only 3s 6d and 3s per day respectively. A full six-day week was the norm, with a minority of workers choosing to work a seven-day week. The number of hours worked per day was about thirteen, resulting in a seventy-eight to ninety-one hour week. The treasured rest day is celebrated in a Yorkshire rhyme:

Setterday neet it is soah sweet
An soah is Sunday morn
But Sunday neet it cum too soon
An soah does Monday morn

Leeds had played its part in the history of political reform and factory legislation. But under the LTC staff were not members of trade unions. The senior members of LTC staff would have been enfranchised by the 1867 Reform Act and made even more confident by the 1872 Secret Ballot Act which protected the secrecy of their vote and made them safe from possible reprisal from employers.

At a national level the Fabian Society was founded in 1884, by such radicals as George Bernard Shaw, H.G. Wells, Sidney and Beatrice Webb and others, to promote a respectable kind of 'evolutionary socialism'. Of importance for our story is that the Fabians were strong advocates of 'municipalisation' and what became know in the early twentieth century as 'municipal socialism'. They published pamphlets, or 'tracts', which had quite a wide national distribution and were an influential source of data and policy ideas at a time when there was little political organisation, let alone 'think tanks' on a truly national scale. A Fabian tract of 1891, which is a date of precise significance for our story, called for the municipalisation of tramways. Other tracts had called for an eight-hour day for all workers, a norm close to twenty-first-century practice, though for a six-day week. Fabian ideas such as these were shared by some radical Leeds Liberal councillors and public figures and by the *Leeds Mercury*.

The issue of wages, hours and conditions of work had been debated publicly from the very beginnings of the Leeds Tramways Company. The *Leeds Mercury* gave encouragement to the debates on its letters page and in editorials and special reports. During the 1880s public criticism and pressure on these subjects grew. Leeds had a bad time in the depression of the late 1870s and early 1880s. Nationally the Trades Union movement was gathering pace. It had been facilitated by the Acts of 1871 and 1876. Significantly in 1873 the employers set up their own national federation. By 1885 there were 207 trades unions in England; ten years later the number was to rise to an amazing 1,330. The Amalgamated Society of Engineers had set up a Leeds branch and was specifically trying to recruit tramway workers among others. It is doubtful whether LTC workers were responsive to this call to any great extent. But it is an open question.

A report in the *Leeds Mercury* on 14 September 1889 focused on the issue of 'workmen's trams'. It referred to Bradford trams, which was a system run partly by William Turton. Bradford had a service 'for the convenience of working people' or 'artisans, mechanics and daily labourers'. The LTC, the *Mercury* editor complained, did not offer such a service and had also rejected the notion of a half penny fare for any stage, type of passenger or section of the car:

'Workmen only' tram, Manchester and Salford.

For a period of seventeen years the working classes of Leeds have had this immense privilege withheld from them. The management of the Leeds Tramways Company will, in all probability, occupy some attention during the approaching municipal contests [council elections].

Two weeks later the *Leeds Mercury* had an editorial which called on the LTC to provide 'workmen's cars' and, significantly, 'relief' on the number of hours worked by tramway employees. Currently, the editorial states, the morning departure times of the trams are from 7.42 to 8.00 a.m., and the last times at night 11.00 p.m., 11.30 on Saturdays. It called for a daily service, except Sunday, from 5.30 a.m. until 11.30 p.m. This eighteen-hour period would permit two nine-hour shifts to be worked. The editorial further raises the question of municipalisation, which they know is on the cards from 1892.

Several interventions at this time refer to the case of Huddersfield Tramways which was the nearest example in the north of a system controlled by the corporation. Apparently a good service was compatible with shorter hours and profitability. The strongest criticisms consistently used the expression 'tramway slaves' to refer to LTC staff – and those of other privately run tramways – especially the more visible drivers and conductors. This was the most intense criticism of the LTC and it goaded William Turton, who was seldom provoked, into a masterly response. Perhaps the final straw – and he knew about overloading horses – was when the Conservative *Yorkshire Post* proposed in its issue of 16 October 1889 a modest change from six days per week with one Sunday worked in two, to six days per week for all workers. It proposed an extra 5s per month to compensate to some extent for the slight reduction in income, if a better return for the work performed. It supported the idea of workmen's cars from 5.30 a.m. Monday to Saturday. The report summarised the average wages per day of LTC staff as follows:

Steam drivers 5s – 5s 4d

Horse drivers 4s – 5s

Conductors 3s – 9s

It reckoned that most drivers earned 30–35s per week and most conductors 25–26s per week. It further pointed out that many of these workers had been with LTC for six years and some for seventeen to eighteen years, from the very start. Interestingly, it says that these wages are higher than 'accomplished clerks, who also worked long hours'.

Turton reacted to this very public and insistent criticism at a special meeting a few weeks later. 'He needed to explain', he said. Since this is an important aspect of the social history of the LTC and Turton's involvement, I record this in some detail. We can be sure that Wharam was responsible for assembling the facts, but Turton's presentation was crucial. The wages and times worked at LTC were as follows:

Wages of Leeds Tramways Company staff
33 horse drivers 8 @ 5s per day working 7 days per week [£1 15s]
22 @ 4s 3d " " 6 " " [£1 5s 6d]
8 @ 3s 6d " " 6 " " [£1 1s]
50 guards 6 @ 3s 9d per day working 7 days per week [£1 6s 3d]
or 6 " " [£1 2s 6d]
14 @ 3s 6d " " 7 " " [£1 4s 6d]
working 7 days per week or
or 6 " " [£1 1s]
30 @ 3s " " working 7 days per week [£1 1s]
or 6 " " [18s]
8 steam tram drivers (Headingley route; others differed slightly)
3 @ 5s 4d per day 7 days per week [£1 17s 4d]
6 " " (£1 11s) 1 @ 5s 2d " 7 [£1 16s 2d]
6 [£1 11s]
1 @ 5s " 7 [£1 15s]

6 [£1 10s]	
3 @ 4s 8d " 7 [£1 12s 8d]	
6 [£1 8s]	

It was not stated how many steam drivers worked seven or six days. Those who worked seven days worked a thirteen-hour day. Those working six days worked a 13.75–hour day. Lower rates were paid to younger and less experienced staff, whose rates would increase in time. Seven day working was voluntary. Steam engine drivers had a weekly 'shed day' for cleaning and oiling which might take only three to four hours. All workers received one paid day's Sunday holiday in three (seventeen days per year). Boys and assistants received 2s per day. If anyone claimed to be working fifteen hours a day, this would be to include time taken to travel to work.

In the special meeting Councillor Petty, a shareholder, said that more should be done to provide time for meals and to reduce hours if possible, but he recognised that supply of recruits outstripped demand and all were voluntary and not 'tram slaves' as some newspapers had said.

Turton's reply reveals a nice detail of social history, and his own close knowledge of conditions. He said that men preferred to eat as they went along and have a day off instead. Their wives came to meet them with hot food at agreed convenient stops.

Leeds Tramways staff c.1899.

Shareholders no doubt included Liberals and Conservatives, even the occasional radical. The directors may likewise have comprised adherents of both main parties. In any case, this is as far as the board and the shareholders were prepared to go. As we shall see the municipalising of tramways led to better service and better wages and conditions.

William Turton knew his drivers and conductors by name. The following anecdote gives a good sense of his direct and hands-on manner together with a friendly intimacy. It was told by W. Taylor, a long-time driver for LTC, in an interview in 1912 (Soper, Vol.3 p.1,181):

> We were not very particular about running to time in those days (1870s) 5–10 minutes either way did not matter. I was once driving down to Hunslet, getting my dinner on the way, when Mr. Turton, Chairman of the Company, who was in the car, opened the front door, and said:
>
> > 'Nah, Taylor lad, hesn't tha time to get thi' dinner at t'far end?
> > I said 'No Sir' and he replied
> > 'Tha's a poor man as cannot knock 5 minutes extra out.'

Although this records the words of the driver as reported or written up by a journalist, it is highly probable that the spelling represents William Turton's own sound and patterns of speech. Thus it is the nearest thing to an original 'sound recording' of the man.

JOSEPH KINCAID

Kincaid was a London based engineer, with an office in Great George Street, London. He was a member of the Institute of Chartered Engineers (ICE). He had several years of experience with trams in London and elsewhere when the Busby brothers asked him to work with them in the North. He was the first engineer of the LTC and stayed with them for many years. He attended early shareholders meetings as well as regular meetings with the directors and council officials and committees. It is likely that in addition to receiving substantial fees he was a shareholder himself in some of the companies for which he acted. He was a skilful and progressive engineer, continually developing and patenting new designs and systems. His 'iron way' went through several stages of development, each one patented. We have already seen something of his work for LTC. He was to remain a strong partner of William Turton and Daniel Busby in many of their ventures in the north of England. Busby's perspicacity in choosing Turton and Kincaid as partners was a major element in the early success of tramways in England.

Kincaid was to work with Turton and Busby in Leeds, Salford, Dewsbury, Batley, Leicester, Sheffield and Newcastle. He also worked in Birmingham, Wolverhampton, Bristol, Hull and London, and in Adelaide, Australia.

GENERAL HUTCHINSON

Major-General Charles Scrope Hutchinson RE was the Board of Trade Inspector – an inspector-general – and would therefore tend to favour official government regulatory priorities. All sides respected him and he encouraged and supported private initiatives. He is present at so many critical conjunctures in the LTC story and also features in so many of Turton's other tramway ventures in the north of England, that an account is essential.

Hutchinson was born in 1828, in Hythe, Kent. He joined the Royal Engineers in the mid-1840s, so his life and work span are closely comparable with those of William Turton. He served in India. He was just the right age to be involved in the early years of railway development in India, which was of such strategic interest to the military.

Hutchinson returned to England in about 1870/71. Within a year or two he was an inspector of railways in the Board of Trade, London, with the rank of full colonel. This is his rank when he is a guest of William Turton at Hayfield House in 1874 for the opening of the Chapeltown line. His military rank was soon raised to major-general RE and his Civil Service Grade to assistant secretary in the Railway Department of the Board of Trade, a post which he held until retirement in about 1895.

He lived in Blackheath but spent much of his life travelling the length and breadth of the United Kingdom, inspecting mainly railways, and also tramways (horse, steam and electric) and canals. He visited Leeds almost every year during Turton's time as a director of the LTC. In some years he might make two or three visits. He must have been one of the most frequent long-distance train travellers in the country.

One of his tasks was accident investigation. He attended one train crash at Guiseley just a few miles from Leeds in 1892 when five people were killed and twenty-six injured. His most famous 'case' was the Tay Bridge disaster on 28 December 1879 which caused the loss of seventy-five lives, everyone who was aboard the train. The bridge had been completed a little over one year earlier at the cost of the lives of 20 of the construction team of 600 workers. He had inspected the bridge only months before it collapsed in exceptionally strong winds. He was one of the first and most senior of many who inspected the scene of the crash and reported. The president of the Board of Trade, who at the time was Joseph Chamberlain, totally exonerated him. Chamberlain wrote, 'no more competent, conscientious and intelligent officer could have been found to whom to entrust the inspection of the structure in question'.

Given that the period of his work at the Board of Trade (1872–95) corresponded exactly with the life of the LTC, Hutchinson features in the history of just about every early tramway system in the country in that time. He had a special affection for Leeds, which may have been his first tramway experience. When at the end he was asked to help assess the Board of Trade role in the transfer of the company he commented that 'it had always been a pleasure to him to advance the interests of the tramway system in Leeds'.

General Hutchinson, Charles, was a very close colleague of William Turton and became a good friend and companion. They were roughly age mates. Over a period of more than twenty years and in connection with eleven significant tramway companies in which Turton was director or chairman, they could have met on average every month or so. They attended tours of inspection and assessment together; they attended many experimental trials together. They stayed in the same hotels, and for sure they had a great many good lunches and dinners together.

16

GATHERING STEAM

We have already noted the rapid success of the steam-powered railway engine. In 1829, the year of George Stephenson's prize-winning *Rocket*, the Liverpool and Manchester Railway started service, arguably the first regular and reliable model for a passenger system on a significant route. William Turton had seen the first steam train in Leeds leave Marsh Lane station just a few yards from his home in 1834 when he was just 9 years old. Ten years later George Hunt, Mayor of York and known as the 'Railway King', inaugurated the Leeds to York service.

Experimental trials of steam traction engines for use on road and not on rails of any sort began more or less simultaneously with the development of the railway train. Some were separate engines drawing one or more carriages. A few incorporated the engine in the carriage itself. An example of this was a hybrid invention of Sir Goldworthy Gurney in 1827. This used an extended stagecoach frame with the engine situated at the back. Images of some of these experiments survive only in cartoons depicting alarming explosions. Gurney's invention did attempt a few runs on routes such as Gloucester to Cheltenham, Stratford to London and Birmingham to London. They could reach a speed of 15mph compared with the stagecoach maximum of about 10 mph. The service lasted only a short time. Nonetheless a Parliamentary Committee reported in 1831 that steam drawn carriages on roads could be considered practicable and safe.

Thomas Telford (1757–1834), one of the most senior civil engineers of his time, became interested in his later years in 'self-propelled' vehicles operating on highways. He took part in an experiment for a service from London to Holyhead via Birmingham. The pilot scheme started in Birmingham and stopped some 57 miles short of London. The engine travelled at 7 mph. This particular scheme and interest in this form of transport came to a rapid end. The reasons given included mechanical shortcomings, but this would not have held it up for long. More important were the high road tolls and 'vested interests', no doubt the turnpike franchise, stagecoach and railway operators, and landowners.

Gurney's steam carriage, 1827.

The 'Automaton' steam omnibus c.*1835.*

Turnpike charges were high and a large differential rate was imposed on steam engines. In 1840 a new turnpike law regulated the situation by stipulating 4s for horse transport and 48s for steam transport. No competition. Turnpike charges were bad enough in holding up the out of town tram system; they effectively killed off the steam carriage. In addition Parliament decreed in 1861 and 1865 that 4 mph was the maximum permissible speed and even so the engine needed to have a 'vanguard' person on foot with a red flag.

'Static' steam engines had a longer history of use in mines, mills and factories. Some specialised vehicles were allowed on public roads, notably the steamroller (without which the roads would not have been made) and later emergency fire engines. Farms used traction engines off-road for ploughing and other tasks sometimes in pairs drawing equipment across a field. The army was also to use them in a chiefly off-road mode. The *Parliamentary Gazette* of 1842 (p.69) lists the numbers and uses of steam engines in Leeds in 1831:

'Static' steam engine in use, Leeds 1831		
	No. of engines	Total horse power
Manufacturing and finishing of woollen cloth	80	1,884
Dyeing, washing and cleaning cloth and stuffs	23	227
Flax spinning	24	705
Grinding corn	17	282
Ware grinding	5	82
Seed crushing	5	160
Coal pits and locomotives	12	164
Iron foundries	11	145
Tobacco manufacturing	9	25
Machine making	8	68
Pumping water	7	18
Shear-making and grinding	2	12
Sawing wood	2	24
Paper manufacturing	2	42
Silk and cotton spinning	1	36
Worsted spinning	4	57
Carpet manufacturing	1	26
Other minor purposes	12	81
Total	225	4,084

JAMES KITSON, ENGINEERS

Leeds had an early start in the field of steam engineering. The greatest name in the field was James Kitson (1807–85). He is arguably Leeds' most iconic nineteenth-century figure and features large in our story. His engineering works in Hunslet produced its first railway engine in 1838, in which year there were only 490 miles of railway track in Britain. It was also the year of the first Atlantic crossing by a steamship. Kitson soon became very wealthy and a leading member of Leeds civil society, businessman, politician and philanthropist. He was a modern Liberal, alderman 1858–68, mayor in 1860 and 1861. He was a Unitarian and a member of the Ancient Order of Foresters (whose antiquity in Leeds reverts to 1790). He was president of the Leeds Mechanics Institute and the Leeds Philosophical and Literary Society.

Kitson was joined by three of his sons, notably James Kitson (1835–1911), who became the first Baron Airedale, and the firm flourished until well into the twentieth century. He started to build a steam tram in 1876 which was trialled the following year. By 1901 Kitsons had made 300 steam trams that were in use in Britain, Ireland, Scotland, Russia, India, Australia, New Zealand and Argentina.

THOMAS GREEN AND SON, ENGINEERS

Thomas Green (1810–92) set up his wire-making factory in 1835. At first he made simple wrought iron work, especially for fencing and railings and stable fittings. With some help from his apparently wayward sons he developed his steel and white-smithing engineering business at Smithfield iron works in North Street, Leeds. He introduced new specialisations and models continuously and was a close second to Kitson in the Leeds engineering market.

Thomas Green and Son were most famous for their grass mowing machines driven by hand-power, horse and steam and later the combustion engine. These ranged from models for middle-class gardens to those he purveyed to the Tsar of Russia, the Emperor of Japan and the great estates, hotels and golf courses of many lands. He patented a leather horse-boot to protect the fine lawns worked by the horses. He made other horticultural and agricultural machinery, rollers and scarifiers for the construction of roads, reservoirs and later airfields. Stationary equipment included boilers, ranges, cranes and household products such as sausage-making machines, meat safes, washing machines, rollers and birdcages.

Increasingly they specialised in steam engine locomotives especially smaller ones for use in mines and forests. In the twentieth century Greens were franchised agents for Denis motor buses (1905), Italian motor cars (the S.P.A. in 1910) and bicycles. They traded in most parts of the British Empire and other foreign countries such as Japan, Russia, Spain, Java and France. They ceased trading in 1976.

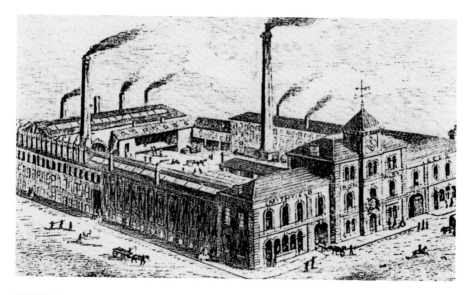

Thomas Green ironworks, North Street.

T.R. Harding's steel pin works in Globe Road; left hand tower 186–66 modelled on a thirteenth-century bell tower in Verona, on right built in 1899 and inspired by Giotto's campanile in Florence, built by Harding's son when Lord Mayor.

William Turton and Thomas Green were neighbours in North Street, close to the Smithfield cattle and livestock market and the Smithfield Hotel. The latter was acquired by Thomas Green in 1925 and is now a listed building, which is all that remains of the site.

In 1876 Turton engaged Green to develop a tram carriage and both their names are on Patent No. 4738 for 'improvements in stopping and starting gear for [horse] tramway cars and other vehicles'.

In 1879 Thomas Green became a limited company. Turton was the leading member of seven non-family shareholders holding five shares of £100. His oldest son, George, was also a shareholder as was his tramway colleague William Baxter (1812–1909) who became the first chairman. Turton became chairman in 1893, when there was a workforce of 600 men. He was a director throughout. Green's stepson, William Penrose Green, was chairman from 1899–1941. He attended Turton's funeral. The title deeds were mortgaged to William Turton.

Turton had a political connection with Green through officeholding in the Leeds Working Men's Conservative Association. Green left property of an unstated value and £63,695 personalty. This may be compared with Turton's estate which comprised £159,932 personalty and £30,760 realty.

STEAM ENGINES GET THE GREEN FLAG

We are of course concerned with steam traction for use on roads for passenger vehicles. This required engines and systems of greater flexibility, versatility and safety. Could the steam engine deliver on road rails? Unlike the train (which was such a British success) but like the horse tram, the steam tram had been trialled and was in use in other countries before the UK. British engineers did not give up however, and some of the technological and other limitations were overcome and circumstances changed. The success of the horse tram was evident, and this spurred the engineers on to design a small steam traction engine suitable to draw the tramcar, maybe even on the same tracks. In April 1879, nine years after Leeds had had its first horse tram, Parliament passed 'The Use of Mechanical Traction on Tramways Act', giving the green flag and removing the obligatory red flag.

The tramway men in Leeds had been keeping an eye on the steam-drawn tram from the start. The *Leeds Mercury* on 4 December 1871, just when the corporation had finally decided to go ahead with the horse tram, reprinted an article on tramways in the *Journal of the Society of Arts* that was strongly in favour of steam trams. It is hard to imagine the first tramway entrepreneurs wanting to change horses, or change horses for engines, in mid-trajectory. But they were realists, pragmatists, and even if it meant re-investment they wanted to keep ahead of competition and provide a better, more profitable service. There was also a general mood that favoured the consideration of innovative technology.

Cartoon of 1831 entitled 'The Effects of the Rail Road on the Brute Creation'. Unemployed horses are shown busking and begging. Concerns that the horse would become redundant were unfounded.

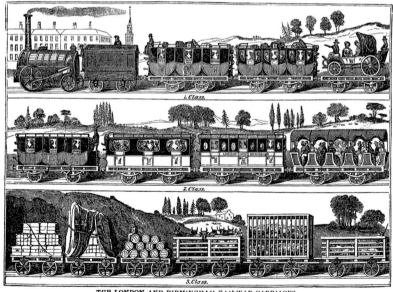

Cartoon of 1837 entitled 'Railway Classes'. Second class passengers are in carriages similar to tramcars; first class passengers are in stagecoach like carriages, with one grand family in its personal carriage on a flat bed trailer while their horses travel third class.

STEAM TRIALS AND TRIBULATIONS

At the February 1877 LTC meeting Turton and Vice-Chairman Eddison are reported to have observed steam trials in Sheffield. They had not been satisfied. Kitsons trialled an engine in Leeds on 24 October that year; Turton and others attended. A modified version of that engine was tried out on the Headingley tramlines in December. A certain interest was becoming manifest. There was no smoke and it was quiet. There was some steam and smut; and it frightened some of the horses. The use of steam by LTC was in abeyance. Meanwhile, undeterred we could say, Kitson produced several new designs and modifications, responding cleverly to the comments and assessments they had heard and solicited. Kitsons then built six new engines which were sold to New Zealand in 1878. One of these was reported to be still working in 1937 and again in 1985. There were still sceptics, including, oddly, the journal the *Engineer*, writing in June 1880 in scathing terms about steam trams as 'faulty copies of the railway locomotive'.

After the passing of the 1879 Act enabling steam trams, things moved fast. The Act was demanding in its requirements, for instance the permanent way was to be constructed with sufficient solidity to bear the increased wear and tear; the engine should be able 'to consume its own steam and smoke'; should be virtually silent, and should show no moving parts above 4in from rail level. A speedometer had to be fitted and also a governor that would apply the brakes if the driver exceeded 8 mph (Soper, 1985).

Major-General Hutchinson of the Board of Trade inspected Kitson's latest engine on 7 May 1880 and again on 5 June. Permission was granted for a trial period of three months on the LTC's Wortley line, from 14 June, and on 17 June 1880 Leeds duly had its first experimental passenger steam tram service. Kitson paid £40 per month for the occasional experimental use of LTC lines. In this way the LTC contributed to the research and development that was to benefit many tramway systems across the world, though they did not need such a grand motive. LTC in turn rented the Kitson engines at £20 per month. It is of interest for our account of William Turton as an entrepreneur that in February 1880, together with Board of Trade people, he observed trials of the Beaumont compressed air engine, which seemed to have some potential and might just have stayed the LTC's hand on steam engine development. But this was not followed up.

Instead, at the sixteenth LTC meeting on 7 August 1880 Turton reported on the Kitson trials on the Wortley line. He had earlier said that he thought the steam tram could only offer a saving compared with a three or four-horse tram operation. But now as chairman he said he 'had seen all the other tramway engines at work in the United Kingdom and none of them were equal to it [the Kitson engine]'. Vice-Chairman Eddison, later a steam sceptic, announced that the board intended to borrow £17,750 to pay for forty engines at £550. By February the following year two Kitson engines were in use on the Wortley line and had been found satisfactory. They were 'quiet and pleasant'. In the event the maximum number of steam engines on LTC lines was to be no more than twenty-six and the engines never equalled, let alone replaced the horses. The Headingley and Chapeltown routes were the next to be mechanised.

Kitson's engine 1880: Boar Lane to Wortley in twenty minutes; the last steam train ran on 1 April 1902.

It was reckoned that 40 steam tram engines could do the work currently being done by 332 horses with 53 cars and 6 buses. Thus we have the approximate equations:

1 horse power = 8 man power
1 tram steam engine power = 8 horse power [64 man power]

The introduction of steam trams in Leeds came ten years after the horse, at an early stage of tramway development nationally but when the system was expanding. The London journal *The Economist* in June 1881 (relayed in the *Leeds Mercury*) reported that the total length of tramway line in the UK in 1871 was 158 miles, and in 1881 488 miles.

The introduction of steam trams, like most transport innovations, had its enthusiasts and its critics. As so often there was a general reluctance to start with, followed by public approval or at least acceptance. Public enthusiasm, or possibly the promoters' public relations message relayed by some newspapers, was often exaggeratedly optimistic.

As we would now expect there was critical comment from the very beginning. A letter from one Octavius Eddison on 13 January 1881 in the *Leeds Mercury* referred to the dangers of the Headingley steam tram, though a few days later an engineer, William Hartnell, is in favour of steam engines as being quieter than 'the clattering of horses'. On 18 July 1881 a new Leeds Tramways Act was passed for the regulation of steam tram operation, and in early August Major-General Hutchinson arrived yet again to inspect the engines with Turton, Baxter and Walker. The Board of Trade imposed a 6 mph limit on some sections and 3 mph on corners. A few days later at the August LTC meeting Vice-Chairman Eddison and Chairman Turton were at odds, a rare public expression of disagreement in the board. Eddison said steam trams were proving more expensive and caused more accidents leading to compensation claims. Turton argues to the contrary that only a quarter of compensation claims result from steam operation. However, the Kitson rental charge for use of its engines rose from the initial experimental £20 per month to £37 8s 4d and by the end of the year to £110. They were in uncharted waters.

Engines were ordered from Thomas Green and Son, Smithfield Works, North Street. The *Yorkshire Post* on 4 December 1882 reports a trial attended by a party of sixteen gentlemen including General Hutchinson; Turton, who was a director and major shareholder in Thomas Green; Baxter, who was vice-chairman of Thomas Green and a director of LTC; William Wharam; and councillors, aldermen and other dignitaries. The trial lasted from 9.00 a.m. to 12.30 p.m. and was followed by lunch in the Queen's Hotel. Two Green engines were purchased and they started work on 1 January 1883, Boar Lane to Headingley. They are steam tram engines Nos 1 and 2 in the surviving Green's order book.

Brakes were an obviously essential part of the new machinery and their initial performance gave rise to serious concern. In April 1883 new brakes on the Green engine failed in Cookridge Street; fortunately 'the passengers had the wit and strength to get out and halt its downhill slide'. On 16 August, General Hutchinson hotfooted it to the scene and declared the brakes satisfactory on a return journey to Headingley, a route he was becoming familiar with. He does, however, recommend further controls including 4 mph on some corners and a compulsory stop at junctions. If it had been the practice not to stop at junctions, we can sympathise with other road users.

The steam trams were the object of close scrutiny by the council. The *Yorkshire Post* published an open letter from Turton to Alderman North on 31 May 1884 reassuring him about the speed of the steam tram. It is a good example of Turton's plain but articulate prose style. He had to do his own public relations work:

> ... we have at the present time four of Messrs Kitson and Co's engines running on the Wortley section, and two of Messrs Green and Co's running on the Headingley section. The two latter will come off in about fourteen days from now, and will be succeeded by six new engines now being made at Messrs Kitson and Co's, and will have all the latest improvement, with automatic brake power, which prevents the engine running at more than eight miles an hour, and when it reaches that speed it will be shut off to four miles per hour. This is self-acting, and cannot be tampered with by the engineer-drivers, so the makers say and has been tested by Major-General Hutchinson on the Dudley tramways, within the last seven days, and spoken of very highly.

Green and Son Ltd engine Wortley to Reginald Terrace, covered double-decker carriage, undated.

The Kitson engine on the Wortley line ran though a largely working-class area, where there were few if any horse and coach owners, and no complaints. The Headingley line, which ran through comfortable suburbs to even more comfortable suburbs and was full of 'carriage folk', was a quite different story. W.H. Maude in the *Yorkshire Post* of 18 January 1883 refers to 'this diabolical machine' sending up 'one continuous stream of sparks 10ft to 12ft long and covering passengers on top with pieces of cinder in so much as some put up their umbrellas to protect themselves'. There are other complaints about frightened horses, 'sickening fumes' and the 'jangling, wheezing, flaring' engines. Other correspondents see the innovation in a different light, hoping that the steam tram will finally put an end to the sufferings of 'that most hard-worked and short-lived animal' the tramway horse.

STEAM TRAMS IN SERVICE, BUT NOT FOR LONG

At the LTC meeting in February 1884 Turton confirms his confidence in steam, especially as being better than horses on gradients. But there had been these issues of brakes and speed. A councillor said he had observed a tram doing a mile in three and a half minutes, or 17 mph. It seems that some gentlemen regularly travelled with a pocket watch in their hand and a notebook to record speeds and the number of times a driver applied the whip.

244

At the next LTC meeting in August, it was reported that six more Kitson engines had been ordered, and soon there were to be ten. Shareholders were encouraged to hear that steam operation cost 6*d* per mile compared with an average 9*d* one farthing for horse trams. For LTC the main issue now was the poor condition of the track.

Times were hard in these years, the chairman said. There had been several years of depression in Leeds. Public soup kitchens had re-appeared. In August 1885 Turton reported a dividend of only 3 per cent, declaring that without steam it would have been nil. On the whole public disapproval of steam trams seems to have been lessening. Conversion to steam was expensive. No more than ten Kitson engines were still in use and the number of horses had not diminished. The next meeting showed a similar low dividend of 3 per cent. LTC was re-investing heavily and by the end of 1886 there was a total of sixteen engines, four of them new. Some fare concessions had been made, ostensibly to help 'the working population', but not by restructuring hours of service. All double-decker trams on steam routes now had a roof to protect passengers – as much against ash and cinders as the weather.

In 1887 things looked up again for the shareholders. Turton expressed the hope in February that they had reached 'a turning point' for the better. The dividends for the year were 5 per cent and 6 per cent. He said, 'they had good plant, a good town to work, and at the expiration of their lease he was confident that they would stand as well as any tramway in the United Kingdom.' 'The shareholders had had value for their money (cries of Hear, hear!).' Eddison, the steam sceptic, was voted off the board. The new Vice-Chairman William Baxter (who was, with Turton, closely interested in the manufacture of steam tram engines through their association with Thomas Green and Son) said that 'there was not a sounder or more efficient tramways in the United Kingdom'. Even omnibus returns, long a sideline, showed some profit though returns were declining year on year.

So the five years up to the time when the transfer had to be addressed were among the best for the LTC. In 1889 a 6.5 per cent dividend was declared. Steam trams looked likely to stay. A double-decker horse tram at this time might seat thirty-eight to forty, while a steam tram could take fifty-four to sixty-six passengers. The maximum fare for anywhere in the system was now 2*d*. This helped increase the number of passengers but still not really 'the working population' though perhaps they might be using the tram a little for recreation. William Turton proclaimed that 'it was wonderful that someone could ride from Boar Lane to Headingley Three Horse Shoes for 2*d*.' And departures to Headingley had increased from seventy-three per day before steam to eighty-two in 1887 and one hundred and five in 1890.

By February 1891, with one year and a half on the lease to run – it was to be four years in the event – the situation was as follows:

Overview of Leeds tramway working 1891	
No. of engines	26
No. of cars	69
Horse tram miles worked (1890)	287,000 (Kirkstall, part; Chapeltown; York Road; Hunslet)
Steam tram miles travelled	160,750 (Kirkstall, part; Headingley; Wortley)
Total miles worked	485,337
Total passengers	4,986,384
Dividend	6 per cent

The vote of thanks included Wharam. The shareholders were content.

This was the high point. In 1891 there began to be a decline in the LTC's standard of operation. At least this is how members of the public and the Highways Committee saw it. Shareholders were upset by the 'grumbling and growling' against the LTC. One wrote a letter to the *Post* on 15 August 1891 recounting that:

The other day I happened to be coming down in a Headingley car when there was a breakdown, and everybody got out amidst general laughter at what they considered a not unusual experience. It was quite humiliating to listen to the amount of abuse poured on to the Company as one travels along the line.

Amid the general concern General Hutchinson steamed in from London to assess the situation. He declares the Headingley line 'fair' and tolerable. The winter was severe and he returned the following March when he found the condition of the track had deteriorated. In January he had already required that steam operation should cease altogether in Central Leeds. At the February meeting Turton tried to make light of his exasperation at the cost of relaying track and the corporation's continual hectoring. He compared the early expectation to laying track with deal, whereas now they were expected to relay in mahogany. This gave rise to much mirth among the shareholders. But it was no laughing matter. On 9 March General Hutchinson ordered the Headingley line, the flagship line, the profitable line, one of the hilly lines, to cease using steam trams.

Bets were now off so to say, and Turton was blunt about the unattractiveness of investing any further in the system before the handover. By early 1894 the steam tram seemed to be doomed. The Highways Committee calculated the comparative costs of tram operation, omitting the horse tram altogether.

Steam system £117,292 per annum
Cable system £101,819 per annum
Electric overhead £90,072 per annum

WEAR JACKSON'S FAMOUS HATS, ALL ONE PRICE AND ALL FUR, 3/9.

THE RIVAL APPLICANTS.
("Which is it to be?")

First City Luncheon Bar, Briggate, Leeds.   W. H. WHITELOCK, Caterer for the People.

Steam or Electricity cartoon, a choice for the council.

The case for the electric tram had been made.

The steam tram had a short life in England. Existing tramway companies were not at first enthusiastic. As with the horse tram, legislation was slow in coming. When it did the engineers and the manufacturers, like Kitson and Thomas Green, were ready to go. The consulting engineers such as Kincaid and Hutchinson were at home with either horse or steam, even more so with the latter. Turton and his directors were ready to innovate and reduce costs. They were not enthusiasts but they assessed the opportunity in a business-like fashion and adopted the new technology to a certain extent. The steam trams were never more than half the total operation. On shorter flatter routes the horse tram could still compete. Steam engines were an expensive investment even if running costs were lower. They were very demanding on track and road surface. As far as I know no town or city ever had a completely steam operated system. Some never went through a steam tram era.

17

MUNICIPALISATION

COUNTDOWN

A new tramline to Roundhay Park seemed to be a wonderful idea to many. The LTC, however, showed no interest in investing. The park was a major asset belonging to the corporation and they wanted to maximise its social use value. The Highways Committee set up a Tramway Sub-committee on 12 June 1889 to consider the matter. It was decided that the council would invest in the track and then invite tenders to run the line on the usual twenty-one-year lease.

The LTC lease was nearing its end and the Tramway Sub-committee was soon tasked with what turned out to be a protracted process of negotiation and contestation. William Turton had referred to the 'expiration of the lease' in a meeting of LTC shareholders in February 1887. He assured shareholders that when that time came the LTC would still be in good shape and something to be proud of. Neither the council nor LTC gave the expiration of the lease much detailed thought for another two years.

The origin of the lease was a condition in the 1870 Tramways Act, which applied to the whole of England and Wales. The lessee obtained a monopoly for twenty-one years, at the end of which they were obliged to surrender the lease to the local authority, who might renew the contract or purchase the operation. In Leeds the Busby brothers had moved quickly and 'their bill' became law on 14 August 1871. They jumped the gun and started laying tracks on 5 June that year. By 13 September the lines were passed fit for use. Two months later the Busbys applied for a second bill to enable the transfer to another company, eventually the LTC. This became the second Tramways Act, which received royal assent on 14 August 1872. Thus in practice the LTC had twenty years of lease, which would expire in August 1892. In the event the final transfer was not to be until some three years after that. William Turton was chairman of LTC for the entire period of the negotiations.

It was not until its meeting on 7 March 1890 that the Highways Committee agreed:

> ... that a special meeting of the Council be called to consider the question of future purchase of the undertaking of the Leeds Tramways Company by the Corporation as the Local Authority in pursuance of the Leeds Tramway Act, 1870, and that the Council be recommended to pass at such a meeting a resolution to exercise its power of purchase as early as they can legally do so.

The town clerk promptly replied that it would be difficult to call such a meeting, and that the Town Council would seek Counsel's opinion. Alderman Firth (chairman of the Highways Committee) and Councillor Harrison were asked to form a sub-committee to follow this up. On 25 April 1890 they, together with Alderman Sir Edwin Gaunt, were to start negotiations with LTC to ascertain the most favourable terms. This was the start of a five-year odyssey.

Two months later the council agreed to purchase 'the undertaking' of the LTC but not 'the land, buildings, works, material and plant'. Each side was to appoint a valuer. 'The basis of the valuation shall be the then value (exclusive of any allowance for past or future profits) of the tramways undertaking or any compensation for compulsory sale or other considerations of the same type.' LTC wanted the valuation to be on a different basis that took account of investment costs.

For the first time the Leeds Corporation had built, at its own expense, 3.5 miles of new track to Roundhay for the use of horse trams. The line was passed as serviceable by General Hutchinson in August 1889, and the LTC was to operate the service while the council started negotiations with the American firm Thomson-Houston International Co. in 1890 to electrify line. The Roundhay line was something of a diversion from the main issue, although the Highways Committee made much of its new direct involvement in tramways.

Parallel to the intermittent negotiations, there was constant harassment, as the LTC saw it, over the matter of repairs to the system. At this time there were frequent complaints from the Highways Committee, the press and the public about the condition of the tramway tracks on several routes. For example the Highways Committee complained about the state of the lines in 1891. Wharam replied as politely and promptly as he could, undertaking to address the works. Later in October, however, he responded a little more strongly. The Highways Committee had requested a specification of track on the Chapeltown route. Wharam replied, 'the Directors are greatly surprised [read: thoroughly annoyed] that the Council should interfere to prevent the LTC repairing the Chapeltown Road ... My Directors are anxious to work amicably with the Corporation.' The LTC went ahead regardless. It had long been established that the council had powers concerning the type of materials used for the roadway but not the tramlines and surfaces immediately adjacent to them. The council replied rather huffily with a similarly demanding set of specifications.

THE YORKSHIRE OWL

TRAMWAY DISPUTE.

WILLIE F-R-N : "Nah then, just lot's hev hod o' that Tramcar !"
JENNIE W-R-M : "Gor art ! What ar' yer baarn to go' me for it !"
MOTHER G-LT-N : "Nar then childer lot me settle this matter for yer."

Cartoon depicting dispute between Leeds Borough Council and Leeds Tramways Company.

This to-ing and fro-ing continued for the next two years. The dilemma for LTC was put by Turton at the LTC meeting on 1 September 1892, when he observed that it would not be worth the company's while to spend a lot on roads if the council were to take over; but that the company was making 'improvements' (repairs?) nonetheless.

The LTC received a major blow in March 1892. The previous summer General Hutchinson, now assistant secretary at the Board of Trade in London, had approved the conditions of the lines. There had followed a severe winter. He was invited to inspect again in February accompanied on the occasion by members of the corporation, the LTC and solicitors Messrs Bond, Barwick and Peake on behalf of several ratepayers of Headingley. The General recommended the immediate cessation of steam trams on the line. It had deteriorated rapidly over the winter. There were broken rails, defective points and crossings, and paving was in some places three inches below rail level and sometimes above it.

On the day after Hutchinson's report was received the *Leeds Mercury* reported:

> As to the Tramways Company, there will not be a meeting of the board of Directors till tomorrow morning. Mr. Turton, the Chairman of the Company, informs us that he is anxious to accommodate the public as much as possible, and to-day he will take arrangements for the transference of the steam cars from the Headingley line to the Kirkstall section, upon which steam haulage is already in use to some extent, and the horse-cars will be removed from the Kirkstall to the Headingley section. At the meeting with the board tomorrow, Mr. Turton will ask his colleagues to sanction these arrangements.

This is a clear and good example of decisive 'chairman's action'. Turton in a sense deflects the blow by expressing concern 'to accommodate the public' and by making practical arrangements without suggestion of a climb-down. This was an astute move and diplomatic press statement in the context of the countdown to the end of lease.

As to the lease, the *Leeds Mercury* seems to have been ahead of the game – or was it flying a kite? – when on 30 September 1889, it reported that there was a council proposal whereby LTC would sell to them and lease back, including 3.5 miles of new Roundhay track at £296 per annum over twenty-one years. The corporation would lay 14 miles of new steel track on other routes. Its editorial on 12 October claims that a new deal, hitherto 'secret', is that LTC sells 22.5 miles of track for £1,000 per mile and leases back. This is in spite of a report that £59,104 is to be the cost of the new 14 miles of steel track. The *Mercury* claims that there is no public support for this alleged proposal. The *Mercury* is still suggesting the following June that a lease-back deal may be done; this time with a fourteen-year lease at £3,000 per annum for the first seven years and £310 for the next seven. Then it reports that talks are 'in abeyance'. LTC responded with a counter-offer, which the council turned down, as announced at the February 1891 meeting of shareholders.

The Highways Committee made another outline offer. On 23 July 1890 the LTC responded, requesting 'that at the end of Clause 1 of the agreement to be submitted to the council, words should be inserted to the effect that the lines of tramway to be valued to the Corporation should include the rails, the pavement and the concrete as laid by the Company'. But at a subsequent meeting between William Turton and the Tramway Sub-committee he withdrew the lesser part of the request regarding the pavement and concrete. The thirty-seventh General Meeting of LTC shareholders on 22 February 1891 was told that the council had not accepted the LTC's revised offer.

By this time the Board of Trade became involved. In April 1891 a substantial joint delegation travelled to London to meet senior officials of the Board of Trade. They included Councillors Firth, Ward, North and Harrison from the Highways Committee and Turton, Hargreaves, Wharam and Kincaid for the LTC. The result of the talks was that a referee would be appointed to adjudicate between the two sides.

In the same month the question of local authority taking over after the twenty-one-year lease was raised at the highest level by the Tramway Institute of Great Britain. The importance of the issue is well captured in a report in *The Times*, on 13 April 1891. Though rather long it is worth quoting in full (paragraphing added):

TRAMWAY COMPANIES AND LOCAL AUTHORITIES

On Saturday afternoon a deputation from the Tramways Institute of Great Britain waited upon Sir Michael Hicks-Beach, President of the Board of Trade, for the purpose of obtaining an authoritative declaration as to the meaning of the 43rd section of the Tramways Act of 1870, enabling local authorities to take over the tramways, or the appointment of a select committee upon the subject.

The President was accompanied by Lord Balfour of Burleigh, Mr. Courtenay Boyle, C.B., Sir Henry Calcraft, K.C.B., Mr. Ingram B. Walker, and Mr. W.J. Howell.

The deputation was introduced by Sir Albert Rollit, M.P., and consisted of Mr. Shaw, M.P., chairman of the Blackpool Electric Tramways Company; Mr. W.J. Carruthers Wain, chairman of the institute; Mr. J. Ebbsmith, chairman of the Birmingham Central Tramways; Mr. S.J. Wilde, South London Tramways Company; Mr. William Turton, chairman of the Leeds Tramways Company; Mr. William Mason, chairman of the Bradford Tramways Company; Mr. S.L. Tomkins, Croydon Tramways Company; Mr. J. Platts, Southport Tramways Company; Mr. G.B. Elliot, secretary of the institute.

Sir M. Hicks-Beach, in reply, said that whatever view the Board of Trade might take, it could not be binding upon the parties in the construction of an Act of Parliament. The position was this – that in 1874 Parliament chose to lay down certain principles upon which compulsory purchase might be carried out, and now that the powers of the Act were beginning to come into force, the deputation came and asked him to give an authoritative interpretation of what Parliament meant. It was absolutely impossible for him to do that. He could not give an authoritative interpretation which would bind anyone as to the meaning of the clause.

Then he was asked to support the appointment of a committee to inquire what the clause meant; but such a committee was not the proper tribunal. The proper tribunal was a Court of Law, and to that they must go. If the result of an appeal to a Court of law should be that the public were convinced that the law was unfair to the one side or the other, then there might be a case for the intervention of Parliament.

As to the difference of opinion amongst lawyers, they get different opinions of different lawyers on every conceivable subject, and he was sorry to say that he could not see his way to help them at all in endeavouring to bring tramway legislation into accordance with modern ideas, that was another matter and one which deserved serious consideration and required ... [illegible], but the period of the Session was now ... [illegible in digitised version] to begin such an inquiry, and he could not ... [illegible] promise with regard to next Session. Looking at ... [illegible] importance of the particular point which the deputation had primarily brought before him, he was ...[illegible] to see how the Courts of Law interpreted the ... [illegible] before making any general inquiry.

The deputation then withdrew.

It is noteworthy that four of the seven tramways companies represented were from the north of England and that two of these were companies in which Turton had a substantial interest: Leeds and Bradford. Turton himself was vice-chairman of the Tramways Institute of Great Britain. I doubt the response of the president of the Board of Trade made them feel that their journey had been worthwhile. But no doubt there was some useful socialising to be done among these leading members of the Tramway Institute of Great Britain.

The year 1892 opened with no agreement in sight and barely eight months to the termination of the lease on 14 August. At the February meeting of the LTC, at which there was 'a large attendance', Turton told shareholders that if the corporation did not take over within six months of the end of the lease, then LTC could continue for a further seven years:

He had no fear in looking forward to next August. The Directors had always dealt with the Corporation in a fair spirit and he could say that there had been no unpleasantness between the two bodies. People however would spread reports about things which never transpired (Hear, hear!).

A few days later there was an important meeting between the TC and the Highways Sub-committee attended by Alderman Firth, Chairman of the Highways Committee;

Alderman Sir Edwin Gaunt, Chairman of the Corporation Property Committee; and Councillor Teale. Finally it was decided to start formal negotiations for the sale and purchase of the LTC undertaking. An open letter from William Wharam, LTC Manager and Secretary, in the *Yorkshire Post* said that the directors were disposed to favour the council's view. But Wharam expressed some substantial reservations to which the council took exception. The Highways Committee said it was 'mysterious, sudden, and unlooked for'. It was not clear whether the directors were unanimous. This was no doubt the case. The LTC seemed to be waiting for the council to show their hand and policy before it made a move. The corporation was in the stronger position. The satirical journal the *Yorkshire Owl* ran a cartoon that indicates the relative strength of the parties, in terms of size, gender and action. It also hints at a bullying manner. The council had the ratepayers to satisfy; the LTC its shareholders.

There was another period of deadlock, until finally on 4 May 1892 the council formally decided to acquire the LTC undertaking in its entirety. A week later all parties met at the Board of Trade in London. Sir Douglas Galton KCB was appointed arbitrator.

At this point the LTC changed its tactic and reinforced its claim for compensation based on past profits, a claim to which, as Turton well knew, the council was totally opposed. The *Yorkshire Post* was unimpressed:

> As a sample of diplomacy, all this manoeuvring may possess interest for those immediately concerned. In the meantime, however, the public are not so much concerned with whether Alderman Firth or Mr. Turton is the more skilled at driving a bargain, as they are anxious to know when the borough tramways will be regulated with some regard to the requirements of the people for whose convenience they are supposed to exist.

Things went quiet once again. The corporation was keeping its eye on events elsewhere. Several of the tramway companies' leases were due to end, including the early starters in London and Edinburgh. The London County Council case was referred to a High Court to decide, based on the terms of the original Act 9, sections 43 and 44). A Leeds councillor was reported in the *Yorkshire Post* (22 February 1892) as saying 'Oh, there is no hurry, the London County Council and the Street Tramway Company are fighting our battle.'

As if to challenge this complacency, the LTC announced through its solicitors that it valued the undertaking at £240,136. This was greeted in council 'with laughter and ironic cheers'. But it seemed to achieve the setting of a date for the arbitrator to start work, in July. The two teams were, for the LTC Sir Richard Webster, QC (a former Attorney General) and Mr Cripps, QC; for the LBC: Mr Lockwood, QC and Mr Lawson Walton, QC. Both sides were supported by solicitors.

Sir Douglas Galton made a detailed inspection of the tramlines and depots. There followed three days of horse and tram trading from 25–27 July 1892. The major part of the valuation was of the lines, the operating system. The minor part consisted of the horses, engines cars, depots, equipment etc. The former was to prove the more difficult. The starting positions of the two sides were wide apart. The council valued it at £46,013 3s based on what it called 'the original cost of the tramway, less depreciation'. The LTC valued it at £155,000, based on 'the rental value of the tramway for 20 years less a certain percentage' (Soper, 1985).

There was great public interest in these negotiations. They made a good story. The humorous and satirical journal the *Yorkshire Owl*, in its 'The Week's Diary' of 2 August 1893, made its own contribution to public understanding:

> The arbitration proceedings were dull. Mr. Douglas Dalton is a perfect demon for facts and figures; but there he stops. The subject matter was too deadly even for Mr. Frank Lockwood's pretty wit; and his sketches in court were few and not at all spirited. The only thing cheerful about the matter was the big fees. Sir Richard Webster nets 400 guineas with his brief, and 100 guineas a day as a 'refresher'; the next Q.C. gets two-thirds and the junior two-thirds of his fees. On the other side Mr. Lockwood's fee is put at 300 guineas and 60 guineas a day as daily refresher; with the others in proportion. The Arbitrator of course gets more than counsel. The solicitors also collar neat sums, as do the shorthand writers; so the total cost is enormous. And it must be borne in mind that the Award to be made is by no means final. So far as I can gather, all that Sir Douglas Galton is to fix is the basis of settlement, to which both parties are pledged to agree. On that basis the case will be argued before a Lord's Committee, and the expense of that will naturally be still more enormous. But whichever side gets the best of the bargain, you may be sure that the public will have to pay for it.

The process of valuation was distinct from the overall agreement; each had its own timetable. Also in July the Highways Committee complained that the LTC solicitors Barr, Nelson and Barr, had inserted a new clause into the draft agreement. They suspended the agreement. The solicitors withdrew the new clause a month later. The council replied harshly that they would now proceed with a compulsory purchase and therefore there would be no need for an agreement at all. In September the Board of Trade supported the council in its request to use compulsory powers.

At the shareholders meeting in August, when the arbitration was still being awaited, the usually up-spoken Mr Butterfield pleaded for a dividend to be issued, for the sake of 'poor fellows who had nothing to depend on. If the directors were going to get £425, he would not give much for their feelings'. This question of whether the directors should make a sacrifice of their fees was to reoccur more strongly later on.

Meanwhile the Highways Committee was much preoccupied with its plans for electrification. It requested authority from the Board of Trade to convert all track for eventual electric use. We shall return to this in Chapter 19.

By the beginning of September, the arbitrator had reached a provisional and partial decision. He resolved that on the main issue of the value of the track, the sum should be either £58,000 (he had raised the council's figure) if based on the 'present' or 'structural' value, or £119,000 (reducing the LTC figure) if based on 'rental' value. As between £58,000 and £119,000 the decision would wait upon the outcome of the court decisions currently being taken with regard to tramways in London and Edinburgh. *The Leeds Mercury* – in what then passed for a front-page headline – announced: 'Leeds Tramways Award. Decision in favour of the Corporation'.

This was enough for the council to withdraw its threat of compulsory purchase. At the Highway Committee on 12 October 1893, an agreement was back on the agenda. The council then requested the Board of Trade for a thirty-year loan of £130,000 to pay for the full cost of purchase plus expenses, no less. The full council voted for the lower valuation on 9 November. The LTC waited still for the court decisions, which went against their position. On 29 November LTC retained the services of Sir Richard Webster, QC But the advice was not to appeal.

At an Extraordinary General Meeting of the LTC on 16 December 1893, one year and three months after the expiry of the lease, the directors proposed acceptance. A shareholder, Mr Eddison, bemoaned the situation. 'They had brought the tramways to Leeds, and were now asked to sacrifice them at half the cost.' Nonetheless, shareholders agreed to accept the agreement and valuation. LTC would be sold to the Leeds Corporation for a total of £114,590 6s 8d, including track, horses, rolling stock etc. Turton was able to announce a small victory. They had managed to achieve the high price of £35 per horse. Not surprisingly there was a very high number of horses in stock at the time: 368. The sale price was paid to the LTC in full on 2 February 1894, nearly eighteen months after the due expiry of the lease.

The Highways Committee had not yet decided, however, how to run the tramways from now on. The LTC would continue to manage in the meantime. At first they favoured putting them out to tender again. The *Leeds Mercury* was an influential voice urging municipalisation, or direct management by the corporation. It reported a meeting of the Leeds Propaganda Committee of the Amalgamated Society of Engineers, one of the stronger trade unions, which had resolved:

> That this Committee representing the eleven branches of the Amalgamated Society of Engineers in Leeds, learn with regret that the Leeds Corporation intend letting the tramways to another company, and hereby urge upon them the necessity of taking them over and working them themselves in the interests of the community.

The *Mercury* editorial was written to coincide with a public meeting that the mayor had called in Victoria Hall in Leeds Town Hall to discuss the issue. The council view expressed in the meeting was that 'the tramways had not been properly worked' by the LTC, but that with greater controls by the council a new company could work it better. The meeting was attended by 1,500 people. On a motion in favour of municipal management, only twenty votes were recorded against. The *Mercury* reported this was an 'emphatic decision for municipal management'. It was noted that the same issue was coming up in London, Glasgow and Edinburgh. Soon enough all these cities, together with Leeds, opted for municipalisation.

The ensuing half-yearly meeting of the LTC was a relatively calm one, with a good attendance. A dividend of 6 per cent was announced. But the directors anticipated that the final share value would be no more than £4 10s. This was the meeting at which William Turton corrected a shareholder who had called him a 'promoter' of the LTC. No, he said, with proper historical perspective, Daniel and William Busby had been the promoters.

The autumn meeting was reported in the *Mercury* as being 'somewhat noisy'. Turton was in the chair, with William Baxter as vice-chairman. There had been a loss of £307 4s 9d. Shareholders criticised the absence of two directors and expressed concern that there might be disharmony among the directors. Mr J. Busby of Liverpool questioned some items of expenditure. Turton replied that 'every farthing had been expended legitimately, honestly and straightforwardly'. 'But extravagantly,' shouted a shareholder. There was murmuring about the directors paying themselves a fee. Turton promised he would take no fee for the winding up process or during it, other directors must decide for themselves.

Turton explained that although they had instructed counsel to secure the £61,000 difference between the council's £58,000 and the LTC's £119,000 for the system, the result in the London and Edinburgh cases meant that it would be useless to appeal. It was not reported that if the LTC had obtained this amount for that part of the whole sale, shareholders would have received £8 6s 4d for each share.

The Highways Committee began issuing monthly accounts for the tramways. They were proud to report that under this new degree of municipal supervision, the margin of revenue over expenditure had increased, wages had increased and working hours had been reduced. At the same time they had made great efforts to promote electrification. This was part of the background too at the rather gloomy penultimate meeting of the LTC. It was held, exceptionally, in the Corn Exchange. There was a small attendance. One director, William Hargreaves, was absent. A passenger had died in an accident. The family had sued for £1,000 but £212 10s had been agreed as compensation. An old man, a shareholder, spoke up and said, 'It is come to this; I'll have to go to the Union House [the Workhouse].' Turton tried to lift the mood by expressing the hope that there was still an additional sum to be added to the share value, a few shillings perhaps.

Another shareholder once again raised the matter of directors' fees. Turton's response is revealingly frank:

I should have hoped they would have foregone their salaries; but some people think they have a right to be paid for the time they spend .... I think my co-directors ought to forego their fee. I have done my best to induce them to do as I did .... At the end of June 1894 there was £200 due to the Directors and £140 was paid to them. I declined to receive anything. For the past year there was paid to them ... (Wharam answers £80) [i.e. Instead of £200].

At this point the other directors present consulted each other and said they would not receive any *further* fees; there being little work to do now. This was clearly a minimal gesture, intended to save face in the meeting. A shareholder said, 'Then we understand that our directors will charge no more fees.' Turton replied, 'I understand so, but they have never said so before.'

The *Leeds Mercury* reporter obviously had a sense of the occasion, noting that:

> The Chairman again expressed his regret that the shareholders had not, in accordance with their expectations, received the full value of their property, adding that there were people who had invested their all in the concern.

The final scene of the final act took place in May 1895 back in the lecture hall of the Leeds Philosophical and Literary Society, just off City Square. There was a large attendance to hear the chairman's final words.

Turton announced that an additional 11s had been added to the share value, to give a final value of £5 1s. They had been bought at £10. He expressed his sorrow. He had received a letter from a man aged seventy-nine and another aged sixty who had seen the value of their savings halved.

Returning to the formalities, Turton moved that 'the Company do proceed to finally wind up the accounts and affairs of the Company with as little delay as possible'. At this point former Councillor Petty, a long-standing shareholder, spoke:

> Now that the affairs of the Company were to be wound up they wanted a gentleman in whom they had confidence, and he had pleasure in proposing Mr. Turton to be appointed liquidator, with full powers to wind up the affairs of the Company. Mr. Turton had been very generous in his reference to the Corporation. He [Cllr. Petty] did not feel so much of that himself (Hear, hear!).

Turton responded saying that 'he was extremely obliged to them for this vote. He was anxious to get the affairs of the company wound up as speedily as possible. He'd not charged anything for his service these two half-years and did not intend to charge anything to the end (applause).'

His last word as chairman was formally to move 'that 11s per share on the 16,000 shares of the company be distributed on the surrender of the certificates for cancellation'.

A vote of thanks to the chairman for his long service to the company concluded the meeting. In the event it was not until 6 February 1896 that the process of liquidation was completed and the Leeds Tramways Company ceased to exist.

18

TURTON & BUSBY
IN THE NORTH

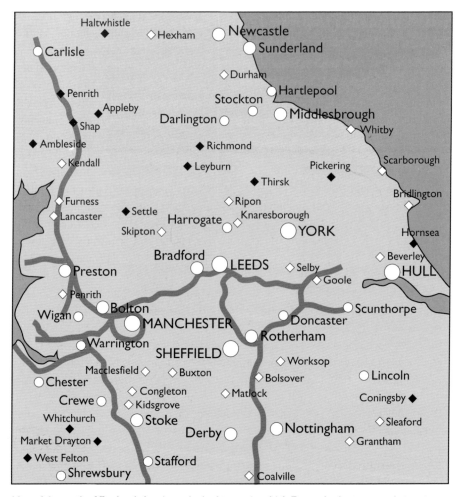

Map of the north of England showing principal towns in which Turton had a tramway interest.

Within a few years of joining the Board of Leeds Tramways Company, William Turton, together with his partner Daniel Busby, had developed tramways in more than ten northern towns in Yorkshire and five other counties. Turton was to become chairman of seven of these companies and a director of all. This was an impressive achievement for someone who had shown resistance to the introduction of tramways by introducing a bill in Parliament. Turton was also a director of the Douglas [Isle of Man] Electric Tramway Company and vice-chairman of the Tramways Institute of Great Britain and Ireland.

It was not trams as such that he was against at first but competition with his own omnibus service. Even before he became a bus and hackney carriage proprietor in 1866, at the age of 41, he had a good idea of transport developments in the towns of northern England. He knew the Leeds operators and supplied some of them with forage. He had heard of omnibus men such as John Greenwood (Senior) who had started the buses in Manchester in 1824, and the Busby brothers, Daniel and William, who started in Liverpool in 1834. He was to know these men and their descendants for the rest of his life.

Daniel Busby and his brother began to take an interest in developing tramways in Leeds in 1869. They soon came across William Turton as he was on the Highways Committee for the whole of the period from the very first mention of trams to the setting up of the LTC. At the beginning of 1871 Busby and Turton were in close touch with each other but in disagreement. By August Turton was on board and on the board. He had seen that he could not beat them, so he joined them, at the top.

Daniel Busby was then aged about 62. He no doubt welcomed a younger partner. Turton was well established as an urban bus owner with control of some of the best routes. He was a wealthy corn and hay merchant and knew all about horses. He was a town councillor with inside knowledge. He had standing and he had capital to invest. Busby appreciated Turton's personal characteristics too, intelligent, steady, cautious but not risk averse, loyal, courteous and affable. He persuaded Turton that there was a future in tramways at a time when not many thought as he did.

SHEFFIELD

Busby had experience of working with local authorities outside his native Liverpool. He also had experience of the complicated Parliamentary processes then necessary to obtain authorisation for each new venture of this sort and scale. His initiative in Leeds in 1869 was one of several across the country that prompted the 1870 Tramways Act, and it was his preparatory work that produced the 1872 Leeds Tramways Act. He knew the lawyers and Parliamentary agents in London. Before the end of 1872, he and Turton had acquired a concession to run trams in Sheffield, one of the biggest towns in the West Riding.

The London *Pall Mall Gazette* announced the flotation of the Sheffield Tramways Company in its issues of 26 and 30 November and 2 December 1872. The details are similar to other such launches, and so are of wider interest:

Issue of 4,000 shares at £10 per share
The Sheffield Tramways Company
£80,000 total capital

Directors
Sir Wilfred Brett K.C.M.G.
Daniel Busby
Meredith Brown
Major W.S. Stuart R.E.

National Provincial Bank of England
Joseph Kincaid, Engineer, 13A Great George Street, London
Office 3 Cheapside, London

The population of Sheffield is 250,000. Rental of the tramline to be £100 per annum for each mile to be increased if dividends pass 10 per cent. Capital for the construction to be paid for by the Corporation. Local authority co-partnership in the profits will secure valuable assistance in the satisfactory working of the tramway.

Messrs Turton (Leeds) and Bulmer (Liverpool) to provide land, stables, horses, provender, cars and harness etc. for £30,500, in a contract between William Turton and William Bulmer and the Sheffield Tramways Company dated 18 November 1872.

Each town tramway system, each concession had its own particular variations and opportunities. Turton was soon enough to become director of the Sheffield Company, but not before he was able to secure and benefit from a substantial contract to supply the company, much of it from his own bus and corn resources. It was such opportunities as these, rather than fees or dividends, that made tramways deals profitable for the few major players.

LEICESTER

Daniel Busby and William Turton were the first tramway entrepreneurs in Leicester, setting up the Leicester Tramways Company. Their first service ran in December 1872. The concession allowed the corporation to acquire the company after only twelve years. However, the company was to last until at least 1900 when Turton was still an active director. He had earlier been its chairman. Electric trams, run by the corporation, started in 1904. This company seems to have had a peaceful and successful life. One interesting condition of the lease was that the council would operate its sanitary, or refuse collection service, on the rails at night. Another was that they would call on profits over 12.5 per cent. This degree of initial optimism was not uncommon. Leeds, we recall, had promised 11 per cent but rarely reached the highest 6.5 per cent.

The service expanded steadily as follows:

Expansion of tramways in Leicester 1877–1900		
1877	17 trams	83 horses
1887	45 trams 228 horses	228 horses
1900	39 trams, 30 buses	375 horses

A quarter-hour service from 8.00 a.m. to 10 p.m. by 1874 was improved to 7, 10, 12 and 15 minute services between 7.30 a.m. and 11.00 p.m. by 1888 with a lower one penny fare. The popularity of the tram was marked by a pub changing its name from The Artilleryman to The Tramway Inn.

DEWSBURY, BATLEY AND BIRSTALL

The following year, 1875, Turton and Busby promoted and won the concession for the Dewsbury, Batley and Birstall line, just south of Leeds. This is an example of a tramway network linking smaller towns. They held steam trials here as early as 1876, well ahead of Leeds, and on 10 April 1880 inaugurated the first steam on-street tramway in England. The company was sold in 1902.

LIVERPOOL

The years 1877–79 saw more ventures successfully started. Liverpool was Busby's hometown; he had run a bus service there since 1834 and as early as 1860 had tried to get permission to start a railway bus service, setting up the Liverpool Road and Railway Omnibus Company Ltd. This company had eight family shareholders who together with the Busby brothers held 80 per cent of shares between them. They eventually started a small service in 1869. A new company was formed in 1878, The Liverpool and District General Omnibus Co. Ltd, which was to take over and develop all of Liverpool's trams. The promoters included Turton, Bulmer, Carson and Scott. Daniel Busby was a shareholder. Bulmer was a Liverpool man who had been until then the manager of the LTC. J.B. Horne, author of *Liverpool Transport 1830–1900* (1975), writes that Busby found Turton 'an energetic and enthusiastic ally'. He also notes that by 1895 Turton was 'by far the most senior director in the tramway industry'.

NOTTINGHAM

Nottingham was the next town. This took three years or so to get off the ground. After initial discussions in 1875 Turton and Busby founded the Nottingham and District Tramways Company Ltd and started a service in September 1878. An orderly take over by the Nottingham Corporation ended the standard twenty-one-year lease.

BLACKBURN

Blackburn's tramways had a rather different story. Blackburn did not even have a regular horse omnibus service until 1870. It was a late starter and moved directly to the use of steam trams. The corporation finally consented to the Blackburn and Over Darwen Act of 1879. Busby, Carson and Co. of Manchester and Liverpool contracted to operate the system as the Blackburn and Over Darwen Tramways Company Ltd. with offices in Castle Street, Liverpool. The tramway was operated on behalf of the Over Darwen Council. The track, which reached a length of 5.5 miles, was constructed by 'William Turton and Company Limited' of Leeds – an unusual formulation. Thus Blackburn with Over Darwen became the first tramway in the country to be authorised solely for the use of steam without passing through a horse-drawn stage. There were seventeen engines: ten from Kitsons and seven from Thomas Green & Son. There were twenty-three trailers: eight open top, eleven enclosed bogie cars and four open top workmen's cars.

The company experimented with motorbuses as early as 1898, when Turton was still chairman. It chose electric traction in 1901. It is likely Turton would have been involved in the discussions leading up to the switch to electricity. He was thus involved in the introduction or trial of three tram traction systems, none of which, in this case, directly involved horses. But 'the company led a stormy life and were in almost constant trouble with both Darwen and Blackburn corporations and with the law.' The causes of dispute included accidents, over-loading and allowing one engine to pull two trailers when one was authorised. Time may sweeten the memory: a 'tram reversing triangle' in St Peter's Street, Blackburn, has been preserved as a heritage feature.

MANCHESTER AND SALFORD

We have an excellent history of the Manchester and Salford tramways in the nineteenth century (Gray, 1977). In spite of the differences between cases that I have emphasised, this can usefully stand as a more detailed case study to give an idea of many comparable aspects of systems in other towns. Many tramway systems in Britain were promoted, or soon taken up, by men who were established omnibus proprietors. Just as Liverpool had its Busby brothers, Leeds had the Atkinsons and then Turton, so Manchester had its John Greenwoods – three generations of them.

In 1880 the board of the Manchester Carriage and Tramways Company included a formidable list of tramway notables: William Busby, William Turton, John Greenwood, John Howarth and Daniel Busby.

John Greenwood senior, 'owd John', was a tollgate keeper on the Bolton-Manchester road. He started a twelve-seater passenger bus service in Manchester in 1824; at 6d a mile it was a very expensive ride. By the time he died in 1851, his son John (b.1818) was running a fleet of 64 buses with a stud of 387 horses. In 1852 he introduced a double-decker bus service and a 3d fare. By about 1860 he introduced an extraordinary, indeed one-off innovation. This was John Howarth's 'patent perambulator', a 'three-rail omnibus' steered by a double-flanged smaller wheel running on the central rail. It was so novel and such a curiosity that there are several rather well known pictures of it, one of which is a colour painting of 1872. It is at the Victoria Arch of Peel Park, Salford, on its way to Manchester. There are ten passengers on top. It is drawn by two horses. It lasted ten years or so but was found unsatisfactory. The central rail was a dead end in transport history. It gave rise to an expression that was common in the Manchester area until the end of the century 'about as useful as a five-wheeled bus'.

Trams were introduced rather late in Manchester. Perhaps Manchester was content with Greenwood's omnibuses or he and others prevailed to keep trams off the agenda. But in 1875 a Salford Tramway Improvement Act and a Manchester Tramway Order were approved. By 17 April 1876 the corporation had accepted a tender to construct a line from Pendleton to Kersal made by Busby and Turton, to start on 31 May 1877 on a twenty-one-year lease, the rent being 10 per cent of the cost of laying the tracks. Interestingly, Manchester Corporation opted to build the tracks itself so that it could control the streets and their surfaces, get a better rental and have more leverage on fares and services. There was a raft of specifications and requirements. It was one of the strictest leases Busby and Turton had to deal with. The company had to provide workmen's cars at a halfpenny per mile. The sign on workmen's cars were removable at times in between the morning and evening use by workmen. Maximum fare was to be 3d or 2d on top. Children on the lap under three went free; children between three and seven, half-fare (allowed inside only). Morning departure was to be not later than 7.00 a.m., last journey not before 6.00 p.m. corporation permission was required for placing advertisements and for the type of freight carried.

Opening the Manchester and Salford tramways coincided with the opening of the new Manchester Town Hall where on 17 May 1877 William Turton, Daniel Busby, their associates and municipal worthies took refreshment after their 'inaugural journey'.

John Greenwood (the second) did not join the initial tender, but when an extension was agreed in 1878 – which led to the construction of another 20 miles of track –

he joined Busby and Turton together with Benjamin Whiteworth, MP and others. They were incorporated as the Manchester Suburban Tramways Ltd., later the Manchester Carriage and Tramway Company.

When Turton and Busby found the Manchester Corporation slow to approve expansion of the urban system, they adopted a cunning strategy. The local 'Boards of Health', which were the authorities in the districts outside the borough boundary, were keen to have a tram service. They encouraged Busby and Turton in every way to develop tramways in their districts up to the borough boundary, for example in Stretford, Gorton, Moss Side and Old Trafford. This spurred demand for extensions into the city centre. In a way this was a reversal of the process in Leeds, which saw a steady extension outwards from the centre.

There was a long period of friction between the Manchester Carriage and Tramway Company and the municipal authority. The most troublesome issue was the corporation's refusal to allow Turton and Busby to transfer their lease to another company. The two sides were still in dispute in 1887. Another cause of disagreement was the corporation's insistence that the company paid 10 per cent rent on any line the corporation chose to construct, regardless of whether the company thought it profitable. Nonetheless, when a Manchester Council sub-committee met in 1896 to consider the impending moment of option to municipalise they concluded that 'there was no town in the Kingdom so well supplied, and the tramway worked to such advantage, as was the case in Manchester'. It had been 'very profitable for the corporation' despite the usual challenge posed by the independent horse omnibus services.

Manchester did not switch to steam. At the turn of the century Manchester had 66 miles of tramway, ten of which still owned by the MCT Company. There were 15 tram depots, 366 cars and 3,876 horses. In the Greater Manchester and Salford area there were no fewer than 145 miles of track, under the control of fifteen different local authorities. Together with the Liverpool area, which it abutted, it formed the largest regional tramway system in the country. Electric power had been initiated in 1901, a year before the corporation takeover. The last horse trams were withdrawn in 1903, and by 1906 motorbuses were being trialled in Manchester.

A few days after the opening of the Manchester tramway in May 1877 the *Salford Chronicle* contained a lyrical, even ecstatic leading article which is so evocative of the excitement and optimism that attended the early days of the horse tram, that it is worth quoting in full:

We congratulate our readers on the notable circumstance of the opening of the new tramway communication between Salford and Manchester. It is undoubtedly the beginning of a great work, and we look forward from this auspicious commencement to the time when the main roadways of this vast civic and municipal settlement known as Manchester and Salford, will be interlaced with tramways, through which the teeming population can easily, and conveniently, and comfortably pursue their multifarious avocations. What a vast improvement on the shut-up, slow-going, crawling, clumsy things of a best forgotten past, which trudged from Pendleton to Manchester Exchange at three-hour intervals. Just so much comparatively favourable is the smooth railway roll of what we are to know henceforth as the cars, an improvement on the rumble and roll of the omnibuses. Delicate ladies can now, or shortly will be able to glide to town without encountering the danger of headache; frail old age, of either sex, can sail along the streets, as comfortably easy as if in a sedan chair [ah, the really good old days!]; while the commercial man, rushing hither and thither with his bag, the laggard telegraph runner with his impatient message, the homeward bound rustic late for the train, and many more in emergencies can take a lift by the way in the accomplishment of their pressing purpose with increased facility, expedition and despatch. The present foretaste of convenience and comfort will make the public in less favoured districts than are embraced in the regions of Pendleton and Higher Broughton impatient to exchange the easy-going locomotion of the cars, for the tumble and noisy roll of the buses, with their straw-litter matting, their intolerable noise, their plush cushions, and their noisy signals for stoppage or advance, and it is impossible that the consummation we have pointed out can long be delayed. (Gray, 1977)

NEWCASTLE

The *Newcastle Courant* of 27 December 1878 had an exceptionally full report of the opening of the tramway in Newcastle. The new system had been leased to Turton and Busby, whose interests in other northern towns are listed. The rent over the 21 years is 7.5 per cent of the £30,000 cost of the track, which the corporation had invested in, and the company was to repair the tramline section of the roads.

It further reports the inaugural procession of six cars each drawn by two horses, at 1.00 p.m. on Monday 23 December. William Turton and Daniel Busby had provided lunch at the Neville Hotel, Central Station, for some sixty to seventy ladies and gentlemen, including the mayor and the sheriff.

Mr Turton proposed the health of the mayor and corporation. He spoke in some detail – as he was wont to do – about the routes and their use and value to the public. The mayor responded:

Today the Mayor and Corporation with Messrs. Turton and Busby, had done that which prudent men ought always to do: at a time of depression they had prepared themselves for the day of prosperity. My friend Mr. Turton had talked about the water and the gas, he would say nothing about the water, but he would venture to say that if Mr. Turton was in the Town Council there would be no shortage of gas (Cheers and laughter).

A Mr Gray spoke:

> Although the lessees and himself were opponents for the lease, he wished them
> every success (Cheers). He knew them well, and the work they had done in Leeds
> and other places. He had pleasure in knowing them individually, especially Mr.
> Turton; and he knew that in every town in which they had worked tramways, they
> had given great satisfaction not only to the Corporation, but to the inhabitants. In
> every case they had worked the tramways honestly and to the public advantage,
> knowing that the public advantage was also to their private advantage; and he was
> sure that what had been done by them in other towns would be done here.

BRADFORD

Bradford was a very different story. Turton was part of an initiative with several other
promoters to start a horse tram service in November 1872. It was a natural early move
by the Leeds partnership. Leeds' close neighbour Bradford was a fast growing town;
it had already surpassed Leeds in the wool trade. It had had its eye on a tram system
for some years. As early as January 1857 the *Bradford Observer* had discussed the
matter, 'horse railways are popular in America, why not England?' Again in April
1862 the *Observer*, in a piece headed 'Mr. G.F. Train and his Tramways', argued for a
similar system in Britain. Several ideas surfaced; dividends of up to 15 per cent were
imagined. Nothing happened. Then in November 1872 Turton and partners advertised
a Parliamentary Bill for tramways in the Bradford area, mostly outside the borough
area. Their 'Bradford and District Tramways Company' would operate a superior sort
of 'Tramcar' and not the unpopular 'street railway', with the raised rails, of G.F. Train.
However, the ultra-cautious Bradford Corporation insisted on financial guarantees that
the promoters found unacceptable and in 1874 the project was abandoned.

Bradford, so close to Leeds and yet so distinct, was eventually to be served by the Turton-
Busby partnership. They were joined by William Mason, the former director of LTC with
whom Turton was to have long-standing dealings. Bradford Corporation finally got round
to deciding to build a tramway system in July 1881. It was let to Busby and Turton for the
usual twenty-one years, at a rental of £290 per annum rising to £300 after ten years.

In January 1882 the town clerk, borough surveyor, chief constable and William
Turton inspected the line in their handsome nut brown and yellow liveried cars. The
cars had eighteen seats facing inwards downstairs and twenty 'knifeboard' seats',
back-to-back, facing sideways. These were to be replaced by more popular 'garden
seats' in rows facing forwards. A few days later the inevitable inspection by Major-
General Hutchinson took place. He admired the state-of-the-art 'spring operated joints'.
There was a 'triumphal procession', by all of two cars. This was followed by lunch at
5.00 p.m. The service started on 2 February with sixty horses and five cars, soon
increased to seven. Three of the favourite teams of horses have their names recorded

forever: Violet and Fairy, Maggie and Daisy, Tom and Doctor. But already by October that year a steam tram service had begun. There was a cautious expansion of the whole system and the use of steam traction. At the end the company had thirty-three steam engines, twenty-nine of which had been made by Thomas Green and Son, of which firm, as we know, Turton was a director and major shareholder.

Bradford had soon made up the ground it was slow to occupy in the early years of the tram. There was a public demonstration of electric tramcars, with overhead wire and trolley poles, on 16 March 1892, in a snowstorm. Major-General Hutchinson attended; he was no shirker of duty in any weather conditions or in any part of the United Kingdom and Ireland. A trial electric service started in May that year. One of these trams was captured on a historic piece of ciné film in 1896. It was good for Turton's local reputation that the Bradford tramway was such a fine example. In 1894 the Bradford Tram and Omnibus Company was said to be a 'progressive' company paying 'handsome dividends'. William Turton was still chairman at the time of his death; the Bradford Company sent a wreath to his funeral. Daniel Busby had died in 1889, his older brother William died two years later. William Mason, the last surviving promoter, took over the chair from Turton.

SOUTH SHIELDS

The Turton-Busby partnership's final success was in South Shields and came after a gap of several years. No doubt they had kept an eye on this town from their Newcastle and Gosforth office. The South Shields Tramways Company was more of a salvage operation compared with the others. The corporation had laid an unusual 3ft 6in gauge track in 1883. The system had run into difficulties. There seems to have been poor management; and the managers were underpaid and poorly qualified, one being a former chief constable. The receivers tried unsuccessfully to interest Turton and Busby in buying up the old company. Instead they formed a new company, the South Shields Tramways and Carriage Company, with £10,000 capital, and on 29 June 1887, obtained a fourteen-year lease at £500 per annum rising to £600 after seven years. The corporation, grateful to have new tramway management, built new stables and car sheds at a cost of £4,000. There were 22 cars and so probably about 264 horses.

The people of South Shields had had to do without trams for a year. The *South Shields Daily Gazette* reported on 2 February 1887:

> [T]hroughout the town, there is an aching void. The absence of the cars has at least provided a little fun. An old lady addressing a workman asked the question 'what time's the next bus, hinny?' 'Six weeks time, mum' is the blunt reply.

Turton and Busby filled the aching void and ran what was judged to be a 'highly successful' company. It was sold in 1894 to the British Electric Traction Company (BET).

ADVERTISEMENTS ON TRAMS

Since this is a chapter on Turton and trams within a wide region, this is a good moment to append a brief generic essay on the topic of advertising in and on trams. Pictures of nineteenth-century trams increasingly show advertisements on the exterior. They are quite intrusive, but although we see them in the illustrations, they are seldom mentioned in the texts, and only in passing. I know of no attempt to reflect on this commercial and cultural phenomenon. I mentioned the case of Manchester and Salford tramway where the corporation stipulated it should be consulted and approve any use of advertisements on trams. Gray's valuable work includes two references of inter-est. There is a record of Turton and Busby meeting the Salford Highways Committee in May 1886 specifically to request the council's agreement to allow advertising. On another occasion John Greenwood (the third) showed the corporation some sample advertising boards for external use and assured them that they would neither obscure route names nor the windows. I imagine the authorities were also anxious to exclude 'political' messages – except of course patriotic ones at times of 'national' celebration – or otherwise offensive causes, products or wording.

The main advertisements were usually on either side of the upper deck, filling the whole upper side panel. Smaller advertisements appeared on spiral staircases and the front corners. Even so the company's name and route were prominently displayed. I have no knowledge of what income this practice may have brought in, but the fact that Turton should go in person to seek permission suggests that it was of significance. The images were almost entirely textual, no pictures, but the lettering, trade names and style were eye-catching and attractive. They were positioned and were of a size such that any passer-by could read them; and it was an increasingly literate society after the education reforms of the 1870s. What is more, they were moving images, slow moving.

The advertising was intended for the general public. This meant promotion of many products that everyone was likely to buy quite regularly, even if in 'penny packets', and which were being manufactured on a mass scale. Incomes were rising in real terms, with inflation low or non-existent; working people also had a little more lei-sure time. A famous Leeds merchant, who was just starting up, used the slogan, 'Don't ask the price; everything's a penny.' He was Michael Marks of course.

Some of the advertisements were very simple. The shortest was that lovely palin-drome *OXO*. The wordiest I have come across was this – some readers might not have read it all before the tram was past:

Neave's Food
Best and cheapest since 1825
For infants, growing children, invalids and the aged
"Admirably adapted for the wants of infants." Sir Chas. Cameron M.D.
"Highly nutritious." *The Lancet.*

At the end of the century, on 22 April 1899, there was an 'Advertiser's Exhibition' held in London. The list of participants included: Mr Joshua Sheldon, Chairman, Sheldon Ltd Leeds, omnibus and tramway advertiser; Mr James W. Courtney, tramway-advertising contractor, Leeds. So there was already a specialist niche, in Leeds alone, for tramway advertising within Turton's lifetime, a felicitous 'unintended consequence'.

In conclusion, for general interest, it may be fun to see some of the products advertised. It was usually for consumables and consumer durables rather than for services or entertainment such as are more common as I write.

Processed foodstuff
Cocoa   *Van Houten* 'best and goes further'
Cadburys 'absolutely pure'
Fry's pure cocoa
Tinned milk   *Milkmaid*
Nestlé 'the richest in cream'
Bread   *Bermaline*
Jam   *Ogden's* fruit and honey
Chivers jellies and jams
Bovril 'invaluable for invalids', 'a most delicious beverage', 'liquid life'
OXO
Colman's mustard
Borwick's baking powder

Patent medicine
Beecham's pills
Andrew's liver salts

Household, cleaning etc.
Soap   *Sunligh*t (Lever)
Hudson
Mother Shipton
Compo 'for washing everything'
Brasso
Oakey's Wellington knife polish
Nixey's black lead for grates and ranges
Zebra grate polish
Reckett's blue
Blakey's boot polish
Bryant & May matches

Clothing, shoes and furniture are commonly advertised and, especially in Leeds, are mainly by local manufacturers, rather than national brands. Advertisements for cigarettes and alcohol are infrequent, especially in the earlier years. Exceptions were *'Cameo'* cigarettes and *'E.Y.O'* whisky. Some minority interests are captured in *'Archibald Ramsden's Organs and Pianos'*; *'Walker Bros. The Leeds Cycle Experts'*; and *'Cycling School and Skating Rink'* on the Roundhay Park route.

19

ELECTRIC SHOCK

In the streets of Leeds the gas lamps were alight, competing with the gases and smoke from the same fuel that lit them and blackened all around. Inside the Lecture Theatre of the Philosophical and Literary Society the lights were out; not a gas bracket turned on, not a mantle burning. In the expectant audience sat William Turton with his eldest son George, aged eighteen in that year, 1867. They were about to see, for the first time in Leeds, the production of electric light.

Electricity had been 'discovered', in a limited sense, long before. The Greek *elektron*, meaning 'amber', indicates an awareness of properties of static electricity. A much-mythologised milestone in the history of electricity is the discovery in AD 1752 by Benjamin Franklin, with the help of a kite, of the electrical nature of lightening. In Britain at least the industrial history of electricity began with the early work of Michael Faraday (1791–1867) at the Royal Institute in London, of which he was director from 1826–62. In 1821 he had built an apparatus that is regarded as the first simple electric motor. Faraday continued experimenting until the 1850s, demonstrating the unification of the forces of electricity, magnetism, heat and light.

ELECTRIC TRAMS ON THE AGENDA

In the 1830s some early electric machines were in industrial use. In 1867, the year of Faraday's death, electric light was being demonstrated across the country. And by 1879 the possibility of electrically powered traction became a reality.

This happened on Turton's watch. Confusingly perhaps for the historian of urban transport, this was also the moment of the steam engine's bid to be traction of choice for trams. We have already noted the slow adoption of steam for passenger transport in towns, while on railways out of towns they were traversing routes thousands of miles long at ever increasing speeds. And when steam came it did not last long. It was to be the electric tram that almost everywhere supplanted the horse tram.

Turton and his partners took note of the development of electric traction for trams from early on. When the Leeds Borough Council began to take electricity seriously for a new line to Roundhay in 1890, it was about to negotiate the end of Leeds Tramways Company's lease, so it was too late for LTC to consider an electric option. But for some of the other tramway companies in which Turton had a decisive voice, electricity was very much on the agenda. In Bradford, where Turton was to remain chairman until his death, overhead electric power was given a trial on 16 March 1892, attended by Major-General Hutchinson, of the Board of Trade, who, like Turton, kept up with new developments. Electric trams were duly introduced to Bradford. Turton would have taken part in discussions about electricity in other towns in which he had an interest, such as Blackburn, Manchester and Sheffield. They went electric just after his death but before municipalisation. South Shields was sold in 1894 to British Electric Traction. As a corn and hay merchant Turton had conflicting interests. However, the market for horse fodder remained buoyant until the early 1920s. An ironic note is struck by the fact that in urban areas with tramway systems, other vehicles had to reduce the height of their loads. This made hay wagons less efficient.

Let us return to the first appearance of the electric tram. The family name and firms of Siemen have a pioneering role in its history. Karl Wilhelm Siemen (1823–83) came to England from Germany in 1843 and set up an engineering company. He changed his name to Charles William and became thoroughly at home in England. In 1883 he was knighted for his services to science and industry. In addition to designing and producing furnaces for the manufacture of glass, iron and steel, the Siemens were at the forefront of discovery and invention in electrical machinery, lighting and telegraph. The Siemens factories were state of the art, they were high technology employers of their time; their staff worked an eight-and-a-half-hour day.

Charles William's brother Werner von Siemen (1816–92) remained in Germany where he produced the world's first 'electric railway'. This was demonstrated at the Berlin Trade Fair of 1879. The scale and power of this model resembled a miniature railway in an amusement park. It could tow a platform with outward facing 'knife-board'-type seats for eighteen adults. Development of the model was rapid. On 16 May 1881 the first electric streetcar, or tramway, ran in the town of Lichtenfeld, near Berlin.

The electric tram attracted engineers and local officials from all over Europe. It was a good time to travel round Europe by train, in Pullman carriages and staying in magnificent new hotels near railway stations. Larger, modernising cities, especially where roads were wide and surfaces were relatively flat, were quick to adopt electric tramway systems. Berlin, Budapest, Madrid and Paris are examples. In 1885 Blackpool was the first British town to inaugurate an electric tram service. It continues to this day. Apart from major cities, seaside resorts were among the early adopters of trams to attract visitors and run along the coastline. Such sites were often also suited to various cable-drawn systems and rack and pinion railways to ascend cliffs and hills. These were introduced at about the same time. Cable traction proved not to be generally acceptable except on certain well-known long gradients, such as the famous San Francisco tramlines. In north London a smaller example was the cable-drawn carriage up to Highgate Village on a 3ft 6in gauge. This short service ran from 1884–1907 when it became part of the electric tramway system. It was not greatly profitable because people were not so willing to pay to come downhill!

Mention should be made here of another form of urban transport that arrived in the late nineteenth century. The bicycle in its modern form arrived from France in the 1860s and soon became popular with members of the middle classes. A Leeds amateur bicycle club was formed in 1876 and later The Volante Club in Leeds was even more middle-class, with patrons such as Sir James Kitson, Sir John Barran and Sir Andrew Fairbairn. Walker Brothers, a Leeds bicycle manufacturers, claimed in 1892 to supply bicycles to 'Leeds City Police, Isabella Ford's Young Ladies Union and the officers of the 8th Hussars'. At first they were not cheap. In 1883 a Penny Farthing bicycle cost £12 10s but by the 1890s a steady proletarianisation of bicycle use began. Until the combustion engine the pedal bike was the fastest form of travel after the train. The Leeds to London journey could be made in a day on a Penny Farthing, aptly named as the larger wheel was 60in and the smaller 15in in diameter. The capital cost was less than half that of a pony; its maintenance cost a tiny fraction and it could travel as far and fast as the rider could pedal.

William Turton lived at the most exciting and innovative time for urban transport in Britain, and indeed Europe as whole. Within the decade of the 1870s alone the horse tram started, steam trams were trialled and news came of a new electric form of traction.

ELECTRIC TRAMS ON THE STREETS

The need for urban transport had grown on a mammoth scale throughout Europe and elsewhere. Late developing countries were now industrialising and becoming highly competitive. Urban population was increasing at an unprecedented, and not fully anticipated rate. In Britain at least, the middle-classes had expanded greatly. They had the wealth and leisure, but not yet the private transport, to need to reach the new shopping arcades, parks and seaside resorts. Many members of the working class, and clerks and tradesmen, were receiving better real wages and more leisure hours. Attractive opportunities for spending leisure time and money were multiplying. These were often at the end of a tram journey.

New entrepreneurs and old were ready to seize the advantage in promoting urban transport. The British Electric Traction Company (BET) was set up as early as 1886. It was to become the major player and investor in electrically powered transport. The American firm Thomson-Houston was active in the development of Leeds' first experiment with electric trams on the Leeds Centre to Roundhay Park route, which started in 1891: 'the first electric tram operating on the overhead wire system in Europe' (Soper,1985). This was built on steel tracks similar to those used by horse-drawn trams. A proposal for an elevated electric railway had been considered and rejected.

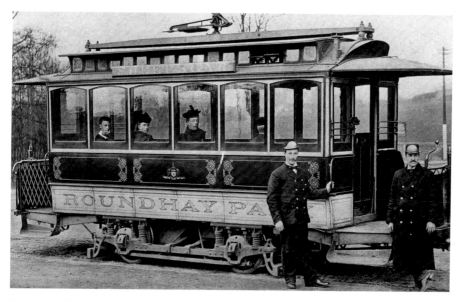

Thompson– Houston electric tram, 1892.

The early years of the electric tram are also those of great municipal activity all over the country. New municipal areas were declared. Local authorities were keen to take over infrastructural services. 'Municipal socialism' became a widespread reality. In the field of urban transport this momentum was of course helped by the government's requirement of twenty-one year leases for the original horse tramways. These began to fall in throughout the 1890s. Most local authorities took the opportunity to take over the tramways, and this coincided exactly with the newly available electric technology. Politically too, they had to be ever more responsive to the needs and demands of their electorate as regards transport facilities and working conditions in the transport industries. They invested more, paid their staff more, improved working conditions and the quality of service to services to passengers. This is not to say they satisfied everyone. They needed to respond to the claims of newly powerful trades unions. In Leeds transport workers held their first strike soon after municipalisation.

Several towns and cities in England experimented early on with a single line or so of electric tramway. The only systems of any size by 1892 were Blackpool, South Staffordshire and Guernsey. The latter was soon to be followed by another island attraction, Douglas in the Isle of Man, which is one of the very few old tramways still operating both horse-drawn and electric trams. The period 1892–99 saw the inauguration of electric tramway systems in twenty-six towns and cities, a high proportion of them in the north of England. Port cities such as Glasgow, Aberdeen, Liverpool, Hull and Bristol were among the earliest.

As with the tram, government legislation was necessary to enable full development of the new technology. In 1896 a Light Railway Act was passed. Ominously, in the same year a Locomotive and Highways Act was also passed. This has been called 'the emancipation of the motor car', and, one might add, the emancipation of speed on roads.

THE TRAM IN THE TWENTIETH CENTURY

From the perspective of the twenty-first century, there is a tendency to regard the start of the twentieth century as the beginning of 'the modern', with such iconic phenomena as Einstein's theory of relativity, cubism and the music of Stravinsky. By contrast the nineteenth century to the very end is seen as Victorian, vintage, old-fashioned. It is therefore appropriate to recall how much of what we consider modern technology, especially in the field of transport, was already in early stages of development: telephones, electrically powered engines, lighting and traction; the internal combustion engine and even the dirigible airship.

There is no disputing, however, that the period 1900–40 was the golden age of the electric tram. In 1900 to celebrate the new millennium, an 'International Tramway and Light Railway Exhibition' was held at the Agricultural Hall in Islington, north London. By this time there were some twenty-nine tramway systems in Britain. Between 1900 and 1905 no fewer than 127 sprang into being. By 1909 some 95 per cent of all British tramways were in service.

This is not the place to tell the twentieth-century story of the tramways, but we will allow ourselves a glimpse of the future. The following selective figures give an idea of the great expansion of tramways after the age of the horse tram:

Expansion of tramways in Leeds and England 1870–1927			
Date	Length of tramway (miles)	Passengers carried on trams	
		Leeds	England
1870–80	233	–	–
1895	982	10,500,000	885,200,000
1901	1,840	–	2,912,110,000
1909	2,526	–	2,659,891,136
1914	93,700,000	–	
1927	2,554 [Number of tramcars 14,481]		

Leeds Tramways	No. of daily services	
Date	Horse trams	Horse buses
1895	750	1,100
1900	1,500	750
1905	nil	<50

It is a truism that each stage in the development of urban transport systems overlaps the previous ones. The internal combustion engine was trialled for buses as early as 1898 and was taken up by some local authorities even before the end of the nineteenth century. A few adopted it almost from the start, just as a few late-starting authorities bypassed the horse tram entirely and opted for steam.

The first electric tramway system to be abandoned in favour of the combustion engine was as early as 1911. Over the following years the petrol or diesel powered motorbus was to replace the electric tram. In 1960 only eight tramways were still in operation. Fuel crises in wartime (1914–19, 1939–45, 1956) slowed down the process of closure only slightly.

Closures of urban electric tramways 1920–1959	
1920–29	33
1930–39	99
1940–49	23
1950–59	17

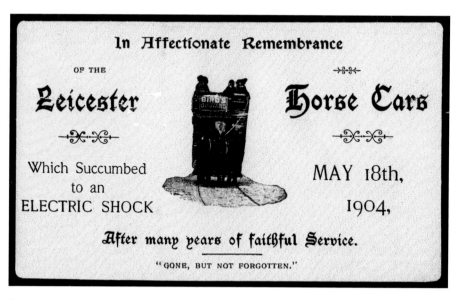

Epitaph for the horse tram; Leicester was one of Turton's tramway companies.

The demise of almost all British tramways by the 1950s gave rise to a spate of publications in which enthusiasts and local authorities celebrated their passing with varying degrees of nostalgia or optimism for the future of diesel-engined buses and the private motorcar. It was not fortuitous that in 1959, the year in which Leeds City Tramways ceased to run, the National Tramway Museum was founded at Crich in Derbyshire.

Prince Charles, the Prince of Wales, famously described the demise of the tram as 'utter madness'. A few cities, notably Manchester and Sheffield, have reintroduced trams in selected areas of town, which would have greatly pleased Turton; Leeds itself had high hopes of a new 'Super Tram'. In 2001 a £500 million scheme was authorised. The town maps showed the new routes, totalling 28 km., mainly the north, east and south of Leeds. It would carry 2.2 million passengers a year. It would greatly reduce the number of car commuters. Work was to start in 2004 and a service would be running by 2007. But government backing was not forthcoming and the scheme was dropped. This was widely felt as a missed opportunity.

There are now a growing number of voices and organisations, local and national, arguing a new case for the use of tramways, light rail or similar urban passenger transit systems. As with the horse tram, continental Europeans are more advanced than the British in maintaining or re-adopting tramways systems in their towns and cities.

PART V

SUCCESSION

1900-25

Robert Turton in his private carriage c.1910.

William Turton (1880–1965) at the wheel of a French Gladiator, going to a wedding c.1905. Turton was an early adopter of the combustion engine. He remodelled the coach house at his house, Bankfield. North Park Road, Roundhay, as a 'motor house' complete with a service pit. He had his initials carved in stone above the doorway.

20

PASSING ON

RETROSPECT

On New Year's Day 1 January 1900 William Turton had reason to be content and optimistic. He was fit enough and had never had any prolonged illness or disability. He was seventy-five, with a birthday in a few days' time. It was against the odds that he had survived the smoke of Leeds for so long. Even on the occasions when he left Leeds, which was quite frequently, it was usually to go to another smoky old city in the North. He'd never been far. London was about as far as he'd got, and he was not too fond of that place, all bankers and lawyers. He was a Leeds man. He'd done his best by Leeds. The city had expanded and improved no end, and in ways he could not have imagined when he was a lad, starting up the business back in 1844, as it said carved in stone on his warehouse. He'd been part of it all, what with the corn and hay business, and then coal and buses, and finally the trams. They still kept him busy, even if his near fifteen years in the Leeds political arena was well in the past. His public appearances were fewer, but he still attended meetings as an overseer of the Leeds Union.

Queen Victoria was still on the throne, as she had been for most of his life. It was sad that Britain seemed to be fighting more wars than any time he could recall. The Crimean had been the last big one and he could not remember much about that except the extraordinarily high price of corn. Now the Europeans were all up against the Chinese; there was the usual war against rebellious natives, this time the Ashanti. But the really big one was against white men in South Africa, the Boers, they called them. The papers were full of it. With the horse trams being decommissioned, perhaps there would be more horses to send to the front lines.

The electric tram was clearly the thing of the future. It had been pioneered in the north and in Leeds in particular. The Germans had started the ball rolling. They seemed to be making a lot of the running these days. Their new chemical processes were challenging the long established Leeds dyeing industry. There was Siemens developing electric engines of all sorts; and now Daimler with the petrol engine. And to cap it all there had been a photograph in the paper of Graf von Zeppelin's mighty airship.

William Turton was known as a horse man above all. He knew just about all there was to know about horses: breeding, selection for purpose, training, feeding and general care and management. He certainly knew everything to do with all forms of horse transport. But he was also a modern man. He was always keen to see new mechanical inventions and give them a trial. He had after all started as a machine maker's apprentice; he might have become an engineer of sorts. Many of his friends and associates were engineers: Kitson, Green, Kincaid, Hutchinson, Marsden and so on. He had shared with them many moments of excitement, testing innovations. There had been a few false starts, such as the 'compressed air' engine, but Turton had eventually become enthusiastic about steam traction, so long as it was in a balanced combination with horse traction. One of his companies had introduced the internal combustion engine in 1898.

For many years the name William Turton was synonymous in Leeds with the omnibus. 'Turton's buses', bearing his name in elegant paintwork, were familiar on most of the best routes in the town and the outer townships. They had a high reputation. Even after he had started with the trams, his buses kept on serving the town for many years. But for nearly thirty years trams were his chief preoccupation. It was only five years since he'd finally wound up Leeds Tramways company. He was still chairman of Bradford Tramways, deputy chairman of Manchester Tramways and a director of Leicester and some others. It was not just horses and their fodder: he knew how to run a transport company. He was the most experienced and respected figure in urban transport in the north of England.

He was fortunate to have two surviving sons: George William, now 51, and Robert, 43, both in good health. He regretted that neither had any children. George had been more or less running the corn and hay business for a few years now, and Robert managed the coal business. They had known nothing else. It looked as though the firms he had founded had a good future in the new century.

Who knows what might have become of young John, his second son, if he'd survived as long as the rest of them. As it was he died in 1888 at the age of 34. He was a bit more like his father. He had married young, moved away from home and started his own business, with a bit of support from his Dad. And he was one of only two of the five siblings to have children. The older son was christened William, a proper respectful and dynastic choice. William was born in 1880. He has a special place in this narrative as he and his wife are the first people to be mentioned who were personally known to the author being his paternal grandparents.

Young William, my grandfather, was a bit of a lad. For nearly eight years he was old William's only grandchild, and he had the full attention of his mother and father. They lived close to Hayfield House until John, his father, died, when they moved even closer. He was favoured and indulged. He used to boast that he usually got his way, memorably in demanding a pony before he would go to school. It is not clear which school that was. He was enrolled at Giggleswick School for Boys, a boarding school in north-west Yorkshire. He stayed there for two years. He must have had fun growing up in the mid-nineties. Living with his mother and little brother at No. 17 Sholebrooke Avenue, he could pop into Hayfield House any time or travel on the tram into the centre of town. Gradually he started to work in the family corn and hay business. By the age of 17 or so he was be becoming quite the young gentleman, well dressed, socially adept, athletic and with many friends and companions.

Among his friends was Clifford the son of Joseph Roberts a well-to-do dye merchant who lived at No. 47 not more than a hundred yards up Sholebrooke Avenue. He had an older sister, Felicia, a beautiful, educated young woman, about three years William's senior. They fell in love. So determined were they to marry, that they eloped. The family story, which they themselves seem to have cultivated, was that William took a ladder, placed it up against the wall of Felicia's house, probably at the back where they could sneak off down Reginald Road. Felicia climbed down and joined him for the next sixty-five years. The exact date of the elopement is not known. In any case they were soon married at the registrar's office, on Sunday 31 December 1899. Perhaps they thought there was something romantic about this date. It was also William's nineteenth birthday.

And so life continued for the first half of the first year of the new century. Then some time in July William felt the onset of a bout of bronchitis. It quickly worsened and within a week or so he died, 'suddenly and at home', as death notices say, on Sunday 5 August 1900. *T'owd man 'ad popped 'is clogs.*

MOURNING

The death was announced on Tuesday 7 August in the *Yorkshire Post*, the largest provincial newspaper with a national readership second only to *The Times* and the *Scotsman*. London newspapers (*The Times* and *Daily News*) also reported the death of William Turton.

The funeral was held on the following Friday 10 August. As an Anglican William Turton had been worshipping at St Martin's Potternewton after leaving the parish of St Peter's. The announcement requested 'No cards'. The funeral at St Martin's, at 11.45 a.m. was conducted by Canon Wood, assisted by the Vicar Rev. J.S. Addison and the Curate Rev. A.H. Kennedy.

The list of mourners given in the *Yorkshire Post* was presumably authorised by the funeral directors on instruction from the family, so it is of interest to read who is mentioned. The list starts in order of family seniority:

Mrs. Turton [widow], Mr. George Turton, Mr. Robert Turton, Mrs. George Turton, Mr. and Mrs J.B. Pegler [daughter and son-in-law], Mr. and Mrs. G. Fillingham [daughter and son-in-law], Mrs John Turton [widowed daughter-in-law], Mr. Willie Turton, Mr. and Mrs. E. A. Robinson [daughter and son-in-law of his widow by her previous marriage], Master John Turton, Mrs. Robertshaw [mother of Mrs. John Turton], Miss Nora Fillingham, Master Alan Fillingham; and the nurse and household servants.

The dozens of close friends and associates who attended included: members of the Hepton family, the wife of a former Mayor Alf Cooke (printer), Mr and Mrs Penrose Green (The Thomas Green and Son), Mr Samuel Busby, Mr Charles Mason, Mr William Wharam, Mr Whittington (Messrs. Clarke, Son, and Whittington, the family solicitor), Mr Wm Green (Thomas Green and Son), Mr, J.W. Heals (the Committee of the West Riding Trades Protection Society).

The service at the graveside (plot no. C−502) was conducted by the vicar of St Martin's. The coffin was of polished oak with brass furniture, and a plate with the following inscription:

William Turton, born January 2nd, 1825, died August 6th, 1900

The body was encased in a metal shell, hermetically sealed. There were a great many wreaths, sent by, amongst others, the Bradford Tramways employees. Others who could not attend 'sent their carriages' as was the custom of the period. If the church was full as reported, then at least two hundred people attended the funeral service and at the very least some sixty people attended the burial service.

A curious absence is the Roberts family. Felicia, who was of course already married to 'Mr Willie Turton', was not there; nor were her parents or adult brothers. Or at least neither detailed newspaper report included their names. It is a considerable mystery as to why they did not attend. It seems possible that the Roberts family did indeed still feel some sense of rancour, and that Willie was in disfavour, for a while at least, for having abducted their daughter.

LEGACY

Probate was quickly granted, and on 15 September 1900 the *Yorkshire Post* published some details of 'The Will of the late William Turton'. The total value of the estate was £190,692 15s 11d of which £159,932 14s 9d personalty, £30,760 1s 2d realty. The proven will was dated 14 June 1899, with a codicil dated 14 September 1899. Either Turton kept up-to-date with his will or he had some special premonition that it was time to make his final will and testament.

The *Post's* summary is useful so I will give it full:

The bequests include the following charitable legacies, viz.: -

Leeds General Infirmary − £200
Leeds Parish Church Sunday School − £200
Leeds Dispensary − £100
Leeds Women and Children's Hospital − £100
Leeds St. James Sunday School − £100

The testator leaves in trust for investment a sum sufficient to provide £500 per annum for his wife during her widowhood. On Mrs. Turton's death, or remarriage, the principal is to form part of the residuary personal estate. Mr. Turton also leaves his wife a horse and carriage, wines etc. The warehouses, offices, and stable at Crown Point and The Calls are devised to Mr. Turton's son Mr. George William Turton, absolutely. The coal wharfe, stables, offices, sheds, engines, plant, and fixtures at Crown Point go to another son Mr. Robert Turton, absolutely.

The residue of the real estate is bequeathed to the Trustees, who are to receive the rents for five years after the testator's death, and to divide these proceeds equally among the testator's children living, and the issue of his deceased son, John. At the expiration of the five years the Trustees are to sell the residue of the real estate as they may think fit, and divide the amount accruing therefrom equally among Mr. Turton's four children and the issue of his deceased son, John. The daughters' shares are settled.

The residue of his personal estate the testator leaves to his trustees to call in and convert at their discretion, and after payment of certain expenses they are to divide the residue accruing between his four children living at the time of his death and the issue of his deceased son, John. Here again, the daughters' shares are settled. There are specific legacies of pictures to members of the family, and legacies to old servants and others.

The trustees and executors are George William Turton and Robert Turton (sons) and Thomas Boyne Pegler and George Fillingham (sons-in-law). Each executor proving the wills receives £50.

The list of individual legatees is as follows

Step-daughter Ann Robinson £100
son of my late half-sister Grace Carver Charles Carver £100
Percy Carver £100
son of late cousin George Turton John Turton £100
son of late cousin William Robinson
formerly my foreman at Crown Point Percy Robinson £100
former cashier, now cashier to GWT Thomas Gaines £200
former manager of my depot at North Street William Whalley £50
former clerk George Thomas Tuke £25

The legacy to Thomas Gaines, a former clerk to William Turton, was mysteriously deleted in the Codicil.

The individual gifts of pictures provide us with an interesting detail. I suspect it was on the basis partly of value and also previously ascertained preference. There were many other paintings in Hayfield House:

  Robert the picture by [John] Leech of my first wife
  George the picture of myself by the same artist
  Mary Ann the Trial of Queen Catherine by Leech
  Elizabeth Pegler the painting 'Hyde Park in 1851' [also probably by Leech]
  grandson William the painting of Calais [also probably by Leech]

Intensive efforts have failed to find the whereabouts of any of the paintings. Leech painted few portraits and most were for family or intimate friends. Thus the portraits, such personal records of William Turton and his wife, remain a particular mystery.

21

INHERITANCE

The old man had bequeathed an extraordinary legacy to his family. The Turton family moved on. We need now to become better acquainted with his immediate successors to see what they made of the wonderful hand they had been dealt. Let us look at first at the corn and hay business which had been inherited by his oldest son.

GEORGE TURTON AND THE CORN BUSINESS

George William Turton was born on 27 March 1849. He was the first child of young parents; he had no surviving grandparents. His future was by no means secure or predictable. His name George was probably from his great uncle who helped his father in setting up in business on his own. By the age of ten he had two brothers and two sisters. They were to remain a close family, living together into their twenties. His father became more established and wealthier by the year. He would remember his mother always having at least one resident domestic servant to help look after the children and the household. They lived in modest but basically comfortable circumstances in a small terraced house in the middle of one of the worst areas of Leeds.

George went to Leeds Grammar School when he was just thirteen. The school, where his father in turn had spent just six months, had recently moved to its grand new building on a site near Woodhouse Moor. The family had just moved to live in North Street, so it was not too far to walk. Life was more comfortable now. His father was a well-known figure in town and was thinking of going into politics. He stayed at school for two years, above average for the time. He would have met the sons of many of the prominent families of Leeds, many of them non-conformists, many of them sons of large merchants, senior professionals and local politicians. Soon after he left the grammar school, he began to become familiar with his father's business. He started with some clerical work. By the age of 18, in 1867, he was working full-time in the corn and hay business. This was just the moment that his father began to be involved in the omnibus business, and he would have been well pleased to have the extra help.

By the time his father started in the tram business, both his two brothers had joined the family firm.

One of the earliest biographical traces of George is a mention in the local papers reporting his presence at the reception given by his father in Hayfield House on 11 November 1874. This was to mark the opening of the Chapeltown tram service. It was attended by the Mayor, Colonel Hutchinson and other notables. Two years later his mother died, in January 1877. He was to remain at Hayfield House until after his father had remarried in November 1883, when he himself finally married at the age of 35.

George Turton's first entry in a Leeds Directory shows that he was running the omnibus business for a while. He was based at the Royal Hotel Yard, No. 161 Briggate. He was continuing the old coaching inn tradition. He had married Annie, daughter of John and Bessie Maude. The Maudes were steel and timber merchants, and a prominent Leeds family. They owned property in the Calls and Calls Lane, close to William Turton's Warehouse; Maude Street, which abuts Turton's building, is named after them. The two families would have known each other for some years before this marriage.

George and Annie set up house at No. 1 Newton Villas. This was a one-off pair of large semi-detached houses on the east side of Chapeltown Road a little north of Hayfield House. The house, now much sub-divided, still stands, as Nos 198–200 Brandon Grove, Chapeltown Road. They remained here until William's death when they moved immediately into Hayfield House. They were to stay there until 1920 when George died. They were the 'sponsors', or godparents, of my father George, who in family fashion gave me the middle names George William.

The value of George's estate at his death in 1920 suggests in itself that he continued to manage the William Turton Corn & Hay firm efficiently and profitably on at least the same scale as when his father was alive. This estate was finally dispersed at the death of his widow Annie Turton on 11 November 1925, nine months after Robert. They had married in 1884 and had no children. For twenty years after the death of William Turton they had been the senior members of the successor generations. They lived at Hayfield House and continued the business and lifestyle of the old man. On the death of her husband Annie continued living for while at Hayfield House. She was still resident in April 1921 when in a deed in which she acts as a trustee in the conveyance of No. 157 Chapeltown Road (Milton House), her late mother Bessie Maude's house. She was sharing Hayfield House with two other widows, Mary Ellen Nickson and Emily Tinsdale. She then moved to Harrogate, renamed the house at No. 8 Leeds Road 'Hayfield House' and spent the last few years of her life in comfort and in frequent touch with her nephews and nieces. She was the last member of the family to be buried in the family tomb in Chapeltown that had first been the resting place of Sarah Anne, the mother-in-law she never met. Her name was inscribed next to that of her husband.

Annie left an estate valued at £74,524 of which 'net personalty' was £42,227. Her charitable bequests amounted to only a little over one per cent of the total, but in early twenty-first century terms might be compared with sums of from £10,000–£20,000. These were reported in detail. The main beneficiaries were women: Leeds Maternity

Hospital, Leeds Unmarried Women's Benevolent Institution, Leeds Hospital for Women and Children, Leeds Victoria House for Invalid Ladies; and children, Marguerite Home for Crippled Children, Leeds Children's Convalescent and Summer Holiday Fund, Leeds Poor Children's Holiday Camp Association. Like William, she also gave to the Leeds Dispensary and also to the Leeds Tradesmen's Benevolent Institution, in which William had been particularly active and generous.

Leaving the real estate aside, her personal estate was worth say £40,000 after small bequests and expenses. This was divided into four equal parts to Nora Turton Inman (aged 37) and Alan Fillingham (aged 35?), children of William Turton's daughter Mary Anne, and William (45) and John (37), children of Turton's son John. Due to William's bankruptcy his share passed directly to his three sons: Ralph (aged 23 in 1925), Robert William (21), George (19).

Hayfield House is no longer. It was demolished in 2002 by order of the council and then rebuilt as a multi-purpose health centre. The Turton family had built it and lived in it for more than fifty years until the early 1920s. Two or more subsequent owners had let it as private accommodation until the 1960s when it was converted into a hotel, the Hayfield Hotel. It later also had a pub sign with a picture of a haymaker and it was generally known just as The Hayfield. By then the area had a high proportion of people of Afro-Caribbean origin, especially from Jamaica. It became a popular local pub and acquired a nationwide reputation as a centre for live music with a Caribbean flavour. Sadly by the mid-1970s The Hayfield began to become notorious for hard drug dealing, including crack cocaine, and there were incidents of assault, rape and murder. One of the 'Yorkshire Ripper's victims, whom he mistakenly thought to be a prostitute, was killed just outside The Hayfield. Fights between rivals increased, involving the Jamaican Yardies. A massive police raid in 2002 led to arrests, imprisonments and deportations. There was considerable local opposition to the demolition of what many thought to be the finest house along the whole length of Chapeltown Road.

ROBERT TURTON AND THE COAL BUSINESS

Uncle Robert remains a bit of a mystery. He was William Turton's youngest child, born in 1857. He would have remembered little of the East Street days. He was active in the family businesses from about 1877 at the latest, a year of maximum activity for his father and the year his mother died. He was no doubt a bit pampered as a youngest child in a house with two older unmarried sisters and several female servants. He never married and lived at home until his forties.

Robert gravitated towards the coal business at an early date. He was more or less in charge when his father left him the entire business in his Will. The summary of the bequest read, 'The coal wharfe, stables, offices, sheds, engines, plant and fixtures at Crown Point.' At various times the coal business also had addresses in Water Lane and Black Bull Street, both close to Crown Point. Robert ran the business until some time before his death in 1925, when it had been taken over by Turnstalls, Leyssel and Limmer Rock Asphalt Co. Ltd. He was nominated chairman of the new company, now a subsidiary of a large national company. Limmers and Trinidad Asphalt Co. continued trading until the 1970s.

Soon after his father's death, when George and Annie returned to Hayfield House, Robert had moved to Harrogate. This was a common move for wealthy Leeds businessmen. His first address was a hotel. After looking around he bought one of the most desirable houses in the town, No. 25 North Park Row. This faces the 200 acres of open land known as The Stray in central Harrogate. This house still stands. It is a corner house of some distinction. It has a large coach house at the rear with accommodation for a coachman and family. In later years his then widowed sister-in-law Annie lived virtually within sight across the park at No. 8 Leeds Road on the western edge of The Stray.

Robert's obituary mentioned his distinguished father William. It also reported that both he and one of his sisters had each endowed a cot for £1,000 in Leeds Infirmary in memory of his mother (Sarah Turton 1825–1877).

Robert Turton's will has a rather peculiar status since it was made in 1909, sixteen years before his death, and not revised. Some of those named in it are deceased or very elderly by 1925. Apart from a few smaller gifts and legacies, personal and charitable, he leaves everything to the trustees to hold or invest. He leaves the freehold of his coal business at Crown Point to Alan Fillingham, when he attains the age of 25. All other property, after payment of expenses, goods, shares etc. was to be invested and the income to be divided into four equal parts, namely to George William Turton (who predeceased him by five years), Elizabeth Pegler (*b.*1852), Mary Ann Fillingham (1854–1948) and fourthly the two sons of John Turton, William and John and their successors.

Robert's estate was valued at £58,985 of which £45,605 net personalty, the rest being real estate. The following specific legacies were reported:

> £200 each to the Leeds General Infirmary, Leeds Dispensary and Leeds Hospital for Women and Children.
> £100 each to Leeds Parish Church (St. Peter's) Sunday School; to William Whalley, formerly manager to his father; to Thomas Gaines, family clerk to his father; and Mrs. Elizabeth Muscroft, formerly servant to his father.
> £50 to his clerk, Henry Arthur Taylor.

Robert's personal legatees included the three sons of his nephew William: Ralph £500, Robert William £1,000 and George, my father, £500. This suggests that Robert may have been a godchild. George was the godfather (or 'sponsor') of the author's father, also named George (1906–44). Various cousins, eight in all, received sums of £100–£200. William himself received 'the close of grassland at Swillington Common [near Leeds], now occupied by Thomas Lawn'.

If we assume that the amount in Robert's will to be invested was about £44,000, then William and John would have each benefited from the income from £5,500, potentially say between £250 per annum. And once again this was from investments that were declining in value. The value of some of the shares plummeted, for instance £100 shares held in the engineering firm of Thomas Green and Son were worth £10 by 1937 and had been subdivided into 10s shares.

The mention of William Whalley in Robert Turton's will is intriguing. I found a cutting in a family scrapbook from the *Yorkshire Evening Post*'s column 'Diary of a Yorkshireman', dateable some time in 1941. In his eightieth year, William Whalley reflects on his years working with the Turton forage business. He joined the firm on 14 February 1876, as a boy of 15. This was the year the new warehouse was opened. It is likely that a brother or other relative was already working there, as there is a directory entry in 1875 for Frederick Whalley living at No. 8 Elmund Street, which was owned by William Turton. William Whalley had worked his way up through the company to become manager. He was also a beneficiary in Annie Turton's will. In the 1941 interview he is referred to as 'Secretary and Director'. He was known as a hard worker, arriving before eight in the morning six days a week. He had great strength and stamina still in 1941. 'Despite his 81 years, his back is as straight as a guardsman's, and when he takes a visitor round the "Chambers" in which chopping, grinding and rolling machines chatter tirelessly, he skips up and down spiral staircases and in and out of lofts, with an agility that would be remarkable in a man twenty years his junior.'

JOHN TURTON 1850–88

William Turton had bought the North Street premises Nos 149, 151 and 153 some time by the late 1860s. He had in a sense been expanding north, following the city's growth, that of his transport network, and also his corn and hay distribution, from Crown Point to Briggate and Harrrison Street to Sheepshanks Yard and neighbouring parts of Templar Street and York Road. In the early 1860s he had moved his residence from East Street to No. 114 North Street, on its eastern side.

At first his son John had managed the North Street operation at Nos 149–53, quite independently it would seem. By 1877, the year before he married, or at the latest 1880, John was trading there as 'John Turton, Hay, Straw and Horse Corn Merchant, Government and Corporation Contractor'. The description 'Government Contractor' suggests that he supplied the army headquarters and cavalry barracks which were located just a few hundred yards north east of the North Street premises.

After John's death in 1888, North Street was still an important part of the Turton business and William Turton is listed as trading there and at Nos 64–66 The Calls in the 1890s. Very interestingly, in 1897, one of the firms of hay dealers listed in the annual directory as working from The Calls and Crown Point Bridge is John Turton and Sons. It seems as if the old man had revived the name of John Turton to provide an interest for the grandchildren to inherit, William, then 17, and John, then 10. The young John first appears as a 'corn factor' in 1906/7 aged about twenty at No. 153 North Street and The Calls, and again in 1911 and 1912. In 1903 the North Street office is described as a 'branch depot'. The fact that the Turton corn and hay business was not a public company presumably meant that these changes were easy to make.

John Turton's sons, William and John, left the family business in or by about 1912. William Turton 'junior' (1880–1965) volunteered in October 1914 and served in the Army Service Corps (ASC) with West Riding 62 Division on the western front, later on the Army's Central Purchasing Board. He was providing, as ever, food for horses. His brother John was conscripted in October 1915 and served as an ambulance driver in the ASC. The brothers were alike in many respects. They both married very young and received a large inheritance very early. They both married exceptionally beautiful women and had a taste for yachting and motorcars, animal breeding and small-scale farming. They also lived in fine houses. William lived in a large house next to Roundhay Park; John had a house in the Avenue des Hirondelles in Poole within convenient commuting distance of Leeds. In 1922 John moved to a dower house and farm in Melbourne, East Riding. He was to have fifteen children by two wives. This must have been a major reason for the dispersal of his inheritance. William started a car and coach business in Scarborough in 1920. His advertisement in the *Scarborough Mercury* 13 April 1923 read:

For smart
Taxi Cabs
Touring Cars
Motor Coach Tours
Garage accommodation
Repairs, accessories
Coach painting etc.

William Turton
Clifton Street
Tel 217   end of Aberdeen Walk

He was 'let down' by his partner in 1921 and separated after a lawsuit. He then made an unwise investment in new coaches. He was also substantially in debt on his horse racing account. He was declared bankrupt in September 1923 and moved with Felicia and their three sons to an only slightly less grand house and smallholding in Bournemouth. The relationship between the two brothers was no doubt coloured by a strong sibling rivalry. John's children recall his annoyance at working with William who liked to travel about visiting farmers and leaving him doing the accounts in the office. It may be that animosity reached a critical point over some financial matter, possibly William being turned down for a loan or investment in about 1920. The feeling on William's side, at least, was so strong that the brothers never spoke again nor was brother John ever mentioned to my own generation. In fact I had no certainty that he existed until I started my research.

A SUCCESSOR COMPANY

The Turton family had no further involvement with corn or coal after 1925. The warehouse at No. 64–66 The Calls, however, remained in the possession of the Turton estate. In 1934 it was offered for sale in a well-publicised auction of Turton properties in Leeds. It was not a favourable moment for the economy and several lots, including Nos 64–66 The Calls, were withdrawn. It was to be sold finally in the 1940s or '50s.

In the *Yorkshire Post* article of 1941 the then managing director is given as Philip Campbell. Campbell was a farmer from the North Riding who dealt with the Turton firm. He was born on 15 February 1876 and moved in 1921 to live at Thorner, just outside Leeds to the northeast. He had started working as a corn merchant in Selby. But by that date he was working for the Turton corn and hay business and in 1921 took over management and ownership of the company, if not the premises. The Turton family relinquished all control but Campbell provided unbroken continuity trading under the name of William Turton (Leeds) Corn and Hay Merchant. The *Post* records his special friendship with and reliance on William Whalley, who by 1921 had thirty-five years' experience with the firm. He handed over to his son-in-law Roland Marriner who died in office in 1964.

The manager of one of Philip Campbell's farms, at Acaster, Selby, was Jock Penty. He had been introduced to the corn business by Campbell. Jock Penty's grandson Andrew Penty still manages the quite separate family firm of Campbell and Penty, of York. Campbell married the daughter of a north Yorkshire farmer, Barton, whose son John Barton helped me with this part of the research. John's daughter in turn continues the family tradition of farming near Boroughbridge in the Vale of York. The Barton family had been a long-standing supplier of corn to the firm of William Turton.

The firm of 'William Turton (Leeds) Corn and Hay Merchant' continued trading successfully. It is from the same *Post* article that we learn that in the early 1940s the firm was still supplying feed for 2,000 pit ponies in Yorkshire. The *Post* commented that this was 'an odd thing to record in this motoring age'. The last date the Turton company's name appeared in any directory is 1968.

William Turton's yacht Gloria, *1905, 15 tons; in 1910 he bought* May Morn, *31 tons.*

William Turton with Felicia behind him, and friends
on the Yorkshire coast c.*1910.*

Captain William Turton ASC c.*1916.*

Felicia Turton c.1916.

John Turton Private ASC, ambulance driver, brother of William Turton ('the second').

22

HERITAGE

LOCAL CAPITALISM

William Turton was a medium to large sized merchant capitalist, deriving his main income from trading animal feedstuffs and coal. He also profited from his bus operations, his numerous tramway directorships and from shares in Thomas Green and Son engineers, and probably some other companies. Although he owned many properties over the years, these were chiefly for business purposes and for his staff, or for his own family. Income from property was probably not considerable.

Croix de Chevalier de l'Ordre du Mérite Agricole, awarded to Captain Turton by the French Government for wartime services.

Turton's operations were examples of what can be called local capitalism. Of course he bought grain from several other countries. Thomas Green sold throughout the world, but this was not 'global capitalism'. It was part of 'national capital' but the firms were not quoted on the London Stock Exchange. Consider these aspects of this notion of 'localism' as it may refer to Turton's businesses:

Employees   100 per cent local
Capital Corn & Hay and Coal 100 per cent family
Capital LTC   high proportion Leeds and West Riding
Horses source   almost entirely from Yorkshire
Corn source   high proportion from northern England
Coal source   100 per cent Yorkshire
Investments   100 per cent UK

The advantages in this form of localism which is more practised in other European countries, notably Germany, are worthy of a discussion beyond the scope of this book.

GREEN AND SLOW

There are ways in which our story resonates with contemporary concerns about localism and environmental issues. These might be local sourcing of food and materials, recycling waste, sustainability and reduction of pollution. Although paradoxical, the image of sheep grazing on the green roof of John Marshall's flax mill in the middle of the nineteenth century is an endearing and enduring image. Other examples of sustainabilty we have come across include the use of 'scavenging' for municipal recycling of waste products, and the encouragement and advice on Turton's invoices about returning sacks for re-use (see the title page of this book).

Most importantly this account may speak to and encourage current debates about urban transport: alternatives that are less pollutant, more environmentally friendly and more sustainable.

THE LEGACY OF THE HORSE-DRAWN TRAM

The last tram ran in Leeds in 1959. Within twenty years, in May 1977, there were proposals for a new tram system. In 1991 Leeds City Council and the West Yorkshire Passenger Transport Authority commissioned a study. A positive decision was taken to build a new system to Headingley, Hunslet, Roundhay and beyond. Funding was approved in 2002. It was intended to start work immediately and complete by 2006–7. In the event the scheme was abandoned mainly on financial grounds, though there was some opposition from those whose areas the new routes would not at first serve. There remains some hope that some form of new tram service may yet be reconsidered.

Today there are a growing number of boroughs that have re-introduced some form of limited tram service, including Manchester and Sheffield. The Isle of Man still has its horse tram service which is a favourite visitor attraction. Alongside these developments there are numerous societies dedicated to aspects of research and understanding of historical forms of transport and their conservation. Outstanding among these is the National Tramway Museum at Crich in Derbyshire. More relevant for our story is the active Leeds Transport Historical Society. This is run by a dedicated, skilled and knowledgeable team.

The Leeds Transport Historical Society has restored 'Car 107'. After decommissioning it had been used as a mess car for the Leeds Highways Department and then as a garden shed or summerhouse. Rediscovered in the 1970s by a LTHS member it was later donated and in 2005 it was decided to restore it to full working order, with all the trimmings, together with newly cast wheels. A sizeable team of expert amateur craftsmen, including Jim Soper, carried out the work. The following brief account is largely based on the website of project manager Jamie Guest.

'Car 107' is the oldest surviving Leeds tram and the only one from the horse-drawn era. It was built during Turton's lifetime but not when he was in charge. It had been made in 1897 by G.F. Milnes at Birkenhead, source of many of the Leeds Tramways Company carriages. In 1897 Leeds Council was phasing out the horse and steam trams and electrifying the whole system. Some routes could not be electrified immediately due to the need to strengthen some bridges to carry the heavier trams. Leeds ordered two batches of double decker horse trams to fill the gap. The cars were designed to be pulled by three horses, with a fourth for steeper hills, such as Woodhouse Lane. The car was in use until 1901.

The restored car ran on rails again pulled by two fine horses on 26 August 2013 at an inauguration by the Lord Mayor of Leeds. It is now housed at the National Tramway Museum in Crich, Derbyshire.

WILLIAM TURTON: A SUCCESSFUL ENTREPRENEUR

The term 'ecology of success' is sometimes used as a way to focus on the circumstances, the complex matrix of factors that contribute to the success of an individual undertaking. This book has attempted to illustrate the value of the term in demonstrating the multiple influences of the political economy of Leeds on the entrepreneurial and pioneering work of William Turton.

In conclusion I should attempt some sort of qualitative assessment of William Turton that underpinned his contributions to Leeds and the wider economy and society of northern England. Turton worked hard for at least sixty years, as an apprentice, working for his parents' firm and then striking out on his own account aged 19. If we except director's fees he never worked for a wage or salary from anyone else. He started with a bare amount of capital and support. He expanded and diversified steadily as we have seen. Here I shall not rehearse what he did so much as consider his styles and methods of work.

He accumulated steadily through trading profits.

He deferred personal gratification at first.

He re-invested his surplus in his business.

He later invested in other local businesses.

He diversified, was innovative and had commercial foresight. By the end of the century he was almost certainly the only tramway entrepreneur to have worked with horses, steam, electricity and the combustion engine and had experimented with compressed air, not to mention mules.

He developed his portfolio systematically: horses, forage, transport, coal and steam.

He operated locally, expanding into neighbouring towns and counties.

He had considerable knowledge and general 'savvy' in matters of horses and forage, transport planning and management, logistics in a wider sense (his wharf and warehouse, lifting and loading machinery etc.) and local politics.

He balanced risk taking (including conflicts of interest) with caution.

He sought the best professional advice (financial, legal, engineering).

He knew how to develop partnerships and business friendships (Atkinson and Busby, Kincaid and Hutchinson, Wharam and Whalley, Green and Baxter).

He had a persuasive manner, firm but charming.

He was a good employer.

He was not greedy (viz. his refusal to accept fees or expenses when winding up LTC).

He was honest and fair, and punctilious in accounting.

He looked after his family well. At the early peak of his fortunes he built Hayfield House and gave his family a comfortable home and social background.

He was averagely generous with his money and time in his pro bono and philanthropic involvements.

He did not go in for 'gentrification' by the usual markers of building a country house or sending his children to expensive 'public schools'.

When I began this book I had no way of knowing how 'low' he started, nor how 'high' he reached. I had this picture of a fatherless lad, living in the slums of the East End and making an early start on his own. Well it was something like this, but it has turned out not to be not quite a 'rags to riches' story. He did not reach the aristocratic heights of those Leeds 'merchant princes', the super rich who were elected to Parliament, knighted and even ennobled. But he was more than a 'shopocrat'. He was among the business élite of the borough.

William Turton left £190,692 15s 11d net in his will. Of this £30,760 1s 2d was realty. This might be worth between £10–15 million pounds today. F. and M.L. Thompson tell us that in the twenty years 1894–1914 there were only 96 millionaires in Britain (about five dying each year) in terms of personalty, who were not hereditary landowners.

Blue plaque.

Most of these fell into one of the following categories, in declining order of frequency: banking and finance (27); manufacture (24); railway and shipping (12) and brewery and distilling (11). There were no millionaires in road transport or corn dealing in the nineteenth century. This gives some perspective on Turton's wealth and financial achievement.

WILLIAM TURTON: PERSONAL STYLE

I have developed an affection for this ancestor whom I had been brought up not to know. This may well be apparent. Try as I may it is hard to play devil's advocate and try to maximise the score against him. Maybe he should have paid his workers and domestic servants more. Maybe he should have charged his customers and passengers less. Maybe at times he was intolerably self-willed and stubborn. Maybe, without wishing to engage in cod-Yorkshire stereotypes, he was not quite that generous but a bit more calculating. Maybe he was a bit self-indulgent. He was certainly a proud and ambitious man.

William Turton had a little formal education. He had a few years of attending Sunday School, six months at the Grammar School and about five years as an apprentice. This was already an above average platform of knowledge, literacy and numeracy. Later in life he and his family joined the Leeds learned societies and libraries that put them in the top 400–500 or so of families of good education and social standing. He was intelligent and energetic. He was indisputably a good communicator, especially in meetings and negotiations but also in writing business letters.

I believe that one of his most laudable and useful bag of skills and dispositions was what we might sum up as diplomacy. This started with a capacity for empathy and understanding of people. He listened and involved himself in the personal living conditions and circumstances of others, of higher and lower estate. He was tactful and polite, not antagonistic or querulous. He was a mediator and conciliator.

William Turton was blessed with wonderful support from his wife Sarah Ann and their children, and his second wife Mary Anne who was his companion until his death.

Behind all this lay a deeper personality that revealed itself in openness and affability, charm and kindness. People came to rely on him, depend on him, trust him. He was dependable and loyal. As a co-director said at the final LTC shareholders meeting in 1895, he was 'a gentleman we can depend on'. And as his obituary was to say 'men liked him'.

BIBLIOGRAPHY

Adams, M., *The firebringers: art, science and the struggle for liberty in nineteenth-century Britain* (London, Quercus, 2009)

Anderson, W., *Self-made men* (London, John Snow, 1861)

Anning, S.J. and Walls, W.K.J., *A history of the Leeds School of Medicine over one and a half centuries 1831–1981* (Leeds, Leeds University Press, 1982)

Anon, *The stranger's guide through Leeds* (Leeds, Henry Cullingworth, 1831)

Anon, *An historical guide to Leeds and its environs* (Leeds, Fenteman & Sons, 1858)

Anon, *The poll book of the Leeds Borough election November 1865* (Leeds, C. Kempley, 1865)

Anon, *The poll book of the Leeds Borough election November 1868* (Leeds, Edward Baines and Son, 1868)

Anon, *The architects, engineers and building trades directory 1868* (London, Wyman, 1868)

Anon, *The Leeds Official Yearbook* (Leeds, Charles Goodall, 1876)

Anon, *Memorial to Edward Baines on the completion of his 80th year* (London, Hodder and Stoughton, 1880)

Anon, 'The family of Denison of Great Woodhouse and their residences in Leeds', *Thoresby Society Journal* Vol.15. pp.251–73

Anon, The Leeds Steam Carriage Company, *Thoresby Society Journal*, Vol. 37, pp.132–44 (1945)

Anon, *A history of Manchester tramways* (Manchester, Manchester Corporation Transport Department, 1949)

Anon, *The tramway era in Sheffield* (Sheffield, Sheffield Transport Department, 1960)

Anon, *Saint Michael: a history of Marks and Spencer* (London, Weidenfeld and Nicolson, 1969)

Anon, *The Irish in Leeds, Thoresby Society Miscellany*, pp.1–20 (1979)

Arnold, J.H., *Leicester City Tramways* (Leicester, The East Midland Area Omnibus Enthusiasts Society, 1972)

Barber, B., 'Municipal government in Leeds 1835–1914' in Fraser, D. (ed.), *Municipal reform and the industrial city* pp. 61–110 (Leicester, Leicester University Press. 1982)

Bellamy, J. (ed.), *Yorkshire business histories (*Bradford, Bradford University Press, 1970)

Beresford, M.W., *The Leeds Chamber of Commerce (*Leeds, Leeds Chamber of Commerce, 1951)

– *East end, west end: the face of Leeds during urbanisation 1684–1842* (Thoresby Society Journal, Vols. 60 & 61, 1988)

Beresford, M.W. and Jones, R.J. (eds), *Leeds and its region* (Leeds, British Association for the Advancement of Science, 1967)

Bett, W.H. and Gillham, J.C., *Great British tramway networks* (Light Railway Transport League, 1962)

Blanchflower, D.G. and Oswald, A.J., *Entrepreneurship* (University of Oxford Allied Economics Discussion Paper Series, No. 125 (1991)

Bodley G.F., *St Matthew's Church, Chapel Allerton* (Newcastle, Oriel, 1897–98)

Bradford, E., *Headingley, this pleasant village: clues to the past* (Huddersfield, Jeremy Mills Publishing, 2008)

Bradley, T., *The old coaching days in Yorkshire* (Leeds, Yorkshire Conservative Newspaper Co., 1889)

Brearly, H., *Tramways in West Yorkshire*, Locomotion Papers, No.13 (South Godstone, Oakwood Press, 1960)

Brears, P., *Images of Leeds 1850–1960* (Leeds, Breedon Books, City of Leeds Museum, 1992)

– *A guide to the history and buildings along eight miles of the Aire valley through Leeds* (Leeds, Leeds City Museums, 1993)

Briggs, A., *The Victorian city* (Harmondsworth, Penguin Books, 1963)

– The eighteen seventies, *University of Leeds Review*, Vol.17, No.2. pp.215–31 (1974)

Broomhall, G.J.S. and Hubback, J.H., *Corn trade measures, recent and remote* (Liverpool, Northern Publications, 1930)

Brown, R.S. (ed.), *Digging for history in the coal merchants' archives: the history of the Society of Coal Merchants* (Seaford, Society of Coal Merchants, 1988)

Buckley, R.T., *A history of tramways: from horse to rapid transit* (Newton Abbot, David and Charles, 1975)

Budge, A., *Early photography in Leeds 1839–1870* (Leeds, Leeds Art Galleries, 1980)

Burt, S. and Grady, K., *The illustrated history of Leeds* (Derby, Breedon, 2002)

Bye, S. (ed.), *A history of the Middleton railway* (eighth edition) (Leeds, The Middleton Railway Trust, 2004)

Campbell, R.H. and Wilson, R.G. (eds), *Entrepreneurship in Britain 1750–1939* (London, Adam and Charles Black, University of Sheffield Documents in Economic History, 1975)

Carter, E.F., *Railways in wartime* (London, Frederick Muller, 1964)

Church, R.A., *An economic and social history of the British coal industry* (London, Social and Economic Research Council, 1983)

Clutton-Brock, J., *Horse-power: a history of the horse and the donkey in human societies* (London, Natural Science Museum, 1992)

Cochrane, R., *Risen by perseverance or, lives of self-made men* (Edinburgh, Nimmo, 1879)

Cook, C. and Keith, B., *British historical facts 1830–1900* (London, Macmillan, 1975)

Craig, A., *Room at the top: or, how to reach success, happiness, fame and fortune with biographical notes of successful self-made men, who have risen from obscurity to fame* (Chicago, Summer, 1883)

Croft, D.J., *The Bradford tramways* (Tarrant Hinton, Oakwood Press, 1972)

– *A century of public transport in Bradford 1882–1982* (Bradford, City Library, 1982)

Croft, D., and Gordon, A., *Source book of literature relating to Yorkshire tramways* (Brora, A. Gordon, 2002)

– *A bibliography of British and Irish tramways* (Brora, A. Gordon, 2009)

Curtis, J.S., *The story of the Marsden mayoralty* (Leeds, Barmby, 1875)

Dalton, R., *Labour and the municipality: Labour politics in Leeds 1910–1914* (PhD thesis. University of Huddersfield, 2000)

Dalton, H., Sunday Schools in Leeds: church associations of children and young people in Leeds, 1836–1851 (*Thoresby Society Miscellany*, Vol.13, pp.67–89)

– Walter Farquhar Hook, Vicar of Leeds: his work for the Church and in town, 1837–48, *Thoresby Society Miscellany*, Vol.19, pp.27–79 (1988)

Department of the Environment Inner City Task Force Unit, *An evaluation of the government's inner city task force initiative.* Vol. 2. Chapeltown and Harehills (Leeds, 1992)

Dickinson, G.C., The development of suburban road passenger transport in Leeds 1840-95, *The Journal of Transport History*, Vol. 4, No. 4, pp.214–23 (1960)

– Stagecoach services in the West Riding of Yorkshire between 1830–40, in Dorian, G. (ed.), 1996, *Road transport in the horse-drawn era* (Brookfield, Vermont, Scolar Press, 1996)

Dove, R.C., *A history of Chapel Allerton*, 2 vols (Chapel Allerton, Robin Dove, 2008)

Driver, C., *Tory radical: the life of Richard Oastler* (Oxford, Oxford University Press, 1946)

Eden, Sir F., *The state of the poor*, III Vols (1797)

Edward, P., *Horse and man in early modern England* (London, Hambledon Continuum, 2007)

Elton, A., Leeds cyclists and cycle makers 1880–1901 (*Thoresby Society, Miscellany,* 2nd series, Vol. 5, pp.110–40 (1995)

Engels, F. [1845], *The condition of the working class in England: from personal observation and authoritative sources* (London, Panther, 1969)

Fabian Society, *Why not municipalise the tram?* (Fabian Tract, No. 33, 1891)

Fairchild, C.B., *Street railways: their construction, operation and management (Trams): a practical handbook for street railway men*, Chapter 3, Horse Trains, pp. 135–163 (New York: Street Railway Publishing 1892, reprinted Brora, Adam Gordon, 2005)

Farrar, M., The struggle for the city: representing the inner city, *Regenerating Cities* [later *Cities*] No. 7 January (1995)

– *The struggle for paradise: constructing and deconstructing 'community' in a British multi-cultural inner-city area* (Lampeter, Edwin Mellen Press, 2000)

– 'The zone of the other: imposing and resisting alien identities in Chapeltown, Leeds during the twentieth century', in Gunn, S. and Morris, R.J. (eds), *Making identities: conflict and urban space 1800–2000* (London, Ashgate, 2001)

Felstead, A. et al., *Directory of British architects 1834–1900* (London, Mansell, 1993)

Fido, R. and Merlo, M., *Chapeltown past and present* (Leeds, photocopied MS, *c.*1992)

Fowler, L.N., *Self-made men: a lecture* (London, Tweedies, 1863)

Fraser, D., *Urban politics in Victorian England: the structure of politics in Victorian cities* (Leicester, Leicester University Press, 1976)

– (ed.), *A history of modern Leeds* (Manchester, Manchester University Press, 1980)

– (ed.), *Municipal reform and the industrial city* (Leicester, Leicester University Press, 1982)

Freelove, W.F., *Victorian horses and carriages: a personal sketchbook* (London, Ventura, 1979)

Freeman, M.J. and Aldcroft, D.H. (eds), *Transport in Victorian Britain* (Manchester, Manchester University Press, 1988)

Freese, B., *Coal, a human history* (London, Heineman, 2005)

Friedman, M., *Chapeltown and its Jews (*Leeds, private, 2003)

Furniss, C., *Leeds waterfront* (Leeds, Leeds Civic Trust, 2011)

Galloway, R.L., *Annals of coal mining and the coal trade* (London, Colliery Guardian, 1898)

Gandy, K., *Sheffield Corporation Tramways* (Sheffield, Sheffield City Libraries, 1985)

Gibson, R. and Lefevre, M., *Images of England: Central Leeds* (Stroud, Tempus, 2006)

Gilham, J.C. and Wilson, R.J.S., *Tramways of West Yorkshire* (Light Railway Transport Association, 2001)

Gill, D., 'The people's carriage', *Buses Illustrated*, Vol.5, No.24, pp.118–20 (1955)

Girouard, M., *The English town* (New Haven and London, Yale University Press, 1990)

Gladwin, D., *A history of the British steam tram*, Vol.3, Ch.13 Leeds (Sutherland, A. Gordon, 2007)

Godward, B., *Leeds waterfront east* (Leeds, Leeds Civic Trust Walkabout Series)

Goodman, D., *The making of Leeds* (Barnsley, Wharncliffe Books, 2004)

Gordon, W.J., *The horse-world of London* (London, Religious Tract Society, 1893)

Gough, J.W., *The rise of the entrepreneur* (London, Batsford, 1969)

Grady, K., and Stringer, J., *Edwardian Leeds in postcards* (Leeds, Leeds Civic Trust, 2004)

Grandy, R.E., *Standard guide for the corn merchant, miller and baker* (Dublin, McGlashan and Gill, 1866)

Gray, E., *The tramways of Salford and Manchester* (Manchester, Manchester Transport Museum Society, 1967)

– *The Manchester Carriage and Transport Co.* (Manchester, Manchester Transport Museum, 1977)

– 'The horse-drawn era', in Yearsley, I. and Groves, P., *The Manchester Tramways*, Chapter 1 (Glossop, Transport Publishing, 1991)

Green, R.M., *Politics in Leeds 1852–65*, MA Thesis (Edmonton, University of Alberta, 1983)

Groves, P., *Nottingham Tramways* (Crich, Matlock The Tramway Museum Society, 1975)

Hailstone, E. (ed.), *Costumes of Yorkshire*, paintings of George Walker, 1814 (Leeds, Richard Jackson, 1885)

Hall, C.C., The horse tramway period in Sheffield, *Transport Review*, 1.5 (1951)

Hall, D., *Far Headingley* (Leeds, Far Headingley Village Society, 2000)

Hammond, C., 'Casework and Conservation', *Journal of the Royal Victorian Society*, West Yorkshire (1985)

Hanham, H.J., *Elections and party management, politics in the time of Disraeli and Gladstone* (London, Longmans, Green, 1959)

Hargrave, E., The formation of the Leeds Yeomanry (1813), *Thoresby Society Journal*, Vol.24, pp.435–68 (1924)

Harrison, J.F.C., *Social reform in Victorian Leeds: the work of James Hole, 1820–1895* (Leeds, Thoresby Society Monograph No. III, 1954)

Hartley, F. (comp.), *A brief history of Bradford's horse and steam trams 1882–1903* (1974)

Heap, A. and Brears, P., *Leeds described: eyewitness accounts of Leeds 1534–1905* (Derby, Breedon Books, 1993)

Hearse, G.S., *The Tramways of Jarrow and South Shields* (Cambridge, Dunkirk House, 1971)

Hennock, E.P., *Fit and proper persons: ideal and reality in nineteenth-century urban government* (London, Edward Arnold, 1973)

Hey, D., *The Oxford companion to family and local history*, 2nd edn (Oxford, Oxford University Press, 2008)

Hibbs, J., *The history of British bus services* (Newton Abbot, David and Charles, 1968 rev. edn 1989)

Higgs, E., 'Domestic servants and households in Victorian England', *Social History*, Vol.8., No.2, pp.201–10 (1983)

Hirsch, F., *Social limits to growth* (London, Routledge and Kegan Paul, 1977)

Hobsbawm, E., *The age of revolution: Europe 1789–1848* (London, Weidenfeld and Nicolson, 1962)

– *The age of capital 1848–1875* (London, Weidenfeld and Nicolson, 1973)

Hobsbawm, E. and Ranger, T., *The invention of tradition* (Cambridge, Cambridge University Press, 1983)

Hole, J., *Light, more light: on the present situation of education amongst the working class of Leeds, and how it can be improved* (London, Longmans, Green, 1860)

– *The homes of the working classes, with suggestions for their improvement* (London, Longmans, Green, 1866)

Horne, J.B. and Maund, T.B., *Liverpool Transport Vol.1. 1830–1900* (London, Light Railway Transport League, 1975)

Houfe, S., *John Leech and the Victorian scene* (Woodbridge, Antique Collectors' Club)

Hunt, T., *Building Jerusalem: the rise and fall of the Victorian city* (London, Weidenfeld and Nicolson, 2004)

Hutton, W.E., *The millers', corn merchants', and farmers' ready reckoner*, 2nd. rev. edn (London, Crosby Lockwood, 1886)

Institute of Corn and Agricultural Merchants, *The trades of corn and agricultural merchants* (Cambridge, Heffer, 1955)

Jarvis, A., *Samuel Smiles and the construction of Victorian values* (Stroud, Sutton, 1997)

Jenkins, E.W., Leeds Grammar School, the Charity Commissioners and education for girls

1870–1901 *(Thoresby Society Miscellany*, Vol.4, pp.98–132, 1994)

Jewell, A., *Livestock in art* (Reading, Museum of English Rural Life, 1964)

Jones, D., *Crime, protest, community and police in nineteenth-century Britain* (London, Routledge and Kegan Paul, 1982)

Joy, D. (ed.), *The Yorkshire agricultural show: a celebration of 150 years* (2008)

Kemp, P., *The housing market in late nineteenth-century Britain* (Glasgow, University of Glasgow, Centre for Housing Research, Discussion Paper No.11, 1986)

King, J.S., *Bradford Corporation Tramways* (Bradford, J.S. King, 1998)

Kinnear, C.D., *Tramways, their construction and working*, with supplementary volume 1884 (London, Crosby Lockwood, 1878)

Kitson-Clark, E., *The history of 100 years of life of the Leeds Philosophical and Literary Society* (Leeds, Jowett and Sowry, 1924)

– *Kitsons of Leeds 1837–1937* (London, Locomotive Publishing, 1938)

Kitson-Clark, G., 'The Leeds élite', *University of Leeds Review*, Vol.17, No.2, pp.232–58 (1974)

Klapper, C., *The golden age of the tramway* (Newton Abbot, David and Charles, 1961)

Landers, J., *The field and the forge: population, production and power in the pre-industrial west* (Oxford, Oxford University Press, 2003)

Lee, C.E., *The horse bus as a vehicle* (London, London Transport, 1974)

Linstrum, D., Cuthbert Brodrick, *Country Life*, Vol.141, pp.1379–81 (1967)

– *West Yorkshire architecture and architects* (London, Lund Humphries, 1978)

– *Towers and colonnades: the architecture of Cuthbert Brodrick* [1821–1905] (Leeds, Leeds Philosophical and Literary Society, 1999)

London General Omnibus Company, *Street tramways 'as they will affect the ordinary users of the roads and householders'* (reprint of a pamphlet by an anti-Metropolitan Tramways Bill lobby, with refutations by the LGOC, 1868)

Lowe, R., The last post, Obituary of William Turton (1880–1965) *(The Philatelist*, Vol.31, No.6, p.134, 1965)

Lupton, C.A., *The Lupton family in Leeds* (Ripon, printer William Harrison, 1965)

Mayhall, J., *The annals and history of Leeds* 1825–59, pp. 316–75 (Leeds, Joseph John, 1860)

McKenzie, R. and Silver, A., *Angels in marble: working class conservatives in urban England* (London, Heinemann, 1968)

Meiklejohn, A., *Charles Turner Thackrah: the effects of arts, trades and professions on health and longevity with an introductory essay on his life and, work and time* (Edinburgh and London, E. and S. Livingstone, 1957)

Moore, H.C., *Omnibuses and cabs: their origin and history* (London, Chapman Hall, 1902 and reprinted Adam Gordon, 2002)

Moore, J. and Rodger, R., *Who really ran the cities? Municipal knowledge and policy networks in British local government 1832–1914*, Roth and Beachy 2007, pp. 37–69 (2007)

Morgan, J. and Joy, D., *A celebration of Leeds* (Ilkley, Great Northern, 2006)

Morris, R.J., *Men, women and property in England 1780–1870: a social and economic history of family strategies amongst the Leeds middle-classes* (Cambridge, Cambridge University Press, 2005)

Murray, H., *The horse tramways of York 1880–1909* (London, The Light Rail Transit League, 1980)

Nuttgens, P., *Leeds: the back to front, inside out and upside down city* (Otley, Stile Books, 1979)

Offley, G., *Guide to the Transport History Collection in Leicester University Library* (Leicester, Leicester University Library, 1981)

O'Leary, C., *The elimination of corrupt practices in British elections 1868–1911* (Oxford, Clarendon Press, 1962)

O'Rourke, Kevin H., 'The European grain invasion', *Journal of Economic history*, Vol.57, pp.775–801 (1997)

Page, W. (ed.), [1913] *A history of the county of Yorkshire*, 3 Vols, The Victoria History of England (London, Dawson, 1974)

Paine, T., *Rights of man* (Harmondsworth, Penguin, 1976)

Pease, J., *The history of Thomas Green & Son Ltd* (Witney, Lightmoor Press, 2014)

Pennock, P.M., The evolution of St James, 1845–94: Leeds Moral and Industrial Training School, Leeds Union Workhouse and Leeds Union Infirmary. *Thoresby Society Miscellany*, Vol.18, No.2, pp.129–76 (1986)

Pollard, J., Thomas Green and Son tramway engineers, Part 1, *Tramway Review*, No. 166, pp. 264–73 (1996)

– Thomas Green and Son tramway engineers, Part 2, *Tramway Review*, No. 167, pp. 225–29 (1997)

Potts, M.S., William Potts of Leeds, clockmaker. *Thoresby Society, second series Miscellany*, Vol.13, pp.25–45 (2003)

Rimmer, W.G., *The Marshalls of Leeds: flax-spinners 1788–1886* (Cambridge, Cambridge University Press, 1960)

Robbins, M., The Balaklava railway, *The Journal of Transport History*, Vol.1, No.1 (University College of Leicester, pp. 28–43, 1953/4)

Roberts, M.,*Villa toryism and popular conservatism in Leeds 1885–1902* (Cambridge, Cambridge University Press, 2006)

– *Political movements in urban England 1832–1914* (Basingstoke, Macmillan, Palgrave, 2010)

Roth, R. and Beachy, R. (eds), *Who ran the cities? City élite and urban power structures in Europe and North America* (Aldershot, Ashgate, 2007)

Rush, R., *The tramways of Accrington, with brief notes on the adjoining system of Blackburn* (London, W.J. Fowler, 1961)

– *Horse trams of the British Isles* (Usk, Oakwood Press, 2004)

Scott, W.H., *The West Riding of Yorkshire at the opening of the twentieth century: contemporary biographies*, ed. Pike, W.T., Pike's New Century Series, No. 6, 1902

Sekon, G.A., *Locomotion in Victorian London* (London, Oxford University Press, 1938)

Senior, D.J.H., Sheffield tramways 1873–1960, *Buses Illustrated* (1960)

Shadwell, R., *Horse omnibus: entertaining and instructive episodes from the history of its horses and the manners of its men* (Craven Arms, Wooller, 1994)

Smiles, S., *Self Help, with illustrations of character and conduct* (London, Murray, 1859)

Smith, D.J., *Discovering horse-drawn transport of the British Army* (Aylesbury, Shire Publications, 1977)

– *Horses at work* (Wellingborough, Patrick Stephen, 1985)

Smith, P.L., *The Aire and Calder Navigation* (Wakefield, Wakefield Historical Association, 1987)

Soper, J., *Leeds Transport* [Five volumes], Vol.1, *1830–1902* (Leeds, Leeds Transport Historical Society, 1985)

Steele, E.D., Leeds and Victorian politics, *University of Leeds Review*, Vol.17, No.2, pp.259–85, 1974

Stowell, G., *The history of Button Hill* (London, Gollancz, 1929)

Taylor, M., *The canal and river section of the Aire and Calder Navigation* (Barnsley, Wharncliffe Books, 2003)

Thackrah, C., *The effect of art, trade, and professions on health and longevity*, 2nd, ed. (London, Longman, 1834)

Thompson, F. and Michael, L., Whigs and Liberals in the West Riding 1830–60, *The English Historical Review*, No. 290, pp. 214–39, 1959

– *Victorian England: the horse-drawn society* [inaugural lecture] (London, Bedford College, 1970)

– Nineteenth-century horse sense, *The Economic History Review*, Vol.29, No.1, pp. 60–81 (1976)

– (ed.), *The rise of suburbia* (Leeds, Leeds University Press, 1982)

– *The rise of respectable society: a social history of Victorian Britain 1830–1900* (London, Fontana, 1988)

– *Gentrification and the enterprise culture, Britain 1780–1980* (Oxford, Oxford University Press, 2001)

Thomson, J., *Horse-drawn carriages: a source book* (Fleet, John Thompson, 1980)

Thoresby, R., *Ducatus Leodiensis: or the topography of the town and parish of Leedes* (London, M. Atkinson, 1715)

Thoresby Society, *Leeds in Maps* in the *Yorkshire Evening Post*, Leeds Library (Leeds, Thoresby Society, 2007)

Thorne, R.C.N., *West Yorkshire: 'a noble scene of industry': the Development of the County 1500–1830* (Wakefield, West Yorkshire Archive Service, 1987)

Thornton, D., *Leeds: the story of a city* (Ayr, Fort Publishing, 2002)

– *Great Leeds stories* (Ayr, Fort Publishing, 2005)

– *A Brief History of Leeds* (2013)

Trowell, F., 'Speculative housing development in the suburb of Headingley 1838–1914'. *Thoresby Society Miscellany* Vol.18, Pt 1, pp.50–118 (1985)

Van Vleck, Va Nee L, 'Delivery of Coal by Road and Rail in Britain' *(Journal of Economic History,* Vol.57, pp.139–60, 1997)

Vickers, R.J., *Leeds Road and Rail in Old Photographs* (Stroud, Alan Sutton, 1994)

Voice, D., *The Age of the Horse Tram: History of Horse-drawn Passenger Tramways in the British Isles* (Brora, Adam Gordon, 2009)

Waddington, H., *The Story of a Family Business, Crown Point Dyeworks, East Street* (Leeds, Typescript, published by the author, 1953)

Wainwright, P., *Opposite the Infirmary: a History of the Thackray Company 1902–90* (Leeds, Medical Museum Publishing, 1997)

Ward, T.J., 'West Riding Landowners and the Corn Laws'. *English Historical Review*, Vol.81, No.319, pp.256–72 (1974)

Wardell, J., *The municipal history of the borough of Leeds* (London, Longman, 1846, reprinted 1896)

Webster, C., *Building a Great Victorian City: Leeds Architects and Architecture 1790–1914* (Huddersfield, Northern Heritage Publications, 2011)

West Yorkshire Archive Service, *An Illustrated Guide to the West Yorkshire Archive Service* (Wakefield, WYAS, 1988)

Wheater, W., *The Horse and Jockey Inn* (the *Yorkshire Owl*, Vol.VIII, 2, date uncertain)

Williams, C. (ed.), *A Companion to Nineteenth-century Britain* (Oxford, Blackwell, 2004)

Wilson, E. (ed.), *Leeds Grammar School Admission Returns 1820–1900* (Leeds, 1901)

Wilson, R.G., *Gentleman merchants: the merchant community in Leeds 1700–1830* (Manchester, Manchester University Press, 1971)

Wiseman, R.J.S., *British tramways in pictures*, Enlarged edn 1976 (Huddersfield, Advertiser Press, 1964)

Wolmar, C., *Fire & Steam: how the Railways Transformed Britain* (London, Atlantic Books, 2007)

Wood, A., *Nineteenth century Britain 1815–1914* (London, Longmans, 1960)

Wood, C., *Victorian Painters*, 2 vols (Woodbridge, Antique Collectors' Club, 1995)

Wordell, J., *The Ownership of Land in the Borough of Leeds* (1896, first edn 1846)

Wrathnell, S., *Leeds: Pevsner Architectural Guides* (New Haven and London, Yale University Press, 2005)

Yearsley, I. and Groves, P., *The Manchester Tramways* (Glossop, Transport Publishing, 1991)

Youatt, W., *The horse*, new edition (London, Chapman and Hall, 1843)

Young, A., *One hundred years of Leeds tramways* (Leeds, Turntable Enterprises, 1970)

ARCHIVES
Yorkshire

Leeds Parish Church Registers
Leeds Local Studies Library (see below)
Leeds City Registers *c*.1800–1930
Leeds Library, *Annual subscription registers*, 1880–84, 1885–96, 1897–1906, 1907–22
West Yorkshire Archive Service (Leeds and Wakefield)

National
National Census
National Archives (Kew, London)

Turton family collections

LIBRARIES
Yorkshire

Leeds Civic Society
Local Studies Library, Leeds City Council
The Leeds Library
Leeds Transport Historical Society
West Yorkshire Archive Service, Sheepscar, Leeds
West Yorkshire Archive Service, Wakefield
Thoresby Society

National
British Library
Tramway Museum, Crich

Leeds Council Committee minutes
LLC1/1/5–6 Finance Committee 8.1868–7.1885
LLC1/3/1 Printing Committee, 5.1869–1892
LLC9/1/9–10, 12,13 Streets and Sewerage Committee, 11.1866–1880
LLC9/5/1–2 Sewage Committee, 1866–1878
LLC10/1/4–6 Markets Committee, 5.1873–8.1877
LLC10/5/1 Weights and Measures Committee, 1876–1880
LLC17/1/5–6 Scavenging and Nuisance, 3.1863–9.1869
LLC17/6/1–2 Night-soil sub-committee, 5.1867–3.1880
LLC17/8/1 Cellar dwellings sub-committee, 12.1868–1880
LLC18/1/2–3 Printing Committee, 11.1843–1892
LLC22/1-3 Waterworks Committee, 11.1873–11.1878
LLC26/1/1–2 Becks Committee, 1866–1873
LLC27/1/2 Purchase of Property Committee, 2.1871–1879
LLC 28/6/1–2 Leeds Council Tramway Committee
LLC32/1–3 Sanitary Committee, 1869–1878

LLC33/1/1–2 Gasworks Committee 1870–1880
LLC35/1/1 1872 Roundhay Committee 1872

LCC36/1/1 Revision of Wards Committee 1872–1881

LLD1/1/A385 Leeds Town Clerk: exchange of land with William Turton
LLD1/11A 385 Transport Committee
LLD1/4/35/1/116 Purchase of land on Hunslet Moor, 23/10/78
LLD1/1/A1065 Bye-laws for steam trams 25/8/89
LLD1/3/43/27 Bye-laws for electric trams 1891
LLD1/3/43/28 Bye-laws for electric trams 1899
LLD1/4/21/46 Counsel re purchase of LTC, February 1892
LLD1/3/57/30 Copy of deposit by Barr and Nelson, solicitors
LLD1/4/21/6 Letter to Nelson and Co. from Highway Committee, July 1892
LLD28/1/1–4 Highways Committee

LC/ENG/BCP/Vol.9a, p.38, 19.10.1874, re Mr Turton's property in The Calls [poor condition, not seen]
LC/ENG/BCP/Vol.11, p.20, 11 June 1875, 64–66, re The Calls, property of Mr Turton (plan)
LC/ENG/BCP/Vol.34, 17.8.1877, re Mr Turton's property in The Calls (missing)

LL2/1/12–17 Leeds Council Minutes 9.1864–6.1880
LL1/2/3–4 Executive Committee 2.1869–9.1877

WYL769 Thomas Green and Son Engineers, Leeds
WYL1208 Kitson & Co, Engineers, Leeds

Newspapers and Journals

Yorkshire
Leeds Daily News
Leeds Mercury
Scarborough Mercury
The Northern Star (and *National Trades Journal*)
the *Yorkshire Owl*
Yorkshire Evening Post
Yorkshire Post

Other provincial newspapers
The *Liverpool Mercury*
The *Newcastle Courant*

National
Pall Mall Gazette
Reynolds Weekly News Paper
The *Guardian*
The *London Daily News*
The *Times*

Websites
www.ancestry.co.uk

www.archives.wyjs.org.uk
www.britishtramsonline.co.uk/leeds107.html
www.firekeeper.co.uk
www.jamaica-gleaner.com
www.latch.org.uk/ls_history
www.leeds.gov.uk/discover
www.Leodis.net
www.maxfarrar.org.uk/mywork_community/html
www.secretleeds.com
www.thoresby.org.uk
www.tramway.co.uk
www.trampower.co.uk
www.yorkshireripper.com

INDEX

Index of Places

Index of Personal names

Index of subjects